Africana Theory, Policy, and Leadership

The Africana Studies Series examines the experiences of Africana people and societies from a Black/African perspective. The series promotes scholarly debate and research on issues relating to the African global experience. It will only publish original scholarly papers and articles that focus on critical issues confronting Africana people and societies and which demonstrate rigorous and thorough research.

Titles in this series include:

The Black Family and Society

Race, Gender, and Identity

African American Consciousness

Racial Structure and Radical Politics in the African Diaspora

Law, Culture, and Africana Studies

Afrocentric Traditions

Africana Theory, Policy, and Leadership

James L. Conyers, Jr., editor

Africana Studies, Volume 7

Transaction Publishers
New Brunswick (U.S.A.) and London (U.K.)

Copyright © 2016 by Transaction Publishers, New Brunswick, New Jersey.

All rights reserved under International and Pan-American Copyright Conventions. No part of this book may be reproduced or transmitted in any form or by any means, electronic or mechanical, including photocopy, recording, or any information storage and retrieval system, without prior permission in writing from the publisher. All inquiries should be addressed to Transaction Publishers, 10 Corporate Place South, Suite 102, Piscataway, New Jersey 08854. www.transactionpub.com

This book is printed on acid-free paper that meets the American National Standard for Permanence of Paper for Printed Library Materials.

Library of Congress Catalog Number: 2015047868
ISBN: 978-1-4128-6319-3
eBook: 978-1-4128-6356-8
Printed in the United States of America

Library of Congress Cataloging-in-Publication Data

Names: Conyers, James L., editor.
Title: Africana theory, policy, and leadership / James L. Conyers, Jr., editor.
Description: New Brunswick (USA) : Transaction Publishers, [2016] | Series: Africana studies ; volume 7 | Includes bibliographical references and index.
Identifiers: LCCN 2015047868 (print) | LCCN 2016020299 (ebook) | ISBN 9781412863193 (pbk.) | ISBN 9781412863568
Subjects: LCSH: African Americans--Race identity. | African Americans--Study and teaching. | Blacks--Race identity. | Blacks--Study and teaching. | African diaspora.
Classification: LCC E185.625 .A387 2016 (print) | LCC E185.625 (ebook) | DDC 305.896/073--dc23
LC record available at https://lccn.loc.gov/2015047868

Contents

Introduction   vii
James L. Conyers, Jr.

1   Africana Literature as Social Science: Applying the Demographic Literary Standard (DLS) to the Works of August Wilson and Suzan-Lori Parks   1
Christel N. Temple

2   Africana Ethnography: How Homeland Eritrea Monitors Its American Diaspora   31
Dawit O. Woldu and Irvin H. Bromall

3   Africana Gender Studies: Toward Theorizing Gender without Feminism   63
Valethia A. Watkins

4   Africana Aesthetics: Creating a Critical Black Narrative from Photographs in South Texas   83
Alberto Rodriguez

5   Africana Perspectives in Criminal Justice: Are Black Women the New Mules of the Prison Industrial Complex?   107
Nishaun T. Battle

6   Africana Studies and Diversity: All Shapes, Sizes, and Colors of HBCU Athletic Programs: The Sporting HBCU Diaspora—Cultural Convergence and Politics of Divergence   121
J. Kenyatta Cavil, Joseph Cooper, and Geremy Cheeks

| 7 | The Afrocentric Idea in Leadership Studies
Abul Pitre | 155 |

Notes on Contributors   165

Index   169

Introduction

James L. Conyers, Jr.

The theme of Africana Theory, Policy, and Leadership as analyzed in *Africana Studies: A Review of Social Science Research* is given importance at a critical time in American historiography. The reasons are twofold: the presidential campaign and criminal justice reform in America. The contributors to this volume attempt to offer insight and alternative approaches to the theme. Comparatively, this volume makes a contribution to the research and study of Africana phenomena from an interdisciplinary perspective, within the disciplinary matrix of Africana Studies.

Christel Temple's essay "Africana Literature as Social Science" extends and stretches the boundaries of conventional research and writing. She offers an alternative interdisciplinary perspective to examining text through the use of literary canons. Conversely, she applies this triangulation and metatheory analysis to reviewing the scholarship of August Wilson and Suzan Lori-Parks.

Dawit O. Woldu and Irvin H. Bromall in their chapter offer an ethnography, which examines the cultural landscape of Eritrea. These two authors analyze the lasting contributions of this nation state comparing and evaluating NGOs. Also, concentrating on their neighbor states in the Horn of Africa, the authors discuss developing countries and their relationship with the Western powers.

Valethia Watkins, in "Africana Gender Studies," provides a critical assessment of the discussion on gender. Notwithstanding the notion of theory, Watkins supplies groundwork to describe and evaluate gender, on the basis of a cultural context. Cultural context refers to examining the continuity of disparity exhibited toward Africana women and their conceptual narrative. Her chapter reviews definitional dilemmas; politics of compulsory of feminism; the invisible magnitude; and, finally, Africana Gender Studies, going beyond the traditional boundaries of area studies research scholarship.

Alberto Rodriguez offers the Africana narrative in describing and evaluating African American aesthetics in South Texas. Beginning with examining the ethos and voice of W.E.B. Du Bois, Alain Locke's concept of the New Negro, and Booker T. Washington's Atlanta Exposition of 1895, he relates this information as a historical overview of this Africana narrative. Texas in particular has the hybridity of being southern and southwestern simultaneously. That is, the state of Texas supported the confederacy of southern states, though, ironically, no civil war was fought on the state's soil. Texas endorsed, supported, and profited from the enslavement of African Americans nevertheless. Rodriguez's chapter provides statistical evidence and photographic imagery of Africana phenomena existence in the borderline southern coastal areas of Texas.

Nishaun Battle focuses on Black womanhood and the criminal justice reform movement in America. Her introduction to the Trayvon Martin case is indicative of the continuing inequality in the criminal justice system. In either case, Battle's analysis of the social construction of race and gender unpacks queries regarding the role and impact of gender characteristics in social reform and public policy.

Kenyatta Cavil, Joseph Cooper, and Geremy Cheeks provide a critical study of the Historically Black Colleges and Universities (HBCU) and their concept of diversity. The authors explain in detail in what way the idea and thought of how federal and state funding are the impediments for the existence and survival of HBCU athletic programs. Pushing this idea further, they offer a quantitative methodological approach, outlining the rationale, purpose, relevance, and significance for the existence and sustenance of athletic programs at HBCUs.

Abul Pitre in his chapter "The Africana Idea in Leadership Studies" establishes a nexus between the humanities, social sciences, and professional studies of education. Pitre points to the interpretative analysis of the researcher as the guiding point to describe and evaluate phenomena. Indeed, he highlights that Leadership Studies is a relatively new cognitive field of study in the field of education. As such his analysis reviews Africana Critical Theory in the context of describing and evaluating Africana phenomena.

1

Africana Literature as Social Science: Applying the Demographic Literary Standard (DLS) to the Works of August Wilson and Suzan-Lori Parks

Christel N. Temple

Introduction

Literary study engaged within the discipline of Africana Studies embraces the objective of demonstrating literature's value and function as a tool of liberation. The discipline aims to create and to foster the engagement of knowledge that transforms consciousness and inspires a shift toward positive attitudes, behaviors, and activism on behalf of the people of African descent. Yet, many of the practices of literary criticism used to decipher and illuminate the meaning of the world's literatures rely on frameworks and theories that deny, minimize, or ignore the practical applications of the art form. Even in progressive approaches to textual analysis, most frequently used in postcolonial, postmodern, comparative literature, cultural, and anthropological studies, literary analysis rarely intersects with social science research in direct and functional ways. Maulana Karenga observes the problem of the "privileging of literature over social science data" and notes, "literature, even as fiction and personal imagination, is used as an alternative to a social science understanding of Black life rather than as a contribution to a holistic understanding of it. In other words, personal subjectivity is privileged over social science study and a novel or short story becomes the most important and at times only way one understands Black life."[1] The analytical processes in academic work related to people of African descent require a balance, and James Stewart, transversely, warns against failing to balance social science work with measures to clarify the interpretive narratives of Black life.[2] He recommends that "a knowledge generation strategy focused around increasing cross-dialogue between artistic/humanistic and social science modes of investigation would seem to be preferable to a unidimensional emphasis on enhancing perceptions of scientific rigor."[3] Defending his suggestion from "conventional wisdom that scientific research should be uncontaminated by political considerations and that theoretical work is superior to applied research because it requires more intellectual acumen," Stewart emphasizes that "the potential benefits from experimentation with alternative approaches to knowledge generation that reflects the field's multiple missions have not been explored aggressively."[4] Guided, then, by Karenga's and Stewart's suggestions and responding to the challenges of new Black literary formats and Black liberation needs, I offer suggestions for social science follow-through in Black literary study based on an approach I describe as the *demographic literary standard* (DLS).

The DLS model radically amends the engagement of the "sociology of literature," wherein literature increases "social awareness and social responsiveness"[5] from its late-nineteenth-century exploratory period and its 1990s rearticulation as cultural studies, both waves that were and are philosophically concerned with relationships between literature and history as well as concerns over to what extent society influences the artist and vice versa.[6] The DLS is also a point of information for literary purists who suggest that culture "can no longer take literary studies where it needs to go."[7] Their arguments completely overlook Black cultural and Afrocentric criteria of literature, much of which is taught directly through or as cross-listings of literature disciplines.[8] Instead, the DLS is an Afrocentric tool that emphasizes the function of enhancing literary analysis with quantitative and qualitative explorations of a text's collective elements and meaning. The DLS model encourages the following procedural treatment of literature.

Procedural Elements of DLS Method of Literary Analysis

- Confirmation that it is possible to demarcate the line(s) between fiction and social science realism presented by and inspired by the text in order to determine that DLS is a compatible tool for textual analysis and application

- Awareness of demographics, generally understood as typical group or population characteristics expressed in variables that should be Afrocentrically formulated beyond the standard national categories of age, sex, race, ethnicity, education, geographic residence, employment, income, marital status, religion, dwelling, language, mobility, or generation cohort
- Creation of an exhaustive list of all *documentable* and *verifiable* topics, themes, situations, predicaments, historical and contemporary events and figures, proper names, streets, addresses, cities, locales, social movements, eras, businesses, and economic references that are based on the various demographic conditions introduced in the text
- Attention to historical-biographical contexts of the work wherein knowledge of author biography, experience, and influence, date/era of publication, and historical setting are even more meaningful than prescribed by conventional literary analysis
- Interpretation of literature as an integrated art form with aesthetic and structural conventions as well as social science implications
- Attention to determining the functionality of the narrative based on comparisons of the text's thematic and causal variables against quantitative and qualitative social science data sets generated through research, polls, surveys, interviews, and statistics
- Willingness to refine or create conceptual and content categories that are not adequately represented or measured in data sets, as a means of generating ideas for new areas of quantitative and qualitative research that could better inform conditions of Black life
- Attention to the cycles of *tradition and innovation*[9] in Black literature to ensure that literary analysis regards advances and shifts in creativity in the context of the historical continuum of the Black literary tradition
- Attention to the text's *location in time and space*[10] with respect to prioritizing an interpretation of chronology and geography, especially for literature structured based on measurable units of time (e.g., Suzan-Lori Parks' *365 Plays/365 Days*, August Wilson's ten plays representing the twentieth century viewed as an Afrocentric Decalogue, or texts structured as journals, diaries, or dated letters)
- Attention to the text's relationship to *ethics and values*[11] with respect to its usefulness in inspiring solution-seeking discourse by encouraging critical thinking for the benefit of contemporary social change
- Attention to literature study's need for *scientific application*[12] concerning especially the use of technology in research and training of content expertise, which also has implications for literary classroom technology and grant funding for community center technology
- Revision of research directives and evidence categories in order to systematically expand literature's function beyond the humanities, which will permit a reliance on research beyond Modern Language Association bibliography for literature analysis and enable a functional multidimensional layering of knowledge that increases the social value of literary analyses
- Opportunities to suspend the format of prose narrative of literary analysis in favor of listing and short description.

The following applications of the DLS will be *generally* applied to Parks' single volume *365 Days/365 Plays* (2006)[13] and *specifically* applied to Wilson's twentieth-century cycle of plays.

Parks' *365 Days/365 Plays*

Historical-Biographical Context

Parks was born in Fort Knox, Kentucky, on May 10, 1964, and attended college at Mount Holyoke College in Massachusetts and graduate school at Yale University in Connecticut. She lived in six states before graduating from high school, spent time in Germany and London, and has lived most of her adult life in Manhattan. She is African American, and her plays have been performed all over the country and the world. Demographically speaking, she is Black, female, wealthy, educated, married in a mixed-race relationship, nonreligiously affiliated, multilingual, and geographically affiliated primarily with the northeast. The data sets related to her personal/regional experience would illuminate more about the author.

Concepts and Themes in 365 Days/365 Plays

In one year's worth of plays—from November 13, 2002, to November 13, 2003—Parks addresses a diverse mix of social, political, historical, and cultural topics ranging from citizenship and nationalism, war, family, gender roles and reversals, heroics, infidelity, the south, class, religion, criminal justice, homicide, death penalty, aesthetics, African American and American historical narratives and their creative reversal, police power, tradition and censorship, masculinity, literature and literary history, marriage, world history and leadership, human rights, language and language acquisition, drama aesthetics, Black music traditions, popular culture and fame, mythology, storytelling, media, White supremacy, race and racism, mental health issues, enslavement and holocaust, literacy, commemoration and holidays, space and alternate universes, urban life, blues, poverty, U.S. presidents, stolen elections and natural disaster, love relationships, unemployment, drug addiction, and failures of legislation,

The power of Parks' play is that she offers a profound critical observation or a set of observations about every day in the year, to suggest that the average person is a critical being who is attentive to the multiple realities of a single day—including individual, local, national, and international realities—and how the past intersects with this single day. Parks' plays differ from what we have come to expect from the dramatic form because they are more like vignettes or scenes that help to define the most pressing concerns of the average person in America. The brief, presentational form functions as a reminder of the need for readers/Americans to spend longer moments philosophically reflecting on the stimulus offered in the play. The result of such reflection on many pressing sociopolitical and humanistic topics is that citizens will be agents of changes, just as Parks' plays are catalysts for inspiring change. This context of her art form implies a shift in behavior, and the social science and research data that correspond to Parks' subject matter become evidence and tools that support the change readers should be inspired to advocate. Every day, members of society have a fleeting moment of inspiration about making the work a better place to be in. Parks captures this inspiration with her collection of daily meditations.

A significant portion of *365 Days/365 Plays* responds to America's, in particular, and the world's, in general, dependency on war, and the plays representing March–April, 2003, are deeply saturated with discussions of Afghanistan, George W. Bush, male and female soldiers, patriotism, and lessons from the world's wars. This topic, in particular, is reminiscent of the polls, surveys, and data sets representing American satisfaction with U.S. foreign policy, Christianity, ageism, violence, abuse, immigration and enslavement, and more.

Traditional Literary Analysis

Traditional literary analysis of Parks' *365 Days* would entail a survey of the published articles and reviews of the play, drawn from academic journals as well as newspapers and Internet sources. Philip Kolin and Rebecca Ann Ruggeach have offered traditional scholarly treatments of the play, while reviews and commentaries on the 365 National Festival and "play-a-day" projects inspired by the collection appear in sources such as *New York Times*, *Amsterdam News*, *Theatre Journal*, and *Diverse: Issues in Higher Education*.[14] The play has its own website, www.365Days365Plays.com, and is a phenomenon in the theater world, in particular, because the country's theaters gave significant energy in 2006 and 2007 to producing the work of a single playwright, "bringing together disparate parts of a far-flung and often disconnected artistic community."[15]

The collection is set mostly in a U.S. American context and reflects historical context, political awareness, and social commentary, and more specifically, Parks defines the collection as a "Black play" that is relevant to everyone.[16] The literary engagement of her collection as readable literature invokes a critical reading of the text within the traditions of African American literature, Africana Studies, and Black women playwrights, in particular. Elizabeth Brown-Guillory's (1987) framework for measuring the tradition of Black women playwrights based on the works of Alice Childress, Lorraine Hansberry, and Ntozake Shange offers a traditional Black literary approach to analyzing *365 Days*. Brown-Guillory observes, "three images which appear most frequently in the plays of these black women are 'the black male in search of his manhood,' 'the black male as a walking wounded,' and 'the evolving black woman.'"[17] These topics reflect sets of themes that appear in Parks' works such as *The Death of the Last Black Man in the Entire World* (1990),[18] *Venus* (1996),[19] and *Topdog/Underdog* (2001).[20] She suggests that Childress, Hansberry, and Shange "provide America with plausible, and in some cases, unique, images of black men and women" and that society will "be different after meeting the characters in the plays of black women."[21] Parks fits in this tradition of Black women writers, and one could add to Brown-Guillory's list a host of observations about the Black women's dramatic images of White men and women whose social, political, and historical roles in the United States have intersected or been viewed by Black people.

Data Sets for Parks' Collection

Parks' choice to create a collection that reflects Black artistic interest and concern in the measurable unit of time of every day for one year demands a social science analysis and measure of Black life experience. She writes, "Every day for the next year I would wake up and ask myself, 'Ok, so what's the play?' and I wrote what came. The plan was that no matter what I did, how busy I was, what other commitments I had, I would write a play a day, every single day, for a year. It would be about being present and being committed to the artistic process every single day, regardless of the 'weather.' It became a daily meditation, a daily prayer celebrating the rich and strange process of a writing life."[22] We can deduce a definition of the artistic process from Parks' words and work. Parks represents the artist's "commitment to putting art at the very center of life—not as a monument but as a commonplace necessity like fire, water, bread or shoes."[23] When Parks relates art to food, shelter, and clothing, her philosophy of art becomes intrinsically connected to sociological measures and social science measures of well-being and problem solving. This

Africana Literature as Social Science   7

collective focus and commitment is what affiliates drama and theater with quantitative and qualitative social science research.

On the basis of Parks' demographics and on the themes and perspectives of *365 Days* several social science data sets become essential to the social activist follow-through demanded by her art. The DLS method ensures that literary criticism arms itself with social science facts and perspectives in its analysis of functionality. From the demographics of Parks and her collection of plays, the following data sets could complement the classroom study of Parks' plays. The sources were located by running a search through electronic statistical resources catalogued through the Odem Institute Data Catalog, the Odem Institute Public Opinion Poll Database, the Inter-University Consortium for Political and Social Research (ICPSR), the Harvard-MIT Data Center, and the Roper Studies using key word searches of "African Americans," "Blacks," and "women" plus other diverse topics, themes, and current events found in *365 Days/365 Plays*:

- Three Generation National Survey of African American Families, Waves 1–4, 1979–1980, 1987–1988, 1992 by James S. Jackson and Harold W. Neighbors (survey investigates neighborhood-community integrations, services, crime and community contact, the role of religion and the church, physical and mental health, self-esteem, life satisfaction, employment, the effect of chronic unemployment, the effects of race on the job, interaction with family and friends, racial attitudes, race identity, group stereotypes, and race ideology based on demographic variables of education, marital status, income, employment status, occupation, and political behavior and affiliation).
- Childhood Victimization and Delinquency, Adult Criminality, and Violent Criminal Behavior in a Large Urban County in the Northwest United States, 1980–1997, by Diane J. English and Cathy Spatz Widom.
- Intimate Partner Homicide in California, 1987–2000, by William Wells and William DeLeon-Granados
- ABC News/Washington Post Poll #2003-932: 2004 Presidential Election/Iraq/Finances
- CSRA/UCONN Poll #2004-FEM: 2004–2005 National Black Feminist Study
- ABC News/Washington Post Poll #2003-909: Iraq/Affirmative Action/Death Penalty/Economy/Abortion/Race Relations
- Impact of Immigration on Ethnic-Specific Violence in Miami, Florida, 1997, by Ramiro Martinez, Jr.
- Symbolic Racism Scale (CAPS-RACISM module)
- Attitudes towards Immigrants by the Roper Center; Princeton Survey Research Associates

In addition, since Parks' daily meditation of plays presents excerpts reflecting personal elements and experiences, the following databases, compatible with Parks' demographic, are also useful:

- New York Times Women's Survey, 1985
- Black Female Leadership Project, 1986–1987 (Log # 01153) by Patricia Reid-Merritt

There are many more data sets that inform topics that appear in *365 Days/365 Plays* such as the following: prejudice and violence in the work place; race relations; monthly polls on the presidency; issues related to the elderly; slavery (enslavement) apologies, compensation, and reparation; social change; maternal and infant health; athletes, coaches, and race in sports; Latino intersections with the Black experience; the U.S. court system; and healthcare/physicians. Using such social science data sets in an Afrocentric literature curriculum to explore the function of Black literature beyond the borders of standard literary convention is the ideal practice of the Afrocentric literary enterprise. Since Parks' volume introduces 365 plays, this current sample of engaging her work using the DLS is an abbreviated exercise intended to convey the basic elements of the process.

August Wilson's Century Cycle of Plays

August Wilson's century cycle of twentieth-century plays represents vignettes of Black life with a balance of urban and rural portrayals of northern and southern Black culture and sensibilities. Since the Wilson century cycle is a collection of ten plays—a repertoire that could ideally be the primary set of texts for a course or academic term—the application of the DLS has implications for pedagogy as well as for literary function and philosophical uses of historical era. These features permit critical, interpretive, reflective, and civically aware engagements of the collective meaning of the Black experience in the United States. Although Wilson did not publish the plays in chronological order, it is appropriate to survey the plays based on chronology of setting. Thus, the century cycle, for the purposes of this treatment in the context of the DLS, consists of (1) *Gem of the Ocean*[24] (set in 1904); (2) *Joe Turner's Come and Gone*[25] (set in 1911); (3) *Ma Rainey's Black Bottom*[26] (set in the late 1920s); (4) *The Piano Lesson*[27] (set in the 1930s); (5) *Seven Guitars*[28] (set in 1948); (6) *Fences*[29] (set in 1957 and 1965); (7) *Two Trains Running*[30] (set in 1969); (8) *Jitney*[31] (set in 1977); (9) *King Hedley II*[32] (set in 1985); and

(10) *Radio Golf*[33] (set in 1997). It is also possible to study the final play, *Radio Golf*, first and then to proceed chronologically because the final play functions simultaneously as prologue and epilogue.

Historical-Biographical Context

Nine plays of the century cycle are set in Pittsburgh, Pennsylvania, Wilson's hometown, and Wilson created a diverse and lively century of characters. His creations reflect exposures to his local community, to the national cast of Black and White Americans representing collective identities and dreams, and a dedicated and spiritual sense of African identity maintained through epic memory and the leadership of African American community visionaries. Wilson was born in 1945 and died in 2005, shortly after completing the century cycle. His plays have received widespread production on Broadway and in regional theaters and accolades such as the Tony Award, the New York Drama Critics Circle Award, and the Pulitzer Prize. One of the most significant aspects of Wilson's work is his belief in Afrocentricity. He clarifies, "We are Africans who have been in America since the seventeenth century. We are Americans. But first of all, we are Africans. There's no way that you can dispute the fact that we are African people, and we have a culture that's separate and distinct from the mainstream White American culture."[34] Wilson also defined himself as a cultural nationalist. He said, "I simply believe that blacks have a culture, and that we have our own mythology, our own history, our own social organizations, our own creative motive, our own way of doing things. Simply that. That's what I mean when I say cultural nationalist."[35] Wilson's commitment to keeping alive the history of African Americans is what drove his creativity, and this characteristic of his work is also what makes the DLS an ideal critical tool to explore the details of the African American "historical situation."[36]

Traditional Literary Analysis

There are several dozen critical books and hundreds of journal articles published on August Wilson's works, and these sources are the usual and customary texts surveyed in an average critique of Wilson's plays to provide useful historical and cultural background for better understanding and contextualizing the time periods. The DLS method relies on similar background sources but goes a step further to additionally prioritize quantitative sources that give statistical data and references for topics and predicaments addressed in the literature. The result is that those who complete a DLS analysis of a work of literature possess a more structured and scientific background of the detailed historical periods and events symbolically represented in the creative work.

The DLS method enables readers and analysts to be more informed and more conversant with acute details of the documented Black experience thus better demarcating the line between creativity and reality that supports realistic applications of the literature toward problem-solving discourses, behaviors, and activism. For example, from the sixteen essays included in the *Cambridge Companion to August Wilson* (2007), collectively the essays make only a couple of references to social science research.[37] In the essay on *King Hedley, II*, Joan Herrington references an article on Black crime, violence, and segregation,[38] and in his essay on *Jitney*, David Krasner references a source on Black residential segregation in Pittsburgh.[39] As an Afrocentric framework for literary criticism the DLS method challenges analysts to not only conduct a literary analysis and critique (which is a type of qualitative exercise) but also to go the extra mile to gather, interpret, and apply the supporting quantitative social science data that makes the literature socially meaningful and relevant. The DLS is compatible with the aspect of dramaturgy wherein for a theatrical production, a historical era specialist provides background for the play, usually as a brief essay in the program. In addition, a dramaturge ensures that the production's artifacts and costumes accurately reflect the play's historical era. The DLS is also compatible with dramaturgical sociology that emphasizes that human behavior is determined by time and place, but adding such elements of dramaturgy to the practice of Afrocentric literary criticism is an original conceptualization.

Sources for Quantitative and Qualitative Exploration of Wilson's Pittsburgh

The DLS expands the expectations of literary criticism by requiring literary analysts to pursue competencies in social-science-oriented quantitative and qualitative data sets that support the content of literary texts. Responding to the Decalogue structure and the cycle's primary setting in Pittsburgh, there is a significant set of localized qualitative sources that are useful in historically, socially, culturally, and politically characterizing this demographic. A brief bibliography includes Black history, museum, and historical society documents on Black life in Pittsburgh,[40] ethnographies on Black Pittsburgh neighborhoods,[41] local Pittsburgh histories that survey

Black and immigrant life and interaction,[42] and documentaries on Black Pittsburgh districts.[43] In addition, online databases and hardcopy versions of newspapers such as the Black publication the *Pittsburgh Courier*, as well as the city press *Pittsburgh Post-Gazette* are necessary references for the study of Wilson's century cycle.

The quantitative and survey sources identified for the DLS application to Parks' *365 Days/365 Days* are the same types of sources used for the DLS approach to Wilson's works. In addition, since Wilson's plays focus on the region of Pittsburgh, the U.S. Census and similar periodic historical surveys such as atlases, almanacs, catalogs, and pricing lists offer useful data for explicating the acute life experience documented in the creative literature.

The DLS and the Century Cycle

Since Wilson's plays are full-length works, compared to the brief, daily theatrical meditations that comprise *365 Days/365 Plays*, they infer greater depth, detail, regional background, and character demographics. The DLS method aids readers in analyzing such details of the Black historical situation, and these details can be explicated only by layering textual analysis with historical and social science data that come from sources not traditionally prioritized in literary analysis. The following section will provide an Afrocentric summary of each play in Wilson's century cycle and a sample of quantitative and qualitative data and analytical directions of inquiry that guide readers in processing the function of the texts.

In the century cycle the Black Pittsburgh community is a symbolic representation of any Black community in the United States, and Wilson layers community, kinship, extended family, history, socioeconomic factors, politics, and cultural tools of survival into overlapping, genealogically rich narratives. The predicaments in Wilson's plays demonstrate to readers and audiences that at any given moment in the twentieth-century Black experience, Black America had to rely on historical and cultural competency in order to frame a vision of survival. The legacy of the century cycle is its emphasis on patterns of Black survival that are dependent upon a constant prioritization of and negotiation of the past with the present and future. In Wilson's plays, the past must be revered, acknowledged, and processed in rituals of healing, epiphany, and communal restoration. In this sense, a death or psychological defeat of a character is not necessarily tragic, as in the popular literary sense; instead there is always an indicator of renewal.

Analyzing each play using the DLS framework shifts interpretive attention away from the play's literary features such as plot, textual stylistics, discursive structures, action, atmosphere, and themes toward an Afrocentric engagement of life experience, historical context and predicament, problem solving, and nature of the struggle for self-determination. Researching and discussing extra-literary aspects of the plays creates a route toward surveying and identifying functional applications of the texts. This process helps to feature and refine the cultural sensibilities of Africans in America, emphasizing that we possess a unique heritage and point of view that must be cultivated with a sense of agency and priority. The DLS highlights matters of history and statistical data that should be active points of reference to use in the daily process of celebrating, practicing, advancing, and defending our culture and heritage. The DLS method, whether in instructional or informal use, benefits greatly from modern Web-based technology, which permits access to a vast amount of data and should be used liberally as a contemporary research tool. The U.S. Census and related statistical sources that share its data are also widely useful and are the general sources for noncited quantitative data given here.

Gem of the Ocean

Set in 1904 Pittsburgh, *Gem* presents the balance of spirituality and survival matters that preoccupied Black America's pursuit of the freedom anticipated in the decades following the end of enslavement. Readers and audiences may be surprised that the strategies of the Underground Railroad and memories of enslavement are so active in the day-to-day matters, identities, crises, and challenges of the characters, but Wilson is accurate in depicting the characters' African-centered and historically aware modes of constantly and critically interpreting the nature of their *pioneering*. Aunt Ester, the century cycle's spiritual matriarch, makes a lasting impression with this first installment of Wilson's vision of African American legacy, and the community's ritualized behaviors of mutual support, in spite of being terrorized by a Black constable, and gives the century cycle a foundation of communalism that links the experiences and identities of people of African descent in the American North and the American South with the gifts and sensibilities of their African heritage and homeland. The play's one of the most prominent themes is that the younger generation has the responsibility to learn, cultivate, and duplicate the practical and spiritual tools of survival that the elders have retained and seek to pass on, in order to sustain the well-being of future generations.

A DLS engagement of *Gem of the Ocean* considers the following:

- In 1900, the Black community in Allegheny County where Pittsburgh is located had a population of 27,753 Blacks.
- In 1900, 3,659 Blacks over the age of ten in Allegheny County were literate. Solly, Aunt Ester's trusted friend and a former conductor for the Underground Railroad, relies on the literate Black Mary to read a letter that arrives from his sister down South.
- Aunt Ester owned her home, which reflects the fact that in 1900 Blacks in Allegheny County paid taxes on property valued at $963,000, which included taxes on homes valued from $2500 to $3300.[44]
- Aunt Ester's address is 1839 Wylie Avenue, and throughout the century cycle this address is commemorated and celebrated as a Black local monument. Aunt Ester's trusted friend and doorkeeper, Eli, answers her door saying "This is a peaceful house." Aunt Ester's home may be a commemoration of the Arthursville section of the Lower Hill neighborhood in Pittsburgh, which was an active Black community of working class and business elite in the early to mid-1800s that is well known for its vigilance in supporting the Underground Railroad.[45]
- The first tragedy of *Gem* is that a Black man is falsely accused of stealing a bucket of nails from the steel mill and is then chased into a cold river where he chooses to die by drowning rather than to remain alive and be condemned for a crime he did not commit. The price of a bucket of nails in 1904 was $2.01. Comparing the cost of the alleged crime to the value of a Black life is a productive philosophical and practical critical exercise introduced by the text.
- Caesar Wilkes, the Black constable, harasses the Black community with the assumption that Blacks are more prone toward criminality. However, in 1904, in the United States, Blacks were the least likely to be placed in prison. Immigrants had higher prison rates per 1,000 than did Blacks: Mexicans 4.7%, Italians 4.4%, Austrians 3.6%, French 3.4%, Canadians 3.0%, Russians 2.8%, Poles 2.7%, and Blacks 2.7%. This is an informative starting point for a discussion of the history of the contemporary prison industrial complex.
- There were 218,227 washerwomen in the United States in 1900. Aunt Ester's protégé, the unmarried Black Mary, was an industrious entrepreneur who took economic advantage of the predicament that Black women were the primary class of women who did this type of work. In an era of uncertain employment opportunities, these types of facts are reminders of the resilience that helped to increase wealth, businesses, and economic opportunities for early Black communities.
- Another entrepreneurial activity in *Gem* is the collection of "pure" (dog feces). This natural by-product was collected and sold to leather tanners to help cure leather products, but in *Gem* for the sake of freedom, Solly, the former Underground Railroad conductor, put it to practical use to

- throw the paddy rollers' hound dogs off the trails of Africans bound for freedom.[46]
- It is widely known that Underground Railroad agents used quilts to convey messages, but in *Gem*, Aunt Ester has a quilt that is a map to the City of Bones, a spiritual place that commemorates the life, spirit, and courage of Africans lost on the Middle Passage and during enslavement. If in 1904 our ancestors retained and utilized practical artifacts that helped the Black community to remember and to heal, then how much more whole should Blacks be in the contemporary era?
- Aunt Ester possesses her actual Bill of Sale confirming how she was sold for $607 dollars as a twelve-year-old girl in Guilford, North Carolina. In reality, Guilford County was a Quaker region that was among the first in the South to support the Underground Railroad.[47] This textual reference reminds the Black community to commemorate its sacred places and to be aware of the narrative of African history in the United States. Also, stating the actual price of sale reminds readers of the actual court records that could be used to support reparations if we choose to calculate actual economic costs of enslavement.
- Selig, the friendly White door-to-door salesman of metal goods, sells Black Mary a frying pan for $2. In 1904, the average price of a steel frying pan was between $0.10 and $0.75. Wilson may have included this as an example of White economic exploitation. Or, if this figure was the author's estimate, this could also be an example of the DLS' usefulness as a tool to identify the possibility of historical inaccuracies in a text. It is also a reminder of the research that goes into creating a literary text that claims to represent an exact historical period.

Joe Turner's Come and Gone

Set in 1911, *Joe Turner* introduces another set of Pittsburgh characters and journeys whose interactions take place in and around a Black-owned boardinghouse whose revolving-door structure places seekers and witnesses in the right place at the right time for renewal and resolution. The play chronicles the Black community's growing social, political, and spiritual pains during the period of wanderings and relocations characterized by the Great Migration and by the predicament that historian Douglas A. Blackmon described as *Slavery by Another Name* (2009), wherein the convict lease system terrorized Black men from the post-Reconstruction South to the early twentieth century.[48] Wilson presents characters in *Joe Turner* who are primarily paired as couples or who are individuals seeking the stability of love, family, and home. With special attention to intergenerational cultural systems, Wilson introduces Bynum, a lone elder and keeper of African traditions, memory, ritual, healing, and song, who brokers the community's journeys toward wholeness.

A DLS engagement of *Joe Turner's Come and Gone* considers:

- In 1910, there were 34,217 Blacks living in Allegheny County where Pittsburgh is located; 25,623 of this population lived directly in the city of Pittsburgh. The traveling salesman Selig, who was also in *Gem of the Ocean*, was familiar with many of the Black communities in Pittsburgh and the surrounding areas that Wilson's characters mention liberally by geographic name.
- $2 in its 1911 value is worth $22.51 today, thus paying $2 per week at the Holly's boardinghouse is the equivalent of $22.51 per week for room and board.
- Most of the characters in *Joe Turner* are part of the Great Migration of Blacks from the South to the North, and Loomis fled the South after being victimized by the convict lease system. Blacks exploited by this system increased from 33% in 1865 to 58.3% in 1867. The system reached a high of 67% African Americans between 1877 and 1879.[49] Wilson's play accurately depicts a condition that predates the contemporary prison industrial complex.
- In 1910, Black homeownership was significantly lower than White home ownership, and it was not until 1970 that Black homeownership reached the same level of 1900 White home ownership, which was 46%.[50] This invokes a discussion about inequities in wealth and lending.
- Seth Holly, the owner of the boardinghouse, was also a blacksmith who sought to start his own company. The U.S. Census indicates that there were only 17 Black blacksmiths in Pittsburgh in 1910. Seth must get a bank loan in order to secure such a business, but he indicates there are racial barriers that hinder this.
- Seth Holly took great pride in owning his own boardinghouse, and *The Pittsburgh Courier* regularly advertised for Black businesses between 1911 and 1913, including running ads for the largest Black hotel in Pittsburgh (1911–1912). In 1900, only 6% of Black men owned their home.[51] In 1910, 10,000 Black women ran boarding houses, which suggests another entrepreneurial industry for Black women beyond domestic work such as being washerwomen.[52]
- African American marriage rates in 1910 were affected by the high mortality rate of Black men and by the limited categories for describing marriage in the *Census*. In the play, the Hollys have been married for a long time; Loomis is separated from his wife due to time on the chain gang that easily could have claimed his life; and Mattie was abandoned by her companion because he feared whatever caused the infant mortality circumstances that claimed her two babies.[53]
- In 1910, Pittsburgh ranked tenth among large U.S. cities in infant mortality.[54] In 1914, the infant mortality rate in Philadelphia was 89 per 1,000. While Mattie believed a curse was the cause of her misfortune, researchers in 1919 suggested that breast feeding is the best way to limit the number of mortalities.[55] This has implications for contemporary advocacy for pre- and postnatal care. National birth registration did not begin until 1915.

- *Joe Turner* introduces the topic of Black marriage and relationships. In the demographic study of marriage in 1910, scholars suggest that Blacks overreported widowhood, likely as a way to protect themselves from the stigmas of bearing children out of wedlock. In addition, high male mortality (suggested by the perils Loomis and Jeremy face with the law) accounts for the fact that in 38% of Black marriages both partners were alive in the postreproduction years. Around 42% of Black husbands were dead by the time their wives reached 45–50 years of age.[56]

Ma Rainey's Black Bottom

Music, dance, and song feature prominently in Wilson's works, and *Ma Rainey*, though the only play of the century cycle not set in Pittsburgh, itemizes the variables Black musicians managed in 1927 in order to synthesize their experiences, struggles, and dreams into music on their own terms. After multiple journeys and travels through the North and the South on a quest for cultural agency, creative freedom, and control of their art forms, the musicians find themselves in a Chicago recording studio where conflicts of gender, race, capitalism, and competing artistic dreams collide with the underlying harsh realities of race in America. In *Joe Turner*, finding one's song was a path toward healing and soul liberation, but in *Ma Rainey*, White America stakes its claim on Black music, which is one more psychological assault on Black cultural freedom that results in a violent explosion of years of suppressed wrath and racialized pain. The prioritization of the Black music tradition in *Ma Rainey* is prologue for subsequent plays in the century cycle that feature the function of the Blues and other Black music forms for Black sanity and survival.

A DLS engagement of *Ma Rainey's Black Bottom* considers[57]:

- Ma Rainey's real name was Gertrude Malissa Nix Pridgett Rainey, and she lived from 1886 to 1939.
- Ma Rainey had a long concert performance career, but her recording career ran from 1923 to 1928. She was signed with Paramount Records, recording over 100 songs.[58]
- The average annual income in the 1920s was $1,236. In the play, Ma Rainey earned $200 for the recording session, while her nephew and the five band members earned $25 each. This indicates how the music industry, though racially challenging, was lucrative employment.
- In the play Ma Rainey indicates that she bought and paid for her car. An average vehicle such as a Ford Model T cost $290 in the 1920s.
- Out of the 5 back-up band members in the play 4 are illiterate, and this is consistent with the U.S. Census data that indicates that only 1,715 of the 58,721 in Cook County (Chicago) over 21 years of age were literate.

The Piano Lesson

Wilson addresses matters of wealth and inheritance in 1936 in the play *Piano Lesson* as he explores siblings' competing objectives for an heirloom piano. The struggle for possession of this piano appears at first to be the result of a Boy Willie's Southern desire to purchase farmland versus a his sister Berniece's Northern ambition to keep the family piano as the perfect complement to a dignified Black Pittsburgh home. However, since the piano is hand-carved by an ancestor with life-like images painfully reminiscent of the family's history from Africa to America, possessing the piano peacefully requires the family to exorcise layers of pain caused by enslavement, separation, death, loss, and damaged relationships.

A DLS engagement of *The Piano Lesson* considers:

- In 1930, the Black population in Allegheny County is 83,324; 54, 983 of this population resides in the city of Pittsburgh.
- In the 1930s, 50% of Blacks were unemployed due to the Great Depression. Boy Willie and his friend Avery drive from Mississippi to Pittsburgh with a truck full of watermelons for sale and with an objective to sell the family piano in order to get money. There is no indication that either man left a job.
- Boy Willie wishes to buy the farm that his enslaved ancestors worked. According to the U.S. Census, in 1930, there were 182,888 farms owned by Blacks in Mississippi, which accounted for over 6 million acres of land.
- Avery, Berniece's suitor, is a preacher but is also an elevator operator, which was a highly coveted job amidst a limited job market for Black men.[59]
- Berniece works as a domestic in a White home, and this is consistent with data revealing that although Black women were 4% of the labor market, they were 30% of domestic workers.
- The play is named after a Romare Bearden painting/collage created in 1983.
- One of the uncles in the play, Doaker, is a Pullman Porter who reads the Black newspaper *The Pittsburgh Courier*. This paper was one of the most widely distributed Black newspapers in the country with a circulation of almost 200,000, and the paper's owner, Robert Lee Vann, depended on Black Pullman Porters to help with national distribution.[60]

Seven Guitars

Continuing to demonstrate how Black life is intricately intertwined with music, Wilson's *Seven Guitars*, set in 1948, chronicles the lives of six neighborhood friends united by their relationships to the deceased local jazz blues recording star, Floyd Barton. What begins as a sentimental celebration of his life evolves into flashback as readers and audiences have the opportunity to witness the vitality and risk-taking musical personality. With a diverse cast of three eccentric men and three vibrant women characters and with a text full of masterfully constructed dialogues on blues philosophies ranging from topics of love, loss, infidelity, death, violence, health, religion, money, to good times, Wilson suggests that the community is characterized by an interdependence between men, women, and music.

A DLS engagement of *Seven Guitars* considers:

- The Black population in 1950 Pittsburgh was 135,340.
- The median income for Pittsburgh was $2,858, which gives an indication of the value of the approximately $1,200 that Floyd Barton stole in a robbery of loan offices.
- In Act One, Scene Five, the characters listen to a radio broadcast of the Black boxing hero, Joe Louis. Louis participates in 72 fights, losing only 3. The line between fiction and reality is emphasized in the Joe Louis fight scene because the play is set two years after the Louis/Billy Conn fight that actually took place on June 19, 1946. The fight was also not at Madison Square Gardens, as the play indicates, but at Yankee Stadium.[61]
- The men in the play engage in a steady stream of debate, including a disagreement over the price of King Edward Cigars. The cigars were originally ten cents when they debuted in 1918, but by the 1930s, the price dropped to five cents because of more efficient technology. The low price led King William cigars to their popularity in the Black community.[62]
- Savoy Records was founded in 1942 and produced many bebop jazz records. This could be a prototype for the company in the play that produced Floyd Barton's hit "That's All Right," which was a 1947 recording in the play.
- The character Hedley is of Caribbean descent and reveres the Haitian hero Toussaint L'Ouverture and the Jamaican hero Marcus Garvey. Hedley is a rare character in the century cycle because he is not of enslaved U.S. African American descent. Hedley's attention to Pan-African heroics is an example of Wilson's work transmitting Black cultural mythology. In 1950, there were 3,480 male foreign-born non-Whites in Pittsburgh.
- Hedley has tuberculosis, and the text mentions the healing properties of goldenseal, or *Hydrastis Canadensis*, which is a plant indigenous to the Americas that was used by Native Americans to heal ulcers, skin diseases, colds, and other infections. This plant is in danger of extinction because of its popular use. By 1950, TB killed 1 in 20 persons infected with the diseases.[63]
- Canewell has a prison record from the Cook County Jail in Chicago, and this prison from the 1920s to the 1950s was believed to be the largest prison in the free world, with over 3,200 inmates.[64]

- Hedley murders Floyd in a schizophrenic state of mind, and does not recall committing a crime. Hedley is one of the many Wilson characters to exhibit a mental health disorder. Although there is no data for Pittsburgh in the play's setting of 1948, a study such as "Mental Disorder and Violent Crime: A 20-Year Cohort Study in New York State, 1968–1988" would inform the long-term patterns of violent crime for the mentally disordered.[65]

Fences

The relationship between the Black male experience and American sport culture frames the plot of *Fences* as the protagonist, Troy Maxson, constructs a highly individualistic philosophy of life based on lifelong challenges with baseball, prison, women, and his sons. Continuing to feature the prominent theme of Black psychology in his plays, in *Fences*, Wilson introduces issues of anger, defeat, personality disorders, posttraumatic stress disorder, mental illness, transference, narcissism, blended families, and male-female roles and responsibilities. *Fences* is the only play that is set in a two-decade time frame. Most of the action occurs in 1957, but the brief Act Two, which functions as an epilogue, takes place eight years later, in 1965.

A DLS engagement of *Fences* considers:

- In 1960, the Black population of Pittsburgh was 160,845.
- Troy Maxson, a garbage collector, confronted his employer about discrimination and was promoted to a driver. Today, a driver earns a national average of $53,877, which would have been approximately $7,030.12 in 1957.
- In 1959, the average income for a Black family like the Maxsons with a male head of household age 45–64, was $4,270 per year. Troy boasts of owning his home, purchasing furniture, bringing home money for his wife as examples of how this small amount permitted his family to have security.
- Troy Maxson is the caretaker for his brother Gabe who was injured in World War II. There were approximately 2,900 African American casualties (dead and injured) in World War II.[66]
- Troy likely played baseball in the second National Negro League, which was established in 1933 and existed through 1948. The League comprised 18 teams. From the play's timeline, it is likely that Troy played for the Pittsburgh Crawfords that was active from 1933 to 1937.[67]
- *Fences* introduces the topic of maternal death during childbirth. Around 1920, 1 in 100 mothers died during childbirth. In 2003, 12 in 100,000 mothers died during childbirth. Maxson's woman on the side, Alberta, died during childbirth. The rate is three times higher for Black mothers

than for White mothers. Causes of this tragedy in the contemporary era are obesity, older age women bearing children, and complications from Caesarian sections such as bleeding, infections, and blood clots.[68]
- Troy's conflict with his son Corey is that Troy refuses to support Corey's opportunity to get a football scholarship to college. Troy's distrust of organized sport is its racism. In the years leading up to the NFL, Blacks were scattered on various teams from 1920 to 1933. By 1934, there were no Black players due to racism in the league that barred Black players until 1946.
- Troy's son Corey chooses to join the Marines after his father blocks his football scholarship. This opportunity was made available as of June 1, 1942, when Howard P. Perry became the first Black man to join the Marine Corps.

Two Trains Running

Every Black community has its entrepreneurs such as its mortician, restaurant owner, and even agent of the informal economy such as a numbers runner, and in *Two Trains Running,* set in 1969 Pittsburgh, Wilson gives the Black community its economic identity. Illustrating the challenges faced by small business owners, by men and women striving to find their place in the workforce and the world, and by the Black community that must continuously battle the disregard of local government in an attempt to preserve the integrity of its neighborhoods, Wilson lets the energy of the Black Freedom Movement and its debates run free in the setting of a Pittsburgh diner.

A DLS engagement of *Two Trains Running* considers:

- In 1970, the Black population of Pittsburgh was 104,904, a drop from 1960 that reflects the fact that many Blacks had relocated into the suburbs.[69] The Allegheny County population (including Pittsburgh) was 134,122.
- The play acknowledges its setting at the end of the Black Freedom Movement by the mention of the forthcoming Malcolm X birthday (May 19, 1925) march and the possibility of riots. In Pittsburgh from April 5 to April 12, 1968, there were riots after the assassination of Martin Luther King, Jr. which accounts for 505 fires, 926 arrests, and 1 death.[70]
- The central conflict of the play is the City of Pittsburgh's heavy-handed objective to buy out small Black businesses at low compensation in order to redevelop the mostly Black Lower Hill District neighborhood. The redevelopment, while paving the way for the construction of the Civic/Mellon Arena, displaced a significant part of the Hill community.[71]
- Three of Wilson's plays—*Two Trains Running*, *Jitney*, and *Radio Golf*—address the legacy of the redevelopment of the Lower Hill District that indicates the legacy of its catastrophic and monumental meaning to Blacks in Pittsburgh: 1,300 buildings were destroyed over 95 acres of the

district, and 8,000 residents were displaced. This represents 1,239 Black families and 312 White families; 35% went to public housing, 31% to private rentals, and 8% of families secured their own homes. Approximately 90 families refused to move and ended up living in poor housing. This decade-long activity was funded by $17.4 million in redevelopment funds.[72]
- The character Sterling (who reappears with communally redemptive value in *Radio Golf*) earns $1.25 per hour at his construction job. The average yearly salary for this period $4,743, and minimum wage was $1.00 an hour. As a recently imprisoned citizen, Sterling was making more than the minimum wage, which would be a $2,600 yearly salary.
- Risa inflicts herself with "cutting" wounds as a form of self-injury that helps her to resist the way men objectify her. Some suggest that Pittsburgh's Western Psychiatric Institute, founded in the 1950s, would be a source of help for her because it offers treatment for ailments such as anxiety and other more serious forms of mental illness. It is a result of abuse, depression, and trauma. Risa's condition that affects many teens and mostly girls could be illuminated by the study, "A Feminist Qualitative Study of Female Self-Mutilation."[73]

Jitney

Set in 1977, the dramatic action of *Jitney* takes place in a storefront gypsy cab, or *informal* cab, with business comprising Black male drivers, and the play helps readers and audiences consider the intergenerational nature of Black male survival. Wilson created an ensemble of elder, middle-aged, and young Black men whose competing values, assumptions, and philosophies about the notion of "progress" sustain the play's plot and meaning. Wilson continues to feature characters who struggle with the legal system, prison, and local politics, as well as with more personal matters such as fathering and nurturing intimate relationships. At this point in the century cycle, Wilson has introduced the challenges that face Black America, including options of education, military service, careers, home ownership, raising children, and urban crisis.

A DLS engagement of *Jitney* considers:

- In 1980, the Black population of the Pittsburgh metropolitan area was 178,435.[74]
- The jitney industry is an example of Black citizens taking care of the transportation needs of their own communities during an era when legally incorporated taxi and cab companies were afraid to service Black neighborhoods.[75]
- One of the main characters dies in an accident at the steel mill. There were 42 deaths at the mills between 1900 and 2000.[76]

- The youngest jitney driver, Youngblood, worked several jobs in order to purchase a home for his family under the G.I. Bill, which was established in 1944. Around 1970, only 18.9% of African Americans in Pittsburgh owned a home, and the average home value was $12,500. This figure gives an idea of how much money Youngblood had to save in order to make a down payment and explains his willingness to spend his family's grocery money as a sacrifice. Youngblood's character is a model of thrift and hard work that competes with the negative stereotypes of young Black males.
- The men in *Jitney* represent remarkable personal histories, especially Booster who spent 20 years in prison. In the late 1950s, Booster represented the post *Brown v. Board of Education* dreams of the Black Pittsburgh Community. He won the Buhl Planetarium's Science Fair three years in a row and earned a full scholarship to University of Pittsburgh in the late 1950s. Wilson documented the Buhl Planetarium (likely misspelling it Buhel for liability reasons). The Buhl Science Fair was home of the Pittsburgh Regional Science and Engineering Fair started in 1940 for 6th through 12th graders and is the third oldest science fair in the country.[77]
- The crime that landed Booster in prison for 20 years was murder. After his university girlfriend, ashamed to tell her father that she was dating a Black young man, accused Booster of rape, he went to her house and shot her in the face. In the play, Booster was released from jail in 1977, but in reality one year later in 1978 psychologist Panos D. Bardis published a scale to measure "liberalism of attitudes toward dating" that included questions on interracial relationships.[78] If utilized on university campuses, this tool could be a way of measuring racial attitudes before racial fears and insecurities escalate into false accusations of rape that instigate murder.
- Data from the 1970s documents the need for jitneys in the Black Hill district, but even as late as 2004, the University of Pittsburgh's Center for Social and Urban Research noted that 48.6% of Black households in Pittsburgh do not have a vehicle, compared to 22.5% of White households.[79]

King Hedley II

King Hedley II is likely one of Wilson's most painful productions because it offers a hardened view of the state of Black urban inheritance during the Reagan years, namely 1987. Unlike the earlier plays that offered morsels of hope and renewal, *King Hedley II* reveals urban despair with its emphasis on the death of the century cycle's matriarch Aunt Ester, gun violence and crime, mothers fearing their sons, unemployment, alcoholism, and insecurity masked as bravado based on desperate distortions of the past. In this installment of the century cycle, Black music even seems to have lost its power to soothe, calm, and invoke a sense of communalism.

A DLS engagement of *King Hedley II* considers:

- In 1990, the Black population of the Pittsburgh metropolitan area was 178,500.[80]
- In the 1980 presidential election, only 7 million out of a total of 17 million eligible Black voters voted. This low Black voter participation contributed to Reagan's victory over Jimmy Carter.[81]
- The Reagan era that is the backdrop of the despair in *King Hedley II* was a period of sustained losses for Black communities like Pittsburgh. The federal government reduced subsidies that had supported meals served to 94,000 schools throughout the country and reclassified nutrition standards in order to reduce federal expenditures. For example, it was during this period that ketchup and pickle relish became classified as vegetables.[82]
- In Reagan's first year of office the real median income of Black families dropped by 5.2% compared to the 1980 figure.[83] His White supremacist policies affected all areas of Black life, particularly employment and human services.
- King and his friend Mister have a dream of saving and securing money in order to open a Kung-Fu- themed video store. This detail reflects the era's superlative as a prime season for the cults of Bruce Lee and Chuck Norris, as well as feature films such as the *Karate Kid*.[84] However, the escapism embodied in the characters' commitment to this venture suggests a level of escapism that could be better explored by Black psychology research.
- The rate of African American male homicide escalated from 37 per 100,000 in 1960 to 65 per 100,000 in 1980.[85] In the play's timeframe, two African American men are killed.
- In the 1980s, 10% of Black men ages 18–54 were in prison. King and his mother's boyfriend both served jail time. Wilson's century cycle is responsive to the realism of prison's effect on the lives of Black men, their families, and their community at large.
- Aunt Ester dies in this play, and her age is estimated, some say symbolically, as over 300 years old. Regardless of the symbolism or actually age, King informs the cast that they cannot precisely say when her funeral will be held. "They won't give back the body. They trying to figure out what made her live so long."[86] While families may request autopsies and while suspicious deaths may cause the coroner to withhold the body of a loved one, it is an act of exploitation for the coroner to keep Aunt Ester's body indefinitely. This reference makes Harriet Washington's book *Medical Apartheid* (2008) a background source for the topic of Black rights over our bodies.[87]

Radio Golf

The self-destructive and painful glimpse of 1980s Black life that Wilson captured in *King Hedley II* is followed by an aggressively bourgeois, or middle class, version of 1997 Pittsburgh urban renewal. The plot maneuvers through a contemporary landscape of seemingly Black-controlled urban capitalism and gentrification symbolized in the play by plans to build luxury homes and businesses such as a Starbucks coffee shop and a Barnes & Noble bookstore in the historically Black Hill District neighborhood. This version of progress is replete with wealthy Blacks in high corporate positions and those who have the influence and support to even hold public office. However, forces of race, class, and self-hatred erupt into contradictions that threaten this version of urban renewal. Inevitably, Wilson suggests that urban renewal is also a state of consciousness that depends on the community's ability to duplicate the spirituality and communal concern for the souls of Pittsburgh's Black community embodied in the memory of Aunt Ester and symbolized by her dilapidated, yet landmark home at 1839 Wylie Avenue. Aunt Ester's spirit pervades this final installment of Wilson's century cycle in order to remind readers and audiences that her interpretation of the nature of African life transplanted to American soil is the cultural behavioral prototype because it provides a powerful and sustaining legacy of hope, heritage, living memory, well-being, virtue, and decency that cannot be defeated.

A DLS engagement of *Radio Golf* considers:

- In 2000, the Black population in the Pittsburgh metropolitan area was 200,229, numbers well capable of supporting the election of a Black mayor, which the beginning of the play indicates is Harmond Wilks' destiny.[88]
- In 1997, 8.1% of the University of Pittsburgh's students were Black.
- Blacks participated in golf tournaments as early as the 1890s, and the Black community gained familiarity with the sport as the Black press featured instructional columns on golf. Responding to discrimination that prevented them from sharing White-owned facilities, Black golfers established their own clubs.[89] In 1956, the U.S. Supreme Court ended the segregation of public accommodations such as golf courses, playgrounds, public parks, and beaches.
- The play's 1997 setting is approximately 25 years after the end of the Vietnam War, but Harmond still bears the scars of losing his twin brother to the War. During the Vietnam War, Blacks were 11% of the U.S. population but represented 12.6% of the soldiers involved in the War effort.
- As a real estate developer, Harmond's character represents the 140 Black real estate developers in Pittsburgh, as cited in the 2000 U.S. Census. His wife, Mame, represents the 34 Black Public Relations professionals indicated by the 2000 U.S. Census. Wilson's middle-class protagonists are realistic version of the Black elite.

- Roosevelt, Hammond's Black friend and redevelopment partner, is skeptical of the working-class Black population and assumes them to be criminal. A study titled "Development of Crime Forecasting and Mapping Systems for Use by Police in Pittsburgh, PA, and Rochester, NY, 1990–2001" corroborates some of Roosevelt's fears as it documents the types of crimes (burglary, trespassing, liquor law violations, motor vehicle theft, vandalism, etc.) that he fears.[90] Ironically, this study also indicts the types of White collar crimes in which Roosevelt either participates or condones, such as embezzlement, fraud, forgery, and receiving stolen property.
- When Harmond realizes that Aunt Ester's home was obtained fraudulently, he is reminded that the White supremacist power structure controls the processes of the courts with frivolous favoritism. The courts delay ruling on Harmond's requested injunction. As a policy matter, this inclusion in Wilson's play confirms the trends of delays in urban trial courts in Pittsburgh documented in the study on "Caseflow Management and Delay Reduction in Urban Trial Courts of the United States, 1979, 1983–1985" in which Pittsburgh is one of several U.S. cities evaluated for its inefficiency.[91]
- The play mentions Starbucks, Whole Foods, and Barnes and Noble as indicators of contemporary urban renewal. There are ten Starbucks coffee houses in Pittsburgh; eight are located downtown, and two are isolated in other regions of the city; there is only one Whole Foods store and five Barnes and Noble book stores in Pittsburgh.

Limitations of the DLS

The limitation of the DLS is that it may not be appropriate for all literary texts, and the first aspect of the procedural treatment of Black literature addresses this limitation by insisting that readers demarcate the line between fiction and social-science-inspired narrative. One of the functions of literature is to entertain; its other functions are to inform, to inspire a critique of society, to inspire change, and to please the senses with the beauty of language and imagery. If a text is abstract, experimental, or structured as extreme fantasy that significantly diverges from realism, the DLS is not the appropriate framework. The DLS model may also be appropriate for use with single works of literature, provided that it is structured at least informally based on an identifiable and measurable unit of time.

Intellectual/Academic Benefits of DLS

The critiques of Karenga (1993) and Stewart (2005) warn of the imbalance that occurs when either literature or the social sciences are studied in a vacuum. Their initial observations drive the suggestions inherent in the DLS model, and the objective of this model is to formally suggest procedures for merging the study of literature and the social sciences. In conclusion, I wish to review several benefits, observations, questions, and/or recommendations that are related to the application of the DLS model.

Benefits

- Students get exposure to social science research: the need for it, its complexity, the value of statistics; the bias of statistics; the factual information that will support activism in the discipline.
- Creating collaborative exercises between literature courses and social science research is an excellent take-home assessment or project that permits students to respond to literature courses in a more functional way.
- The model's insistence on the compatibility of literature and social science supports university and department demands to use technology in the classroom beyond word processing for writing and revision assignments.
- Students will be inspired to use literature as a catalyst to study current event and historical topics such as the history of the prison system or mental health conditions, topics that are introduced liberally in both Parks' collection and Wilson's century cycle.
- The model gives departments support in demanding proper classification as a social science discipline rather than categorization as part of the humanities.
- The model reiterates the discipline's *multidimensionality,* a term that more appropriately describes what was previously itemized as "interdisciplinary."

Questions/Observations

- Does this model suggest that there should be a collapse of the distinctive curriculum track classifications of "cultural/aesthetic" and "social/behavioral"?
- The model explicitly identifies the difference between taking a literature course in an Africana Studies setting and an English, Comparative Literature, or Postcolonial Literature setting.
- The model encourages students to exhaust all possible routes of research from the formal to the trial-and-error, particularly online and web-based sources and databases that are easily accessible from home, work, and play environments beyond a library setting.
- The model reiterates the significance of the category of "Socioeconomic Realism" suggested in comparative Black literature studies.[92]

Inevitably, the DLS approach is an Afrocentric tool for analyzing the function and value of all Black literature in more social science and scientific ways, as needed, which keeps the discipline's practitioners aware of and naturally conversant with data that inform the life experience, the history, and the public policy concerns of Black people.

Notes

1. Maulana Karenga, *Introduction to Black Studies*, 2nd ed. (Los Angeles: University of Sankore Press, 1993), 428–9.
2. James Stewart, "Social Science and Systematic Inquiry in Africana Studies: Challenges for the Twenty-First Century," in *Afrocentric Traditions*, ed. James L. Conyers, Jr. (New Brunswick: Transaction Publishers, 2005), 87.
3. Ibid.
4. Ibid.
5. See a summative review essay by Kingsley Widmer, "The Sociology of Literature?" *Studies in the Novel* 11 (1979): 104.
6. See Jeffrey Williams. "Toward a Sociology of Literature: An Interview with John Guillory," *Minnesota Review* 61/61 (2004): 95–110, which surveys Guillory's treatment of the sociology of literature in terms of canon formation, the canon of theory, and possibilities of relating the literary to the political. They discuss Guillory's *Cultural Capital* (University of Chicago Press, 1993), but their ideas have little to do with African American literature.
7. See William B. Warner and Clifford Siskin, "Stopping Cultural Studies," in *Profession 2008*, the journal of opinion for the Modern Language Association of America, pp. 94–107.
8. See Chantal B. Dalton, "Teaching Black Literature to Undergraduates: The Problem of a Sense of Perspective," *Black American Literature Forum* 11 (1977): 102.
9. The next several features in italics are aspects of Afrocentric work identified in Molefi K. Asante's "African Betrayals and African Recovery for a New Future," in *Africa in the 21st Century*, ed. Ama Mazama (2007), which offers methodological categorizations . *Tradition and innovation* ensures that "preservation and generation are instruments of the interplay of change and continuity" (p. 77).
10. Asante offers *location in time and space* to address "discovering chronology and geography as keys to interpretation" (p. 77)
11. Asante views this as "enhancing and promoting critical thinking in the area of effective human behavior" (p. 77).
12. Asante's identifies this as using "science and technology to create and enrich the community" (p. 77)
13. Suzan-Lori Parks, *365 Days/365 Plays* (New York: Theatre Communications Group, 2006).
14. See Philip C. Kolin, "Redefining the Way Theatre Is Created and Performed: The Radical Inclusion of Suzan-Lori Parks' *365 Days/365 Plays*," *Journal of Dramatic Theory and Criticism* 22 (2007) and Rebecca Ann Rugg, "Dramaturgy as Devotion," *PAJ: A Journal of Performance and Art* 91 (2009): 68–79.
15. Damaso Reyes, "Public Theater Debuts Suzan-Lori Parks' *365 Days/365 Plays*," *New York Amsterdam News*, November 30, 2006, 20.
16. Ibid.
17. Elizabeth Brown-Guillory, "Black Women Playwrights: Exorcising Myths," *Phylon* 48 (1987): 239.
18. Suzan-Lori Parks, *The Death of the Last Black Man in the Whole Entire World*, in *The America Play and Other Works* (New York: Theatre Communications Group, 1994).

19. Suzan-Lori Parks, *Venus* (New York: Dramatists Play Service, 1998).
20. Suzan-Lori Parks, *Topdog/Underdog* (New York: Theatre Communications Group, 2001).
21. Brown-Guillory, "Black Women Playwrights," 239.
22. Parks explains her inspiration and method in the Introduction to *365 Plays/365 Days*.
23. Bonnie Metzgar and Suzan-Lori Parks discuss the 365 National Festival on p. 401 of *365 Days/365 Plays*.
24. August Wilson, *Gem of the Ocean* (New York: Theatre Communications Group, 2006).
25. August Wilson, *Joe Turner's Come and Gone* (New York: Plume, 1988).
26. August Wilson, *Ma Rainey's Black Bottom* (New York: Plume, 1981).
27. August Wilson, *The Piano Lesson* (New York: Plume, 1990).
28. August Wilson, *Seven Guitars* (New York: Plume, 1997).
29. August Wilson, *Fences* (New York: Plume, 1986).
30. August Wilson, *Two Trains Running* (New York: Plume, 1993).
31. August Wilson, *Jitney* (Woodstock, NY: Overlook Press, 2003).
32. August Wilson, *King Hedley II* (New York: Theatre Communications Group, 2005).
33. August Wilson, *Radio Golf* (New York: Theatre Communications Group, 2007).
34. August Wilson and Bill Moyers, "August Wilson: Playwright," in *Conversations with August Wilson*, ed. Jackson R. Bryer and Mary C. Hartig (Jackson: University Press of Mississippi, 1988), 68–69.
35. Ibid., 74.
36. Ibid., 74.
37. Christopher Bigsby, ed. *The Cambridge Companion to August Wilson* (New York: Cambridge University Press, 2007).
38. Joan Herrington, "King Hedley, II: In the Midst of All this Death," in *The Cambridge Companion to August Wilson,* ed. Christopher Bigsby (New York: Cambridge University Press, 2007), 169–82. Herrington references Edward S. Shihadeh and Nicole Flynn, "Segregation and Crime: The Effect of Black Social Isolation on the Rates of Black Urban Violence," *Social Forces* 74:4 (June 1996): 1325.
39. David Krasner, "*Jitney,* Folklore and Responsibility," in *The Cambridge Companion to August Wilson*, ed. Christopher Bigsby (New York: Cambridge University Press, 2007), 158–68. Krasner references Joe T. Darden, *Afro-Americans in Pittsburgh: The Residential Segregation of a People* (Lexington, MA: Lexington Books, 1973).
40. See Laurence A. Glasco, ed. *The WPA History of the Negro in Pittsburgh* (Pittsburgh: University Press of Pittsburgh, 2004); Ira V. Brown, *The Negro in Pennsylvania History* (University Park: Penn State University, 1970); and David McBride, ed. *Blacks in Pennsylvania History: Research and Educational Perspectives* (Harrisburg: Commonwealth of Pennsylvania Historical and Museum Commission, 1983).
41. See Melvin D. Williams, *On the Street Where I Lived* (New York: Holt, Rhinehart, & Winston, 1981).
42. See John Bodnar, Roger Simon, and Michael P. Weber, *Lives of Their Own: Blacks, Italians, and Poles in Pittsburgh, 1900–1960* (Urbana: University of Illinois Press, 1982).
43. See Doug Bolin and Christopher Moore, *Wylie Avenue Days* (Pittsburgh: WQED Multimedia, 2007).
44. Helen A. Tucker, "Negroes of Pittsburgh," *Chanties and the Commons* 2 (1909): 599–608.
45. Ervin Dyer, "Arthursville Abolitionists Ran Underground Railroad through Pittsburgh," *Pittsburgh Post-Gazette*, http://www.post-gazette.com/blackhistorymonth/19990222arthur.asp.

46. "The Worst Jobs in History: The Pure Collector," www.discoverychannel.co.uk/history/worst_jobs/victorian/index.shtml.
47. See Gertrude Beal, "The Underground Railroad in Guilford County," *Southern Friend Journal of North Carolina Friends Society* 2 (1980): 18–28.
48. Douglas A. Blackmon, *Slavery by Another Name: The Re-Enslavement of Black Americans from the Civil War to World War II* (New York: Anchor, 2009).
49. Randall G. Shelden, "Slavery in the Third Millennium, Part II," *The Black Commentator*, http: http://www.blackcommentator.com/142/142_slavery_2.html.
50. See William J. Collins and Robert A. Margo, "Race and Home Ownership: A Century-Long View," *Explorations in Economic History* 38 (2001): 68–92.
51. Ibid.
52. See Mansel G. Blackford, *A History of Small Business in America* (Chapel Hill: University of North Carolina Press, 2003).
53. Samuel H. Preston, Suet Lim, and S. Philip Morgan, "African-American Marriage in 1910: Beneath the Surface of Census Data," *Demography* 29 (1992): 1–15
54. S. J. Kleinberg, *The Shadow of the Mills: Working-Class Families in Pittsburgh, 1870–1907* (Pittsburgh: University of Pittsburgh Press, 1991).
55. William Davis, "Infant Mortality in the Registration Area for Births," paper presented at the Vital Statistics Unit of the American Public Health Association, October 29, 1919, http: www.ajph.org/cgi/reprint/10/4/338/pdf.
56. Preston, Lim, and Morgan, "African-American Marriage in 1910," 2.
57. Depending on the literature's era, subject matter, detail, and setting, some entries, like *Ma Rainey's Black Bottom,* will have fewer demographic and quantitative topics to explore.
58. Sandra R. Leib, *Mother of the Blue: A Study of Ma Rainey* (Massachusetts: University of Massachusetts Press, 1983).
59. Kimberley L. Phillips, *Alabama North: African-American Migrants, Community, and Working Class Activism in Cleveland, 1915–45* (Champaign: University of Illinois Press, 1999).
60. Doug Bolin and Christopher Moore, *Wiley Avenue Days* (documentary) (2007).
61. Special thanks to Colin Roche-Dutch, one of my student research assistants whose application of the DLS highlighted this discrepancy.
62. Swisher International Group, Inc. "The Great Depression," http://www.fundinguniverse.com/company-histories/Swisher-International-Group-Inc-Company-History.html
63. World Health Organization, "Tuberculosis," http://www.who.int/mediacentre/factsheets/fs104/en/.
64. "Cook County Jail History," http://www.cookcountysheriff.org/doc/doc_history.html.
65. See Henry J. Steadman, Pamela Clark Robbins, and Robin Crincione, "Mental Disorder and Violent Crime: A 20-Year Cohort Study in New York State, 1968–1988" (New York: United States Department of Justice/National Institute of Justice, 1993), ICPSR No. 9978.
66. "Picture This: World War II/Post War Era: 1940s–1950s," http://www.museumca.org/picturethis/4_4.html. Source indicates that the 202 injured and 233 killed in the Port Chicago explosion accounted for 15% of Black war casualties, which puts total war estimates at 2,900.
67. Negro League Baseball Players Association (NLBPA), "Negro League History," http://www.nlbpa.com/pittsburg_crawfords.html.
68. Associated Press, "More U.S. Women Dying in Childbirth," http://www.msnbc.msn.com/id/20427256/.

69. Philip S. Klein and Ari Hoogenboom, *A History of Pennsylvania* (University Park: Penn State University Press, 1980), 494.
70. Carnegie Library of Pittsburgh, "The Hill District: History," http://www.clpgh.org/exhibit/neighborhoods/hill/hill_n4.html
71. Ibid.
72. Ibid.
73. Rosemary L. Ellis, "A Feminist Qualitative Study of Self-Mutilation" (Master's thesis, Virginia Tech, 2002).
74. Data from http://diversitydata.sph.harvard.edu/Data/Profiles/Show.aspx?loc=977&notes=True&cat=1.
75. Carlos Hardimon, "Jitney Taxi Service Keeps Community Moving Ahead," *Pittsburgh Courier* (July 1978).
76. Liz Hayes, "Workers Remembered: Marker Pays Tribute to Ludlum Employees," *Pittsburgh Live* (2003), http://www.pittsburghlive.com/x/valleynewsdispatch/news/s_131807.html.
77. Photo Album, The Carnegie Science Center, http://www.buhlplanetarium3.tripod.com/photoalbumCSC.htm#ScienceFair (Retrieved on July 31, 2009).
78. Panos T. Bardis, "Dating Scale (A)" (Toledo: Donna Bardis, 1978).
79. Glenn May, "Jitneys Remain in the Driver's Seat," *Tribune-Review*, June 20, 2004.
80. Data from http://diversitydata.sph.harvard.edu/Data/Profiles/Show.aspx?loc=977&notes=True&cat=1.
81. Manning Marable, *Race, Reform, and Rebellion: The Second Reconstruction in Black America, 1945–1980* (Jackson: University Press of Mississippi, 1991), 180.
82. Ibid., 183.
83. Ibid., 183.
84. John G. Avildsen, *Karate Kid* (Culver City, CA: Sony Pictures, 1984).
85. AA Studies, "Contemporary African American Thought: The 1980s." http://www.columbia.edu/itc/marable/c1001/weeks/week12.html.
86. Wilson, *King Hedley II*, 85.
87. Harriet A. Washington, *Medical Apartheid: The Dark History of Medical Experimentation on Black Americans from Colonial Times to the Present* (New York: Harlem Moon, 2008).
88. Data from http://www.diversitydata.sph.harvard.edu/Data/Profiles/Show.aspx?loc=977&notes=True&cat=1.
89. Pittsburgh Public Theatre, "Education Resource Guide: *Radio Golf*," http://www.ppt.org/documents/RG%20resource%20guide.pdf.
90. Jacqueline Cohen and Wilpen L. Gorr, "Development of Crime Forecasting Mapping Systems for Use by Police in Pittsburgh, PA and Rochester, NY, 1990–2001" (2006), ICPSR No. 4545.
91. Barry Mahoney, "Caseflow Management and Delay Reduction in Urban Trial Courts of the United States, 1973, 1983–1985" (National Center for State Courts), ICPSR No. 9918.
92. Christel Temple, "Community, Folk Culture, and Socioeconomic Realism," in *Literary Spaces: Introduction to Comparative Black Literature* (Durham: Carolina Academic Press, 2007).

2

Africana Ethnography: How Homeland Eritrea Monitors Its American Diaspora

Dawit O. Woldu and Irvin H. Bromall

The Three Faces of Eritrea

Eritrea presents three interrelated faces to today's world: homeland Eritrea, diaspora Eritrea, and cyber Eritrea.[1] To enter homeland Eritrea is an Orwellian experience of the first order. Independent since 1991 after a 30-year war for liberation from Ethiopia, a ruthless dictatorship rules an intimidated and terrorized citizenry, exercising control over nearly every aspect of its citizens' lives. This uncompromisingly repressive state of approximately 6 million people[2] borders the Red Sea in the Horn of Africa. It is governed by an all-powerful president, Isaias Afwerki, a hero of the revolution, and the only leader the country has ever known, and the ruling Eritrean People's Front for Democracy and Justice (PFDJ).

A recent Human Rights Watch report states that

> Eritrea is one of the world's youngest countries and has rapidly become one of the most repressive. There is no freedom of speech, no freedom of movement, no freedom of worship. . . . Dissent is not tolerated. Any criticism or questioning of government policy is ruthlessly punished.[3]

This bleak view of Eritrea is consistently echoed by the U.S. Department of State's annual human rights reports[4] and by nongovernmental organizations (NGOs) such as Freedom House[5] and Amnesty International.[6]

This chapter is dedicated to a great friend, collaborator, and a sincere philanthropist, the late Dr. Irvine Bromall.

In its 2012 Annual Report, the U.S. Commission on International Freedom again, as it has for eight consecutive years, recommended designation of Eritrea as a country of particular concern because of its stifling of religious freedom.[7] On the 2011 Ibrahim Index of African Governance, Eritrea scored 47th of the 53 countries examined.[8] Reporters without Borders ranked Eritrea the last in its examination of press freedoms in 179 states.[9] No known reputable agency or NGO views the current situation, especially the status of human rights in Eritrea, in any manner other than as portrayed by these sources.

Diaspora[10] Eritrea is a worldwide-scattered entity, comprising about 1¼ million people,[11] with more than half concentrated in states neighboring Eritrea and the remaining numbers in the West, primarily in the urban areas of North America, Europe, and Australia. Reasons motivating Eritreans to seek a better life elsewhere are many. The seemingly never-ending war for liberation from Ethiopia and the later border conflict with that country constituted a major impetus. Internal political conflict, especially between revolutionary factions, played a part. Political repression and general economic hardship were always present. Now, the dreaded national service is a driving push factor. An estimated 3,000 persons, especially youth, flee or desert this "service for life" on a monthly basis.[12] Today, about one in five Eritreans live abroad, many of whom fled before independence was gained. According to UN High Commission for Refugees statistics, since its inception as a state, 252,000 refugees have left Eritrea and have been accorded refugee status by the UN.[13] Such a level of exodus is a by-product of homeland Eritrean political repression, social control efforts, and stagnating economic conditions.

The world of cyber Eritrea is the dynamic pulse of the Eritrean people as well as the official voice of the homeland regime. It is the source of factual information and opinions of all shades—informed and uninformed, and contemporary Eritrean thought. It comprises a wide array of websites, including the official voice of the regime (i.e., http://www.shabait.com), many opposition sites (e.g., http://asmarino.com, assenna.com, http://awate.com), religious sites (e.g., http://tewahdo.rg;http://www.eritreantewahdo.org/), special interest sites (e.g., http://eritreanrefugees.org/index.html), and many others dedicated to differing causes.

Eritreans in America: Population Numbers, Estimates, and Guesses

The Census Bureau estimated that in 2010 there were 29,681 of Eritrean births in the United States.[14] This was an increase over the Bureau's 2000 estimate of 17,520.[15] Before the 2010 data was released, Tricia Redeker Hepner, a scholar specializing in Eritrea and the Eritrean diaspora, and other specialists, argued that the number more closely approximated 100,000. Hepner explains their reasoning:

> This high[er] figure allows for undocumented migrants, unprocessed asylum seekers, children born in the United States who identify as ethnically Eritrean, and those who did not participate in either the Eritrean referendum [2003 Eritrean Embassy estimates placed the number at 30,000–40,000] of the 2000 Census.[16]

Applying the same reasoning to today's estimate, and adjusting for refinements in the Census Bureau's enumerating techniques, the current Eritrean-American population may well be around 150,000.[17]

In the United States, the largest concentrations of Eritreans are found in several major population centers, especially the Atlanta, Baltimore-Washington, Dallas-Fort Worth, and San Francisco-Oakland Bay metropolitan areas. Sizeable clusters of Eritreans are also present in the Chicago, Columbus, Denver, Indianapolis, Los Angeles, Minneapolis, Philadelphia, and San Diego areas. Small Eritrean enclaves exist elsewhere, scattered throughout the American homeland.[18]

American Diaspora Is not a Cross-section of Eritrea

By and large, the Eritrean diaspora in the United States is not a reflection of the sending society.[19] In homeland Eritrea, there is a nearly even division between Christians and Muslims. Highlanders, mainly Tigrinya and mostly Christians, and persons from the lowlands, many of who are Muslim, comprise a majority of the Eritrean population. Although the major ethnic group is the Tigrinya, eight other groups too are officially recognized. Tigrinya and Arabic are the major languages although many speak Amharic, the dominant language of Ethiopia. For many students, English is the language of instruction. In the United States, Christians, highlanders, persons of Tigrinya ethnicity, and Tigrinya speakers predominate.

Characteristics of the Diaspora

First-generation Eritrean-Americans share a memory—itself shaped by time and colored by a new land and culture—of Eritrea. Although many Eritrean-Americans experienced firsthand the liberation struggle, many more have memories of that time and these constitute the stories that are passed on to successive generations. In those revolutionary times, Eritrean society coalesced around the struggle. Old loyalties to ethnic groups and region, many religiously driven, never fully faded away, but were displaced by a growing sense of common struggle, shared sacrifice, and Eritrean consciousness.

The American ambassador to Eritrea from October 2007 to July 2010, Ronald K. McMullen, describes the Eritrean diaspora in America as

> a complex mixture of asylum seekers who fled during the Liberation War, political outcasts who were shunned during the country's formative years, Eritrean youth (some of whom have never seen Eritrea and others who visit mainly during the summer), and current-day refugees fleeing an oppressive regime and increasing poverty levels.[20]

Describing a major diasporic trait, interconnection with the homeland, Hepner implicitly introduces the concept of collective social memory:

> As a population, Eritreans remain strongly oriented towards their home country and share a well-developed national identity, which emerged out of Eritrea's three-decade struggle for independence. Second- and third-generation Eritreans have a more complex identity, which recognizes not only their Eritrean heritage but also their identities as African Americans. The experience of Eritrean Americans highlights how the sending country and government continue to be influential in the lives of individuals and their changing communities in the United States.[21]

Once transplanted to the United States, the Eritrean community—before 1991 not recognized as such, but lumped as Ethiopian—banded together around the support of the revolutionary struggle at home. Those who were fighters, the *yike'alo* ("those who can do all things" in Tigrinya), were exalted, deified, and viewed as role models. Community efforts to further the revolutionary cause at home became an ever-present force in the lives of these new Eritrean-Americans. Much of the collective time of the nascent community—urban pioneers, coming as economic beginners, many from rural backgrounds, and from a society in which communal values were paramount—was devoted to raising funds for the war effort in the homeland. The reality of the Eritrea they had known, and its liberation struggle, stood in stark contrast with the urban America in which they now generally found themselves.

Like newcomers to new lands everywhere, Eritrean-Americans sought out kinship and support groups, looking inward to their own communities. Their bonds as Eritreans in America were forged by ties to and memories of the homeland, the Tigrinya language, Eritrean culture, the Orthodox Church or mosques, and their position in the American socioeconomic structure. In this matrix of cultural bonds and ethnic institutions, each element played a role in providing a safe haven to these newly arrived pioneers, linking their reality of today with that of the past.[22]

Attitudes toward the Regime Held the American Diaspora

If the general diaspora population is united in its patriotic feelings, selective remembrances of the Eritrea homeland, adherence to its culture, and the Tigrinya language, there is little consensus and a high degree of fragmentation on political issues, especially the future of the Eritrean state.

Degrees of support for the current regime range from the enthusiastically supportive through the passively neutral to the strongly opposed. There is no real evidence of an organized and well-funded diaspora political movement for change in homeland Eritrea as we now see developing in the diaspora Ethiopian community where there is significant support of forces in opposition to the current regime. Since many Eritreans in diaspora still have family and hold other stakes in current Eritrea, and these interests are at the regime's mercy, there is little incentive for vocal opposition or expression of antiregime sentiments. It would appear that the course of least resistance for any Eritrean in diaspora is simply to tend one's own garden.[23]

Legacy from the Past: A Political/Historical Cleavage

A continuing cleavage in the Eritrean diaspora is between members of the two major revolutionary groups in Eritrea. The oldest, the Eritrean Liberation Front (ELF), launched the revolution in 1961; the second, the Eritrean Peoples Liberation Front (EPLF), eventually supplanted the ELF after intermittent civil war between the two groups from 1972 to 1980, and carried the revolution to a successful conclusion. The EPLF morphed into the ruling party, the PFDJ. The ELF was seen as tilting toward lowland and Muslim interests; the EPLF was seen as a more inclusive body. Both were Marxist oriented. The cleavages between the two groups, based on narratives brought from the past, the memory of which can be quite selective, persists in the American diaspora.[24]

An Invisible Entity to the Mainstream

Coming from a country that is unknown to most Americans and rarely taught about in American schools, even at the college and university levels, Eritrean communities are barely noticed and certainly not understood by the cultural mainstream, even those who are highly educated. Contact with these cultural isolates is limited to occasional forays into "their" restaurants, admiring their "exotic" dress, or wondering about the exotic lettering of "their" script. These tightly knit ethnic clusters, cloistered by a language few non-Eritreans speak, can reasonably be described as invisible, an underground culture.

A Special Grouping—The Diasporic Elite

Beginning in the late 1950s, Eritrean students, sent by the Ethiopian government in its attempt gradually to modernize the country, began to arrive in the United States. Many became influenced by the forces that were driving American culture at that time, especially the civil rights movement. When the war for liberation began in earnest in 1961, the Eritrean-American student cohort constituted a vital support mechanism for the homeland struggle, through its material and ideological support. Money was raised for the cause through great community sacrificing. The ideological support, heavily influenced by contemporary Marxian thought, began the development of what one scholar calls the *la voix érythrée*.[25] This was effectively used to gain a broad base of support for the Eritrean revolution, both in the United States and abroad. The contribution of this first group of students to the United States was the intellectualizing of the Eritrean Liberation War as a struggle "against all odds,"[26] one that was right, just, and consistent with Western liberal democratic values. Besides, those fighting for the revolution were underdogs for whom many have fond feelings.

Joining these in later years were many educated Eritreans who subsequently fled the country to pursue their studies at American and European colleges and universities, especially graduate and professional schools. Institutions of higher learning are repositories of information and insights into contemporary Eritrea. Opposition to the current regime is overwhelming in these academic concentrations of Eritreans who—along with other professionals, successful entrepreneurs, and noted cultural figures—can fairly be said to constitute an Eritrean sociocultural and political elite. This is a potential force for mobilization of the diaspora, especially if harnessed worldwide, with which homeland Eritrea might someday have to confront.

Theoretical Perspective, Methodology, and Research Goals

Theoretical Perspective

This chapter attempts to explain the political and social problems in Eritrea and its diaspora population using the structural violence theoretical framework advocated by Paul Farmer. He defines structural violence as:

Violence exerted systematically—that is, indirectly—by everyone who belongs to a certain social order: hence the discomfort these ideas provoke in a moral economy still geared to pinning praise or blame on individual actors. In short, the concept of structural violence is intended to inform the study of the social machinery of oppression.[27]

According to Farmer, neither the individual nor the culture is at fault for the existence of the social problems induced by structural violence, but these are the result of historical processes and forces that deny individuals access to basic social needs, and prevent them from attaining the goals to which they aspire.[28] Such is an apt description of Eritrean social reality.

Methodology

While the Eritrean diaspora remains an exceedingly difficult entity to examine systematically, empirically based conclusions can be drawn through carefully used creative methods of social science analysis. Diaspora concentrations are fluid, with high entry and exit rates. Numbers remain estimates, and attitude assessment can be an impressionistic process. Firm studies and reliable statistics are lacking. Even research-savvy Tigrinya-speaking Eritrean-American scholars have difficulty winning the trust and gaining access to the community.[29] In such a situation, creative techniques of investigation—especially participant-observation, unstructured interviews, and following up on leads provided by anecdotal evidence—can be useful tools, if responsibly done.

Our presentation of the techniques used by the Eritrean government to vis-à-vis its diaspora is an amalgamation, not reflective of any one locale, developed from the many sources used in preparation of this document. The opaque nature of the Eritrean diaspora requires the piecing together of many strands of evidence, especially from oral testimony, and the creative application of inference. We rely on what we can observe and, more importantly, on what we can extrapolate. In short, we paint a composite portrait, using a variety of sources as our palate, and logic as our brush.

This chapter draws from academic studies; data from the U.S. Census Bureau and the Department of Homeland Security, and UN sources, especially the UN High Commission for Refugees; World Bank statistics; NGO reports; and other sources. It was supplemented by interviews conducted by the authors over several years with Eritreans in academic and social settings, both formal and informal. Although an interview protocol was developed, it readily became apparent that the sought-after information was unlikely to be found by a formal interview. Therefore, all interviews and discussion sessions were conducted in an unstructured manner. For persons whom we could not contact, interviews were contacted by telephone or e-mail.[30]

Research Goals

Both authors are committed to research with a social purpose and not research undertaken in a social vacuum. Our purposes are simple: to inform others—especially opinion makers and those who influence others—of the Eritrean situation and to advance the Eritrean people's right to choose their own government, develop their own institutions, and freely lead their own lives.

Eritrean Citizenship

The foundation of the regime's control of the diaspora lies in Eritrean citizenship. From the perspective of the Eritrean party-state,[31] its 1992 citizenship proclamation, still in effect, states that any person with one parent of Eritrean origin, regardless of place of birth, is an Eritrean citizen. Citizens have duties and responsibilities to the state, no matter where in the world they live. De facto, the Eritrean state does not recognize dual citizenship and Eritrean citizenship cannot be renounced.[32] For those in diaspora, compliance with the state's policies signifies "Eritrean-ness" and membership in the transnational Eritrean family. A product of the Eritrean revolution, this formulation of the transnational citizen is revolutionary in and of itself.

Methods of Diasporic Control

The regime controls benefits. Concomitant with Eritrea's transnational concept of citizenship, and its policy goal of building national consciousness, is the regime's ability to control—through influence, guidance, coercion, and sanctions—the diaspora in the interests of the revolutionary Eritrean party-state. Controlling every aspect of homeland Eritrean life—ranging from the safety and well-being of residents to the sale of property, the release of transcripts, the issuance of birth and death certificates, giving permission to bury the dead on Eritrean soil (a deeply felt Eritrean cultural need), the issuance travel visas and exit permits, the granting of licenses to do business, issuance of coupons for purchase of scarce goods, and so on—the party-state has formidable powers over those seeking a positive action on its part, on those seeking regime-controlled benefits (RCBs).[33] Since most diaspora members still have family and friends in Eritrea, and hold real stakes there, the regime possesses a powerful weapon.[34]

The threat of retaliation against diaspora members' deepest psychological and physical shares in the homeland is never far from the thoughts of Eritreans abroad. Regime control of privileges and benefits is a potential mechanism that creates a climate of fear in the diaspora, encourages support of the regime, dissuades opposition activity, and silences overt dissent, even in the academy.[35]

One striking example is the recent denial by the Eritrean government of permission to return the body of a former cabinet minister and security chief from the United Kingdom where he had passed away while on medical leave. He was a trusted adviser to Isaias both before and after independence, a veteran of the revolution, and not out of the regime's favor. The Eritrean government gave no reason for denying permission to return the body. The message sent to the diaspora by this action, however, was clear: the regime is omnipotent and even the dead—let aside the living—are not assured a place in PFDJ-controlled Eritrea if the regime so wills.[36]

The Eritrean government's interest is in managing its diaspora wherever in the world it is found. Although our primary focus is on the United States, functional equivalents of the tactics we describe are operationalized in non-Western states, particularly countries neighboring Eritrea, but modified according to local culture and political need. What applies to the United States also applies to the industrialized liberal democracies of the West where Eritreans have sought refuge and build new communities and lives.

The Diaspora Tax and other Levies

To access RCBs, each diaspora member is required to pay a 2% tax on the income earned and is subject to other levies (e.g., payments to disabled veterans, a martyrs' fund, a national defense fund, other special causes, often related to war). All of this is supplemented by voluntary remittances. Together, these revenues constitute approximately "one-third to one half of the country's gross domestic product."[37] These levies are collected through the Eritrean Embassy in Washington and the Oakland, California, Consulate. Issuance of identity cards is also handled by Eritrea's two diplomatic posts in the United States, and Eritrean diplomatic posts in other nations do the same. These operations serve to effect the regime's twin goals of raising much needed money and forging Eritrean national identity. From the individual Eritrean's point of view "being current" on one's taxes and possessing an Eritrean identity card and thus to be registered with an Eritrean diplomatic post are the keys to accessing RCBs in the homeland. For example, the Eritrean Embassy in Washington has placed the payment form on its website and many diaspora members, out of a combination of patriotism, loyalty, and the desire not to incur harm on their interests—and, most importantly, family in Eritrea—do pay the tax. At times, it is inadvisable to rock boats!

A diaspora Eritrean's family or property still in Eritrea gives the regime a strangle-hold.[38] If a person refuses to pay the tax, or vocalizes opposition to the regime, the dissident's family in Eritrea is placed under extreme pressure. State security police may extort monetary payments from the family or refuse it RCBs such as license renewals, coupons for purchase of scarce goods, and the other things over which the state has control. The family is also "encouraged" to bring its dissident diaspora relative into line through whatever pressure it can place on the disfavored individual. In turn, the errant diaspora member loses all access to RCBs.

One witness poignantly described the impact of the regime's policies on his life:

> My longtime girlfriend was in Eritrea; in 2007 I left the country illegally and went to Sudan. From there, I made my way to the United States. I so much wanted her to be with me so we could marry and start a family, but I didn't know how to do it. I was just so upset. I was told by a fellow Eritrean that our embassy in Washington could help me if I signed a document renouncing my actions and pledging loyalty to Eritrea (nai't'asa werket). I also had to pay the 2% tax—make myself "current"—from the day I came to the United States. With so many fears, I had no option. I just signed the document and paid my tax. My fiancée was allowed to leave Eritrea. Both of us reunited in Uganda. There, we got married. The immigration process to get her to America is going well, and I am anxiously waiting to see her, maybe in just a few months. Things will be OK and maybe I can calm down then. You know, man, I just want to live my life, have a family, raise kids.

Other similar incidents are widely reported.

Generally, the regime coordinates relations with Eritreans in diaspora through an office within the Ministry of Foreign Affairs.[39] The issuance of identity cards and tax collection operations are managed through Eritrea's diplomatic posts abroad. One commentator referred to this as a "client/customer relationship" between the Eritrean government through its embassy in the host country and "our Eritrean group."[40] The regime uses these monies for a variety of purposes, including the funding of its military and the financing of foreign-based political movements. Subsidies to Al-Shabaab in Somalia are widely reported.[41]

PFDJ Cells and the Jasus

PFDJ chapters or cells, whose members are zealous party members and supporters of the regime, are sponsored by Eritrean diplomatic posts, and exist in every city with a concentration of Eritrean émigrés. Because these members are already dedicated supporters of the regime, they bring to PFDJ cells a dynamism and self-starting quality. Acting amorphously, PFDJ cell members function as agents of the party-state in the implementation of its diaspora policies, receiving their orders through diplomatic posts in Washington and Oakland, keeping no records of their actions, thus leaving no evidentiary trail. They often function as the conduit between individual diaspora members seeking services and the diplomatic post. Services rendered might include help in securing transcripts from Eritrean educational institutions, securing permission to bury a dead family member in Eritrea, facilitating the issuance of visas for summer travel to Eritrea, and so on.

Known in Tigrinya as *jasus*, these regime agents also serve as informants and monitors of other Eritreans in diaspora. Frequenting places where Habesha[42] gather (e.g., restaurants, social clubs, bars, community centers, etc.)[43] and working for under-the-table cash, *jasus* take notes and "report" remarks and comments that are unfavorable to the regime to their handlers in the diplomatic post. Eritreans in diaspora who speak publicly against the regime are targeted. Antiregime rallies, demonstrations, and other gatherings are favorite venues for these vigilant monitors of ideological virtuousness. Using small digital cameras or videocorders, the *jasus* often photograph or videocord Eritrean protesters. These images, like other "incriminating" reports, are transmitted to Asmara through the *jasus*' diplomatic post contact.

Jasus, many crude in their approach and swelled with their "authority," attempt to "punish" offending Eritreans, oftentimes berating them on the spot for their "unpatriotic and disloyal" behavior. A typical admonishment might take the following form:

> What? You are saying such things about our government? Why are you doing this? What kind of Eritrean are you? Do you not remember the Martyrs, the suffering and the sacrifices of our people, the heroic struggle? Would you waste all of that now? Are you a traitor? How can you say such things?

Said in a public place, with other Eritreans present, such a remark is clearly intended to shame, disgrace, and deter such speech by generating peer pressure on the wayward individual. Sometimes this is coupled with harassing telephone calls to the "offender" after the incident has taken place to remind the person of "proper" conduct.

Over time, individual *jasus* become known in the diaspora community, and their effectiveness to the regime wanes. New party loyalists are recruited, or self-recruit themselves, and the process repeats itself. This particular tactic is highly developed in the Washington, DC, metropolitan area where the diaspora Eritrean community is the largest in the world.

When names of diaspora "violators" arrive at the Foreign Ministry in Asmara, retaliation against family and property in Eritrea usually follows. With total control of its homeland citizens' lives—including leveling false criminal charges as well as the delivery of benefits such as the issuance of exit visas needed, for example, to seek medical care abroad—the regime is unrestrained. As documented in U.S. Department of State annual human rights reports,[44] Eritrean families are often threatened and/or punished—even jailed—on trumped-up or just plain falsified charges for the actions of their relatives abroad. As we have seen before, homeland Eritreans are thus coerced to pressure their relatives in diaspora to fall into line.

"Capturing" Orthodox Congregations

Orthodox Christians are the largest religious grouping in the Eritrean-American diaspora. For many, the Orthodox Church is a major force in their lives, a key to the preservation of Eritrean culture and the Tigrinya language and its Geez (ancient mother language to Tigrinya and closely related Semitic languages), passing these on to future generations, and a major mechanism of attitude formation. The centrality of the Orthodox faith, and the importance of the local congregation, give the church enormous potential leverage in the lives of individual congregants. The Eritrean Orthodox Diocese of North America, established in the United States in 1990 with 4 congregations, had grown by 2005 to 19 congregations, with 5 communities on the verge of establishing their own parishes, and counted about 13,500 congregants. Aligned with the mother Egyptian Coptic Church and the British Orthodox Church, a judicatory under the mother Egyptian Church, the North American diocese mobilized its resources and consolidated itself as a significant power within the Eritrean-American community.

As such, the Orthodox base was also an inviting target attracting "capture" by the party-state. The first assault against the North American Orthodox diocese took place in mid-2005, coinciding with the PFDJ's attack on the homeland Eritrean Orthodox Church. The government's goal was to place both the Orthodox Church at home and in exile in the United States under state control.

In so doing, the "capture" of local Eritrean Orthodox congregations became a key regime strategy to enforce its will on the American diaspora. At home, the church patriarch, Antonios[45]—who had spoken against the government's involvement in church affairs—was first stripped of all power and confined to basic ceremonial duties. Day-to-day control of the Eritrean Orthodox Church was placed under a lay administrator, reporting even now to the PFDJ. Eventually, Antonios was deposed from office, placed under house arrest, later jailed, and finally replaced by a government-picked patriarch, Dioscoros. This was done through shameless PFDJ manipulation of the Holy Synod, the supreme governing body of the church.[46]

At this point, the Eritrean regime dispatched Abune Lukas, Bishop of Gash Barka, to attend—unannounced and uninvited—the annual conference of the North American Diocese, meeting in Washington, DC, in July 2005.[47] At the conference, Lukas requested permission to bring "greetings from the Synod," and he was granted the podium. Lukas then launched into a biting personal attack that, according to the Diocese, had the intent of "render[ing] the leadership of the North American Diocese . . . null and void."[48]

Bishop Lukas was soon joined by another regime-sent bishop, Abune Sinoda, and the two traveled the country in what one pro-diocese website called a "game of cat and mouse,"[49] visiting Eritrean Orthodox congregations, attempting to win their loyalties to a competing North American diocese that Abune Sinoda purported to head. The bishops' visit was most likely orchestrated from Eritrean diplomatic posts in Washington and Oakland, with visitations to individual congregations coordinated by PFDJ cell members in the cities in which the churches were located. When Abune Sinoda crossed swords with the Kidisti Selassie Orthodox Tewahedo Church in Seattle, the governing board stated in a letter, dated August 17, 2006:

> [T]he path you and your cohorts have chosen for yourselves is one of a deliberate and calculated effort . . . to destroy the unity of the faithful of our beloved church, the diocese in North America and of our people at large.[50]

In other venues, he was successful in luring individual congregations away from the established diocese and into the Sinoda camp. This bishops' journey indicates a high degree of sophistication by the Eritrean government in navigating the American sociopolitical landscape.

The North American diocese, with its British and Egyptian Coptic allies, continues to recognize the legitimacy of Abune Antonios and reject the government's puppet, Dioscoros, and the lay administrator. It is now back up to 19 congregations, many newly founded after the Eritrean incursion began in 2005 and the resulting schism. Abba Sinoda[51] heads a rival diocese based at Kdst Selassie Eritrean Orthodox Tewahedo Church in Temple Hills, Maryland, legally registered as the "Eritrean Orthodox Tewahedo Diocese of USA and Canada Inc." Orthodox congregations in the United States, supportive of the Eritrean government, operate in near-secrecy, especially when inquiries are made regarding links with Asmara.

Possibly as many as 13 congregations are affiliated with Sinoda's denomination,[52] although no actual listing is available and next to nothing can be learned about the actual structure and workings of the judicatory. In most communities with any sizeable Eritrean population, there is both an "Antonios" Church and a rival Eritrean Orthodox Church, often progovernment.

Especially sensitive is the issue of the removal and arrest of the church's spiritual leader, Patriarch Antonios, and the government's enthronement of Dioscoros. Persons whom we interviewed became quite uncomfortable when simply asked to name the patriarch of the Eritrean Church. While Antonios has been airbrushed out of the picture, Dioscoros is rarely mentioned. One congregant reported that in his West Coast congregation's Sunday celebration of the Divine Liturgy, the traditional prayers of blessing for the patriarch were no longer included. Other informal conversations with "government" church members suggest that there is a belief among many that Antonios was removed for theological reasons (i.e., he was going pente or Pentecostal) and the process of removal was undertaken by the Holy Synod alone, and without outside influence. Moreover, the church is viewed as independent of the Eritrean government.

Posing questions with political overtones to "government" priests is seen as unwise, possibly resulting in denial of religious privileges in the congregation (e.g., shunning or ostracism, denial of the sacraments, etc.). Political consequences in the homeland are also possible. Money for Eritrea collected in government churches is portrayed as furthering the church's mission in the homeland, and not government causes.

Official visitors from the homeland church are presented as patriotic and church-loving Eritreans. The church proclaims its support for the Eritrean state and its leadership through regularly offered prayers for the country, its government, and its president. This is deeply rooted in Eritrean history, tradition, and culture.

The "government" church views other Eritrean Orthodox congregations as Pentecostal-influenced, funded by "foreign" elements, and a threat to the "real" Orthodox faith. "Government" church members are under a holy obligation not to go to attend churches. While some "government" church members may be truly unaware of the reality of the situation, other congregants clearly understand the situation and know the limits of permitted discussion. A "no-see" posture may be adopted out of self-interest, concern for community standing, and the like.

In some instances, a congregation may chart its own ground between the two fronts. One Eritrean congregation in Florida, with fewer than 15 parishioners, is served by an unpaid priest, but a "worker priest" who holds a full-time blue-collar job. The congregation is not affiliated with any national body. The priest walks a fine line in ministering to his congregation that includes government supporters and opponents. As a general rule, "politics" is never discussed and prayers for the Eritrean government and patriarch are not offered although general prayers for the Orthodox Church and Eritrean nation are said. The number of congregations following this model is unknown.

Community Center Creation

Other tactics used by the regime to monitor and control Eritreans in diaspora include the establishment and funding of Eritrean community centers in areas with sizeable diaspora populations. With funding goes the control of the centers' programs and activities. Community centers do, however, perform many other functions useful to the Eritrean community. These include teaching English as a second language, teaching Tigrinya to heritage learners, job training, conducting other employment-related programs, and other educational activities. For example, the Eritrean Community Center in Boston advertises its job training activities, its library resources, and its sensitivity to its media image.[53] The regime keeps a tight hand over all of these activities, thereby assuring that center programs are consistent with PFDJ "teachings."

In community center classes the story of Eritrea's revolutionary struggle is kept alive for young diaspora members, many born on host country soil. Their knowledge of the homeland is based on the selective narratives of older diaspora members, especially their parents, constituting la voix érythrée.[54] For these youth, the pull of the host country's youth culture is strong and the regime deems it important to contribute to the "Eritrean-ization" of youth in as many ways as possible. The regime tailors youth-targeted community center educational programs to develop regime-supportive attitudes. Diaspora parents are encouraged to involve their children in to community activities and homeland support activities. All of this is done, of course, in the name of loyalty to the homeland. Community centers also serve as the legal vehicle to sponsor refugees thus assuring regime direction in their acculturation process.

Festivals, Sports, and Seminars

Playing on the patriotism of diaspora Eritreans, special cultural festivals in diaspora cities are regularly sponsored by the regime, often on May 24, the Eritrean Independence Day, and June 20, Martyrs' Day, and March 8, Women's Day. Here, contemporary Eritrean artists, loyal to the regime, perform. Large crowds are drawn and feelings of kinship with Eritrea and among Eritreans everywhere are evoked.

Sponsorship of sports teams and events, especially soccer, is another tactic the regime uses to transmit a message of unity and to develop devotion to the regime and pride in Eritrea in diaspora youth. In addition, Eritrean officials often visit diaspora cities, often in conjunction with festivals and sporting events, to conduct "seminars" on PFDJ positions, to urge the diaspora to invest in homeland projects, and to encourage travel to Eritrea. These are widely publicized in Eritrea through the PFDJ-controlled press; the theme of homeland unity with the diaspora is stressed.[55]

Summer Trips to Eritrea

A very important activity organized by diaspora community groups is the sponsorship of youth-oriented summer trips to Eritrea, called Zura n' Hagerka or "Know Your Country Tour." During these trips, seminars are conducted in historic Eritrean venues, especially those important to the revolutionary struggle. Attendance at the annual Eri-Youth Festival at Sawa[56] is a highlight of these trips. At the festival, prominent artists are featured, the narrative of the revolution is told once more, flourishing glorifying the Eritrean party-state are offered, and the intrinsic worth of Eritrean values is emphasized. Youth from abroad have the opportunity to mingle with homeland Eritreans, especially those of their age group.

These trips can, however, backfire on the regime and become an anti-PFDJ learning experience for the visiting youth. Many have been indoctrinated by PFDJ-controlled institutions abroad about the great strides the government is making. Eritrea is portrayed as a virtual paradise—at least a paradise in the making. This stands in sharp relief with the everyday life they see in Eritrea.

Bettina Conrad, who studies the approximately 25,000-member German diaspora, tells the story of the culture conflict that erupted on one such trip by young Eritrean-Germans.[57] Attired in fashionable Western attire, with high expectations about coming "home," they presented a major contrast to their Eritrean counterparts just as the Eritrea of their imagination clashed with the reality of the situation they actually experienced. Called beles, the Tigrinya word for the prickly pear that ripens during the rainy season when many diaspora visit, the youth were shunned by some for the wealth they were perceived to possess, the opportunities that they were thought to have, and the Western tastes and preferences they obviously enjoyed. The reality of everyday Eritrean life that these German teenagers encountered contradicted the narratives they had heard over their short years.

In an unexpected way, these trips can have a lasting impact on families once the traveler returns home. One witness, in an informal discussion, told the authors how his daughter completely changed after her trip to Eritrea:

> My ex-wife—we've been divorced now for several years—had custody of our kids while they were growing up. She is a staunch government supporter and indoctrinated them about how wonderful life is in Eritrea. When I saw my daughter, and she told me these things, I argued with her, and tried to explain the reality of life in Eritrea. However, she was always swayed by her mom's views. Once she went to Eritrea on a trip organized by the youth arm of the PFDJ, she saw firsthand the real Eritrea: the absolute lack of any sort of freedom, economic hardship, and endless national service. Upon her return she called me to apologize. Her relationship with her mother has been getting bad ever since and she is now starting to talk to me again, more often than she used to.

Regime Use of Host Country Resources

Where possible, the regime uses the host diasporic state's systems and processes to accomplish party-state's goals whenever possible. Use of Internal Revenue Services (IRS) reporting forms for the calculation of the 2% diaspora tax is one example. Another is the use of the host state's media for regime gain. Using a time slot provided by Minnesota Public Radio meant to empower refugee communities and accelerate their assimilation into American culture, an Eritrean community group developed a short presentation in Tigrinya that glorified the PFDJ. In Washington, DC, radio station WUST drew the ire of the Eritrean Orthodox Diocese of North America when the station aired an Eritrean community association-produced show accusing the North American Diocese of being a handmaiden of the Ethiopian government—the regime's archenemy. The Diocese's position supporting Patriarch Antonios in the face of his removal by the Eritrean regime was construed as undermining the Orthodox faith and working against the organized church.

In a letter to the Eritrean embassy, the Eritrean diocese in North America protested the accusation against them by saying:

> Accusing us wrongly of joining with forces [i.e., Ethiopia] who have shed Eritrean blood and are daily preparing to continue the bloodshed against Eritrea . . . of campaigning against Eritrea under the cover of human rights and religious rights . . . of being instruments of Woyane, the core ruling party in Ethiopia . . . of being paid agents against Eritrea's enemies . . . of undermining the Eritrean Church hierarchy and its holy ordinances, synods and spiritual rules are all baseless. We categorically deny this false accusations. We are loyal to our church and to our Patriarch, his holiness Patriarch Antonios and we oppose his removal.[58]

Formation of Associations

The regime encourages the establishment of civic associations such as women, youth, and student groups, just as it does chapters or cells of the ruling PFDJ. These organizations sponsor programs relevant to their interest area, providing support systems for their members. Many such organizations form calling trees to alert community members to upcoming regime-sponsored events. Membership in these organizations sometimes overlaps with PFDJ cells and associations join with the *jasus* as informal behavior monitors.

How the Names of Eritreans in Diaspora Are Gathered

Tax Collection and Application for National Identity Cards

The major method used by the Eritrean regime to gather the names of those in diaspora is through records kept in collecting the 2% diaspora tax and other levies. In a similar manner, the name of any applicant for an Eritrean national identity card is recorded and placed in a database.

Applications for Travel Documents

Any time an Eritrean applies for an Eritrean travel document, the applicant's name is recorded. "Papers" are an international necessity for travelers headed across international borders. Not only is this a method of recordkeeping, but also of revenue raising. For example, if an Eritrean passes through Sudan on the way out of the country—as many do by geographical necessity—and applies for Eritrean travel papers, the traveler's name is sent to the Ministry of Foreign Affairs in Asmara. If the person is not significant to the regime, a charge of approximately $1,000 for issuance of a passport is assessed, and the person is cajoled into signing a loyalty pledge (nai't'asa werket) to the Eritrean government promising to support it financially and politically. Then the person is permitted to go on. In addition, once the government has the information about those leaving the country, it goes to the departee's family in Eritrea and asks them to pay an additional rate of approximately $1,000. On the contrary, if the person is important to the regime, Eritrean security forces may kidnap that person, bringing the would-be departee back to homeland Eritrea where imprisonment is the most likely outcome.

Registration of Military Personnel

The Eritrean government tracks its diaspora population through its register of military personnel. The universal national service program, to which all youth are required to serve, generates the major pool of personnel for the armed forces, and a great number of the young people who flee Eritrea are army deserters or youth evading national service altogether. Once a person deserts the military, the Ministry of Defense sends that person's name, through the Ministry of Foreign Affairs, to its embassies abroad. Historically, neighboring governments friendly to Eritrea through which escapees usually pass assisted the Eritrean government to bring deserters back to Eritrea for trial. These include Bashir's Sudan today, and in the past, Kadafi's Libya and Mubarak's Egypt.

Homeland Surveys

Special homeland demographic surveys are another means the Eritrean government uses to keep track of its diaspora population. State agents will descend on a particular venue, usually an urban neighborhood or rural village, and families will be asked to list all of its members and their places of residence. During these surveys, the consequences for nonparticipation are severe and family members are severely pressured to name its members who live abroad. Most of the time, families report and pay whatever amount of penalties the government levies, so that they do not lose their land, licenses, or other RCBs.

Final Thoughts and Conclusion

We offer four conclusions and three suggestions for further research.

While other migrant-sending countries engage their diapsoras in a variety of ways,[59] the scope and intensity of Eritrea's efforts to control its diaspora in the interests of the revolutionary party-state—through influence, guidance, coercion, and sanctions—makes Eritrean efforts different. The party-state's actions suggest a need for total control—or, at least, for the greatest possible suppression of dissent or the pacification of dissenters—and its targeted universe is Eritreans worldwide.

Since Eritrea is an all-encompassing authoritarian state, and many Eritrean-Americans still have psychological and physical stakes in the homeland, the regime's control of homeland benefits, what we have termed RCBs, means the state is in a hegemonic position vis-à-vis its diaspora.

For most of the world's states, homeland-diaspora interaction patterns involve reciprocity of duties and obligations. For fulfilling one's duties, there is a payback of some sort; the flow moves in both directions. In Eritrea, this is not the case: the flow between homeland Eritrea and its diaspora is one way and one way only—from the power center to the periphery. Fulfillment of duties does not lead to reciprocal rewards.

The ideological underpinning of the Eritrean regime's diaspora control efforts are grounded in the concept of transnational citizenship. This is a unique ideological contribution to the concept of transnationalism and to political theory.

Future Research Directions

Although we have touched on the administration of the Eritrean state's diaspora control tactics, we have not examined the cost. Undoubtedly, the proportion of state funds expended on diaspora control efforts, given the Eritrean poverty levels, is remarkably high. Further research is needed.

It would be interesting to build a computer model of the Eritrean diaspora in the United States, using the statistical information and analytical constructs available.

The apparent climate of fear and its chilling effects detected by us in the Eritrean-American community—two Americans, one of whom is a native-born Eritrean, fluent in Tigrinya—were both unexpected and not readily explainable. Interviews with Eritrean diaspora members suggest—or the interviewers sense—a collective climate of weariness, of hopelessness, even of post-traumatic stress. There is a sense of resentment against the world community for its inaction in the face of Eritrean repression at home, as well as hopelessness for international rescue.[60] Many Eritrean-Americans feel that the Isaias government is held accountable by the United States only when it acts counter to Western interests, for example, for its support of al-Shabaab in Somalia. The other dreadful acts that it routinely commits seem to go unnoticed and thereby tacitly approved. These thoughts deserve much further research.

Notes

1. We first saw this conceptually useful trifold typography in the work of Donald N. Levine, Professor Emeritus of Sociology at the University of Chicago and noted Ethiopian scholar.
2. The projected population estimate for July 2011 provided by the CIA *World Fact Book* is 6,086,495. https://www.cia.gov/library/publications/the-world-factbook/geos/er.htm Accessed March 17, 2012. The U.S. Census Bureau International Data Base estimates the midyear population (July 1) in 2011 as 5,939,000, and projects 6,086,000 for 2012, 6,528,000 in 2015, and 7,987,000 in 2025. http://www.census.gov/population/international/data/idb/region.php. Accessed June 20, 2012. The U.S. Department of State. "Background Note: Eritrea" places the July 2011 estimate at 5.9 million. http://www.state.gov/r/pa/ei/bgn/2854.htm#people Accessed June 20, 2012. The United Nations, "Environment Statistics Country Snapshot: Eritrea" for 2011 places the population at 5,245,000. http://unstats.un.org/unsd/environment/envpdf/Country_Snapshots_Aug%202011/Eritrea.pdf. Accessed June 20, 2012. While the current official State of Eritrea population estimates are not available, historically, Eritrean-generated population estimates are lower than Western estimates.
3. Human Rights Watch "Service for Life: State Repression and Indefinite Conscription in Eritrea." April 16, 2009, 29. http://www.hrw.org/sites/default/files/reports/eritrea0409webwcover_0.pdf. Accessed June 24, 2012.
4. See U.S. Department of State, Bureau of Democracy, Human Rights, and Labor. "2011 Human Rights Report," country report on Eritrea. May 24, 2012. http://www.state.gov/j/drl/rls/hrrpt/humanrightsreport/index.htm#wrapper/. Accessed July 19, 2012.
5. Freedom House. "Freedom in the World 2012." http://www.freedomhouse.org/sites/default/files/FIW%202012%20Booklet_0.pdf. Accessed August 12, 2012.
6. Amnesty International. "Amnesty International Report 2012: The State of the World's Human Rights." May 21, 2012, 142. http://www.amnestyusa.org/sites/default/files/air12-report-english.pdf. Accessed August 12, 2012.
7. U.S. Commission on International Religious Freedom. *Annual Report 2012*, March 2012. USCIRF (U.S. Commission in International Freedom) in its 2012 Annual Report again, as it has for eight consecutive years in the past, recommended designation of Eritrea as a country of particular concern. See pp. 70–77. http://www.

uscirf.gov/images/Annual%20Report%20of%20USCIRF%202012(2).pdf. Accessed August 12, 2012.
8. Mo Ibrahim Foundation. "2011 Ibrahim Index of African Governance." On the 2011 Ibrahim Index of African Governance, "a composite index, constructed by combining underlying indicators in a standardised way to provide a statistical measure of [good] governance performance in all African countries," Eritrea scored 47th of the 53 countries examined. http://www.moibrahimfoundation.org/en/section/the-ibrahim-index. Accessed August 12, 2012.
9. Reporters without Borders. "Press Freedom Index 2011–2012." January 25, 2012. http://en.rsf.org/press-freedom-index-2011-2012,1043.html. Accessed August 12, 2012.
10. We use Gabriel Sheffer's definition of diaspora: "Modern diasporas are ethnic minority groups of migrant origins residing and acting in host countries but maintaining strong sentimental and material links with their countries of origin—their homelands." See Gabriel Sheffer. "A New Field of Study: Modern Diasporas in International Politics." In Gabriel Sheffer, ed. *Modern Diasporas in International Politics* (London: Croom Helm, 1986), 3.
11. Although making an estimate of the diasporic population is exceedingly difficult, one million is the number used by many scholars. Other estimates are higher. For example, Ethiopian journalist Argaw Ashine places the number at 1.6 million. Given escalating rates of exit from homeland Eritrea, population growth, and the tendency to undercount diaspora numbers, we estimate 1¼ million as a realistic approximation.
12. The figure of 3,000 is widely quoted and attributed to the United Nations High Commission for Refugees. For example, see Phoebe Greenwood. "Eritrean Regime Cashes in on Arms and Human Trafficking, Says UN Report." *The Guardian*. July 17, 2012. http://www.guardian.co.uk/world/2012/jul/17/eritrean-regime-arms-human-trafficking. Accessed July 23, 2012. In the authors' review of UNHCR documents, the figure of 3,000 could not be found.

"Service for life" is a term coined by Human Rights Watch. See Note 3.
13. United Nations High Commission for Refugees. *A Year of Crises Global Trends in 2011*, 14.http://www.unhcr.org/4fd6f87f9.html. Accessed July 4, 2012.
14. With a plus/minus error of 4,628 persons.
15. For the 2010 estimate, see U.S. Census Bureau. By Elizabeth M. Grieco, Yesenia D. Acosta, C. Patricia de las Cruz, Christine Gambino, Thomas Gryn, Luke J. Larsen, Edward No. Trevelyan, and Nathan P. Walters. "The Foreign-Born Population in the United States: 2010." American Community Survey Reports. May 2012. For the 2000 estimate, see Table FBP-1. Profile of Selected Demographic and Social Characteristics: 2000. U.S. Census Bureau.
16. Hepner. "Eritrean Immigrants," 630–3, and Tricia Redeker Hepner. *Soldiers, Martyrs, Traitors, and Exiles: Political Conflict in Eritrea and the Diaspora (The Ethnography of Political Violence)* (Philadelphia: University of Pennsylvania Press, 2011), 631.
17. We arrived at this estimate simply by cross-multiplying and adjusting as follows: 17,520/100,000:: 29,681/x = 169,312.1; factoring in refinement of its estimating techniques by the U.S. Census Bureau since 2000, the purported underestimate is thereby lessened. Although we are neither statisticians nor demographers, our hunch—and that is all it is, a hunch based on experience—is that the real number of Eritreans living in the United States is about 150,000.
18. This mapping of the Eritrean diaspora within the United States was inferred using statistics from the U.S. Census Bureau and the U.S. Department of Homeland Security, Office of Immigration Statistics. These are probably the most reliable sources. Since we know that religious affiliation is a key component of Eritrean culture, it was logical to gather information on congregational locations from the websites

of the Eritrean Orthodox Church, Diocese of North America, and the Byzantine Catholic Church in America. Internet searches of major cities for individual Eritrean congregations, especially Lutheran- and charismatic Protestant-affiliated groups, and other independent churches were also done. Tricia Redeker Hepner's "Eritrean Immigrants." In Ronald H. Bayor, ed. *Multicultural America: An Encyclopedia of the Newest Americans*, Vol. 2. (Santa Barbara, CA, Denver, and Oxford: Greenwood Publishing, 2011), 617–35, summarizes these sources and provides an excellent overview of the Eritrean diaspora in the United States.

As an anecdotal example of diaspora concentrations and growth, Dawit Woldu, coauthor of this article, currently resides with his wife, a native of Eritrea, and son, born in the United States, in the Midland-Odessa, TX, Combined Statistical Area (estimated 2010 population, 274,002). Two of his wife's coworkers are Eritreans— single men, both geologists, all working, as is she, in the oil industry in the Permian Basin. Just recently, an Eritrean family of five relocated to the area bringing the total known Eritrean community to ten.

19. See Hepner. "Eritrean Immigrants," 630–633, and Hepner, *Soldiers, Martyrs, Traitors, and Exiles*, 631–632.
20. Revelations. "Engaging the Eritrean Diaspora: Wikileaks." *Ethiopian Review*. http://www.ethiopianreview.com/forum/viewtopic.php?f=2&t=29059. June 30, 2011. Accessed December 17, 2011.
21. Tricia Redeker Hepner. "Eritrean Immigrants." In Ronald H. Bayor, ed. *Multicultural America: An Encyclopedia of the Newest Americans*, Vol. 2 (Santa Barbara, CA, Denver, and Oxford: Greenwood Publishing, 2011), 617–655, 617. This provides an excellent overview of the Eritrean diaspora in the United States.
22. For an excellent discussion and summary of the literature on these points, see Amanuel A. Teklemariam. "Understanding Abyssinian Immigrants in the U.S.: Socio-cultural Background and Contemporary Experiences." *Western Journal of Black Studies* (Summer 2005). http://findarticles.com/p/articles/mi go2988/is 2 29/ai n29240859/. Accessed June 14, 2012.
23. For an equally excellent discussion and summary of the internal politics of the ELF and EPLF, see Chapter 2, "A Tale of Two Fronts: Nationalism and Political Identity in the ELF and EPLF" In Tricia Redeker Hepner. *Soldiers, Martyrs, Traitors, and Exiles: Political Conflict in Eritrea and the Diaspora (The Ethnography of Political Violence)*. (Philadelphia: University of Pennsylvania Press, 2011), 26–62.
24. See Chapter 6, "A Painful Paradox: Transnational Civil Society and the Sovereign State." In Tricia Redeker Hepner. *Soldiers, Martyrs, Traitors, and Exiles: Political Conflict in Eritrea and the Diaspora (The Ethnography of Political Violence)* (Philadelphia: University of Pennsylvania Press, 2011), 183–219.
25. See Olufemi A. Akinola. "Politics and Identity Construction in Eritrean Studies, c. 1970–1991: The Making of *Voix Érythrée*." *African Study Monographs*, Vol. 28, No. 2 (July 2007): 47–86.
26. Indeed, this was the title of a later book presenting the revolution in very favorable terms. See Dan Connell. *Against All Odds: A Chronicle of the Eritrean Revolution* (Lawrenceville, NJ, and Asmara, Eritrea: Red Sea Press, Inc., 1993 and 1997).
27. Farmer, Paul. "An Anthropology of Structural Violence." *Current Anthropology*, 45, no. 3 (2004): 307.
28. Paul Farmer. *Infections and Inequalities: The Modern Plagues* (Berkeley: University of California Press, 1999), 13. His book is a complete exposition of this thesis.
29. For example, an Eritrean-born PhD candidate in cultural anthropology at the University of Florida is examining diaspora Horn of African (especially Eritrean) entrepreneurs in the Washington, DC, metropolitan area. He possesses native fluency in both Tigrinya and Amharic. To collect his data, he designed a questionnaire

asking basic questions that focused on "how," "why," and "when" kinds of issues in order to assess entrepreneurs' attitudes and experiences, and to chart business trajectories. Sensitive to the cultures of the ethnic communities he was studying, he took great care in constructing a questionnaire that was straight forward, nonthreatening, and transparent. Using ethnic-based business associations and an Amharic version of the yellow pages, he compiled a list of potential interviewees. He found that these members of the diaspora business communities he was studying were quite suspicious of written surveys and loathe to participate in them. After many attempts to break through the barriers his potential interviewees put up, he analyzed the ways in which his research would be of potential benefit to diaspora entrepreneurs. Developing this as his *shtick*, he thus gave them a stake in participating and by doing so, found that members of his target groups were much more forthcoming. He also found that highly unstructured, nonstressful, and informal interview situations conducted entirely in Tigrinya or Amharic, often over beer and snacks, created ideal interview situations.

30. The interviews, involving as many Eritreans as possible, are ongoing, and were begun in August 2005. Interview situations included after-class exchanges; relaxing with students in the student union; holiday celebrations; shopping in Eritrean-owned stores; socializing in public places where Habesha gather; interviewing service personnel such as parking attendants, cab drivers, and servers, and such others. Although interview notes are kept, they are not associated with a person's name or the date of the discussion. Particularly notable was the authors' interaction with a group of Habesha who gathered at a Gainesville pub on Friday and Saturday nights for beer and discussions, sometimes intense, but always about "home."

It was our distinct feeling that despite our best efforts to assure interviewees that our intentions were not for malpurposes but were designed to produce a study that, ultimately, would be of benefit to the Eritrean-American community, many of those we approached showed great reluctance—even fear—in discussing diaspora matters with us. We are tempted to add pervasive fear as a cultural characteristic of Eritrean-American diaspora members, especially those of the first generation. Notes 29 and 35 support this contention.

31. Hepner appears to have coined this term, which we find analytically descriptive in *Soldiers, Martyrs, Traitors, and Exiles*, 631, xii. Ruth Iyob terms Eritrea a "diaspora state." See her article: "The Ethiopian-Eritrean Conflict: Diasporic vs. Hegemonic States in the Horn of Africa, 1991–2000." *The Journal of Modern African Studies* 38, no. 4 (2000): 660.

32. Eritreans who hold American citizenship are warned by the U.S. Department of State that they may be detained by the Eritrean government if they travel to Eritrea. An April 18, 2012, Travel Warning states:

> A number of Eritrean-U.S. dual citizens have been arrested and some are currently being held without apparent cause. Once arrested, detainees may be held for extended periods without being told the reason for their incarceration. . . . The Eritrean government does not inform the U.S. Embassy when U.S. citizens, including those who are not dual nationals, have been arrested or detained. Should the U.S. Embassy learn of the arrest of a U.S. citizen, the Eritrean government rarely allows consular access, regardless of the reason the U.S. citizen is being held.

See U.S. Department of State, Bureau of Consular Affairs. "Travel Warning." April 18, 2012. http://travel.state.gov/travel/cis_pa_tw/tw/tw_5698.html. Accessed August 12, 2012.

33. In its interactions with the diaspora, the Eritrean regime often acts without finesse. For example, an Ethiopian-American whom we interviewed stated that when the Ethiopian government relates to its diaspora, it clearly offers "carrots," hoping for infusions of cash and access to Western-educated talent. On the contrary, this respondent stated: "[t]he Eritrean government uses a heavy stick and is simply coarse and offensive in its approach to Eritreans abroad. Ethiopia takes a 'kinder and gentler' approach."
34. For example, an Eritrean woman, with whom the authors are familiar, recently sought and was granted political asylum in the United States. Her brother, who was serving his national service in the Eritrean military, had deserted and was granted refugee status in Eritrea. The acts of both siblings are seen as treasonous by the Eritrean regime.

    The siblings' father, who owed a grocery business in Eritrea, was denied the renewal of his license to do business. At a later point, he developed a life-threatening medical condition requiring treatment abroad. He applied for an exit visa on which the regime failed to act; the father died shortly thereafter from his condition. Both actions by the regime against the siblings' father can, by any stretch of the imagination, be seen as retaliation.
35. For example, the authors invited an Eritrean-born diaspora scholar to participate in preparing this article. This person declined, citing fear of retaliation by the Isaias regime against family members still living in Eritrea. Thus, in a real way, the Eritrean government has successfully silenced an opposing voice, circumventing this person's First Amendment rights.
36. This incident was reported on March 2, 2012, in *Horn of Africa News*; his name was Naizghi Kiflu.

    http://hornofafricanews.blogspot.com/2012/03/no-respect-even-for-dead-in-eritrea.html. Accessed July 23, 2012.
37. Hepner. *Soldiers, Martyrs, Traitors, and Exiles*, 24.
38. As part of the University of Florida's process to award master's degrees, the coauthor of this book, Dawit Okubatsion Woldu, a native of Eritrea and former undergraduate student at the University of Asmara, was asked for his transcript to certify that he held a bachelor's degree. The Eritrean institution refused to release it to Mr. Woldu. A University of Florida official telephoned the president of the University of Asmara who told the Florida dean, "It's out my control."
39. Policy decisions regarding diaspora relations are made at the top of the governmental hierarchy, with input from senior officials. The office designated to coordinate Asmara-diaspora relations is the Office for Eritreans Residing Abroad, housed in the Ministry of Foreign Affairs. The responsibility of this office is to translate policy into program with procedures for implementation and administration. This entails all aspects of diaspora monitoring (e.g., name gathering, list keeping, channeling of the 2% tax and other levy revenues from points abroad to Asmara and from there, to designated homeland recipients, control of community centers, coordination of regime visits to diaspora communities, and similar activities). The current director general is Ambassador Hanna Simon whose CV indicates that one of her specialties is "Diaspora Management Issues." Ms. Simon has served in the Eritrean diplomatic corps.

    Tesfamariam Tekeste, currently Eritrea's ambassador to Israel since December 2004, initially held this position, then termed commissioner for Eritreans Living Abroad, after independence, and was instrumental in establishing the structures and processes through which homeland Eritrea coordinates its relations with diasporic communities. U.S. Eritrean community members tell us of biannual visits to this country to receive reports from Eritrean diplomatic personnel and his "lieutenants" in the field.

40. "Eritrea and Its Unusual Embassies." Gedab News. October 21, 2010. http://awate.com/eritrea-and-its-unusual-embassies-2/. Accessed March 17, 2012.
41. An Assenna.com article, dated July 23, 2012, tells of an Eritrean immigrant's attempt to obtain permanent residency in Canada. Canadian immigration services required that he present a valid Eritrean passport. In order to get the passport, he had to pay the diaspora tax, plus other assessments, one of which was earmarked for the "Eritrean defense fund." The man indicated to the Eritrean consulate in Toronto that he would pay the tax, but not the portion earmarked for the military. Eritrean consular officials demanded the entire sum while Canada continued to require the man to present an Eritrean passport. The man paid the tax. See Stewart Bell. "Eritrea, Repressive African Dictatorship, Using Toronto Consulate to Bankroll Military: UN Report." July 23, 2012. http://assenna.com/eritrea-repressive-african-dictatorship-using-toronto-consulate-to-bankroll-military-un-report. Accessed July 24, 2012.

The article leaked a previously unreleased UN Security Council report by its Somalia and Eritrea Monitoring Group. The report stated:

> According to a recent Royal Canadian Mounted Police assessment, which is consistent with the Monitoring Group's own findings, refusal to pay the tax often results in denial of service or threats against, or harassment of, family members still residing in Eritrea, or possible arrest of the individual should they travel to Eritrea without paying the taxes alleged to be owing.

See UN Security Council. *Report of the Monitoring Group on Somalia and Eritrea Pursuant to Security Council Resolution 2002 (2011)*. July 13, 2012, 23.

The report also stated:

> Eritrean officials and party agents routinely resort to threats, intimidation and coercive measures in order to elicit payment. The most common tactic is the denial of unrelated services until taxes have been paid. Other measures include harassment, intimidation and the threat of retribution in Eritrea: individuals who refuse to make payment may have their inheritance rights voided; their family members may be penalized; and they may be subject to detention or denial of an exit visa if they return to Eritrea. (p. 22)

42. A widely used generic term for Eritreans and Ethiopians.
43. The role of public gathering spots is of special significance in immigrant communities where, almost by definition, population densities are high and housing often crowded. Single rooms and apartments are shared by several persons; in some dwellings, residents sleep in shifts. Such a life can be overwhelming, with personal space at a premium. Basic personal hygiene is difficult. Public places (e.g., bars, restaurants, social clubs, community centers, etc.) are welcome venues and outlets for satisfying basic needs, securing nutrition, and providing a space for socialization. As an example, in Washington, DC, those who work in blue-collar and service-related jobs (e.g., taxi drivers, parking garage attendants, etc.) often congregate over their lunch hours for a meal in one of the many Habesha restaurants in that city. This may be the only decent meal they have in a day. Habesha of one ideological persuasion or another often congregate in certain clubs that then attract other patrons of similar political views. These places of recreation and socialization are, as it were, "community living rooms," or recreations of the traditional Eritrean village, the *'adi*.
44. See U.S. Department of State, Bureau of Democracy, Human Rights, and Labor. "2011 Human Rights Report," country report on Eritrea. May 24, 2012. http://www.

state.gov/j/drl/rls/hrrpt/humanrightsreport/index.htm#wrapper/. Accessed July 19, 2012.
45. In the Eritrean Orthodox Church, the patriarch or *abune* is the equivalent of a presiding bishop. The Eritrean Orthodox Church is one of six churches that are called Oriental Orthodox, stemming from a doctrinal dispute after the 451 CE Council of Chalcedon. Traditionally within this family of churches, the Egyptian Coptic Church is viewed as *primus inter pares*. After Eritrea achieved de jure independence in 1993, the Eritrean Orthodox Church formally became independent. (Formerly the Eritrean Church was a diocese of the Ethiopian Church.) A protocol was signed with the Egyptian Church and the Orthodox Church in Eritrea became a full-fledged member of the Oriental family of churches, a process through which the Ethiopian Church had gone through in 1959. Since then, the patriarch of the Egyptian Church customarily ordains the Eritrean patriarch. The governing body of the Eritrean Church is the Holy Synod, or meeting of bishops of the church.
46. As an example of the extent that the state would be willing to go in silencing the Eritrean Orthodox Church, one incident of January 2007 is of great significance. On the orders of the lay administrator, Yohafte Dimetros, two priests, accompanied by three government security agents, confiscated personal effects from Abune Antonios' residence and his sacred symbols of office: his patriarchal vestments, scepter, ceremonial chins, and several other items of great spiritual value, especially the Holy Myron.

Holy Myron (from *"myron,"* a Greek word meaning "fragrant perfume" or "ointment") is the oil used in the Sacrament of Confirmation administered immediately after Baptism. To the Orthodox faithful, it is an item of great significance—a real, physical, and visible link between humankind and the Deity and a symbol of the church's spiritual power. Its seizure, especially for nonliterate Eritreans for whom such physical symbols are of immense importance, was a heinous act of humiliation. Unordained hands are not permitted to touch such holy things. Such an officially sanctioned action of this magnitude of degradation of holy things had never before transpired. This was equivalent to the spiritual rape of the legitimate Patriarch of the Eritrean Orthodox Church, stripping him of all dignity and from the Orthodox faithful all sense of assurance of the church's institutional stability.

Such stripping of the visible emblems of spiritual authority is a message of deep significance—both to the educated elite and to the lesser-educated majority of citizens—in Orthodox Eritrean culture. Dissent and independent thought were not to be tolerated by the regime and that message was clear.

In analyzing the cloudy politics of a country like Eritrea, we should not understate the importance of seeing symbolic political acts as indications and signs of deeper political currents. Small actions are often windows into the deeper processes of the regime's thinking. In a political culture in which over two-fifths of the population is illiterate, and many of those classified as literate are barely so, such symbolic actions and statements carry an intense cultural and political meaning.
47. Eritrean Orthodox Church, Diocese of North America, "Resolutions on the Dangerous Developments in the Eritrean Orthodox Church." July 15, 2005, 2.
48. Ibid.
49. Chains for Christ.org. "An Eritrean Bishop's Game of Cat and Mouse—'Special Report.'" October 20, 2011. http://www.inchainsforchrist.org/index.php?view=article&catid=35%3Aarticles-&id=103%3Aan-eritrean-bishops-game-of-cat-and-mouse-special-report&option=com_content&Itemid=54. Accessed June 22, 2012.
50. Eritrean Orthodox Church, Diocese of North America. "Seattle Board Responds to Abba Sinoda's Illegal Interference in the Administration of the Church." August 17, 2006.

51. Abba Sinoda, first an agent of the Eritrean regime, sent to the United States in 2005 to disrupt the legitimate church, himself later sought and was granted political asylum in the United States. How this plays out in the body he heads and in its political stance is not at all clear.
52. This number was established by the Internet searches of church listings in the cities known to have sizeable numbers of Eritreans. Websites, where available, as were congregational Facebook pages were also examined. Most are vague and focus on purely church matters. A listing of current "Antonios" congregations provided by an administrator of the diocese was compared with a list posted on the church's website prior to the 2005 schism.
53. See http://www.eccboston.org/index.html.
54. See Olufemi A. Akinola. "Politics and Identity Construction in Eritrean Studies, *c.* 1970–1991: The Making of *Voix Érythrée*." *African Study Monographs* 28, no. 2 (July 2007): 47–86.
55. See, for example, the front page lead of the August 11, 2012, edition of *Eritrea Profile*, "Festival of Eritrean Community in Scandinavian Countries Conducted with Patriotic Zeal." http://74.63.78.28/feb2012/eritrea_profile_11082012.pdf. Accessed August 11, 2012.
56. The Facebook link to the 2012 festival scheduled for July is: http://www.facebook.com/pages/5th-Eri-Youth-Festival-SAWA-Festival-2012/221719847893061#!/photo.php?fbid=320877571310621&set=a.320877557977289.78895.221719847893061&type=1&theater.
57. Bettina Conrad. "When a Culture of War Meets a Culture of Exile: Second Generation Diaspora Eritreans and Their Relations to Eritrea." *Revue Européene des Migrations Internationales* 22, no. 1 (2006): 59–85.
58. Letter from Eritrean Orthodox Church, Diocese of North America, to the Embassy of Eritrea, Washington, DC, dated February 9, 2008. The letter incorrectly identifies the station as FM.
   http://tewahdo.org/Diocese/To%20Embassy%20of%20Eritrea%20Radio%20011808.pdf. Accessed June 22, 2012.
   On its webpage (http://tunein.com/radio/WUST-1120-s23436/), the station describes itself as "The Multi-Cultural Voice of the Nation's Capital" "broadcast[ing] to diverse ethnic and international communities throughout our capital region in English and other languages." http://www.wust1120.com/WUST/Welcome.html. Accessed June 22, 2012.
59. For example, a recent edition of *The Economist* ("Diaspora Politics: Returning Officers." *The Economist*, June 2, 2012, 74) reports that "[a]around a dozen countries ... give non-resident citizens their own advocates in parliament." The article cites Columbia, Croatia, France, Italy, Morocco, and Portugal where parliamentary seats are set aside for diaspora members. Eritrea need not be challenged by this development. Although Eritrea does conduct local elections, national elections have never been held since independence in 1993. Such elections were planned for 2001, but were cancelled. The referendum on independence was UN organized and supervised.
   Dovelyn Agunias, of the Washington-based Migration Policy Institute, surveys the institutions developed by homelands to interface with their diasporas and provides case studies of Mexico, Mali, and the Philippines. (See Dovelyn Rannveig Agunias, ed. *Closing the Distance: How Governments Strengthen Ties with Their Diasporas* (Washington, DC: Migration Policy Institute, 2009.) Sonia Plaza and Dilip Ratha look specifically at the developmental aspects of homeland-diaspora relations. (See Sonia Plaza and Dilip Ratha, eds. *Diaspora for Development in Africa* (Washington, DC: World Bank Publications, 2011.) The picture that emerges is one

of vibrant interaction between the homeland government of the sending country and the diaspora residing in receiving countries. Sheffer, in his classic 1986 collection of articles, sharpens our conceptual notions about diasporas. (See Gabriel Sheffer, ed. *Modern Diasporas in International Politics* (New York: St. Martin's Press, 1986.)

60. This is in contrast to Sandra M. Chait, author of *Seeking Salam*, who interviewed Eritrean community members in the Seattle-Portland areas between 2004 and 2008. She found "loyalty and sadness" to characterize their responses. E-mail from Dr. Chait to Irvin H. Bromall, dated July 2, 2012.

References
Books

Agunias, Dovelyn Rannveig, ed. 2009. *Closing the Distance: How Governments Strengthen Ties with Their Diasporas*. Washington, DC: Migration Policy Institute.

Berlin, Ira. 2010. *The Making of African America: The Four Great Migrations*. New York: Viking.

Chait, Sandra M. 2011. *Seeking Salaam: Ethiopian, Eritreans, and Somalis in the Pacific Northwest*. Seattle: University of Washington Press.

Cheah, Pheng and Bruce Robbins, eds. 1998. *Cosmopolitics: Thinking and Feeling beyond the Nation*. Minneapolis: University of Minnesota Press.

Connell, Dan. 1993 and 1997. *Against All Odds: A Chronicle of the Eritrean Revolution*. Lawrenceville, NJ, and Asmara, Eritrea: Red Sea Press, Inc.

Farmer, Paul. 1999. *Infections and Inequalities: The Modern Plagues*. Berkeley: University of California Press.

Hepner, Tricia Redeker. 2011. *Soldiers, Martyrs, Traitors, and Exiles: Political Conflict in Eritrea and the Diaspora (The Ethnography of Political Violence)*. Philadelphia: University of Pennsylvania Press.

Iyob, Ruth. 1997. *The Eritrean Struggle for Independence: Domination, Resistance, Nationalism, 1941–1993*. New York: Cambridge University Press.

Plaza, Sonia and Dilip Ratha, eds. 2011. *Diaspora for Development in Africa*. Washington, DC: World Bank Publications.

Sheffer, Gabriel, ed. 1986. *Modern Diasporas in International Politics*. New York: St. Martin's Press.

Journal Articles and Chapters in Books

Agunias, Dovelyn Rannveig. 2009. "Institutionalizing Diaspora Engagement within Migrant-Origin Governments." In *Closing the Distance: How Governments Strengthen Ties with Their Diasporas*, edited by Dovelyn Rannveig Agunias, 1–54. Washington, DC: Migration Policy Institute.

Akinola, Olufemi A. July 2007. "Politics and Identity Construction in Eritrean Studies, c. 1970–1991: The Making of Voix Érythrée." *African Study Monographs* 28(2): 47–86.

Bereketeab, Redie. 2007. "The Eritrean Diaspora: Myth and Reality." In *The Role of Diasporas in Peace, Democracy and Development in the Horn of Africa*, edited by Ulf Johansson Dahre, 79–96. Lund, Sweden: Social Anthropology, Department of Sociology, and Department of Political Science; Lund University & Somalia International Rehabilitation Center. Research Report in Social Anthropology (Printed by Media-Tryck Sociologen, Lunds Universitet).

Conrad, Bettina. 2003. "When Neverland Meets Otherland: Virtual Communities and Real-Life Divisions in the Eritrean Diaspora." In Siegbert Uhlig. "Proceedings of the 15th International Conference on Ethiopian Studies." Hamburg, 2003, 58–65.
Conrad, Bettina. 2006. "When a Culture of War Meets a Culture of Exile: Second Generation Diaspora Eritreans and Their Relations to Eritrea: Revue Européene des Migrations Internationales." 22(1): 59–85.
Conrad, Bettina. 2005. "'We Are the Prisoners of Our Dreams': Exit, Voice, and Loyalty in the Eritrean Diaspora in Germany." *Eritrean Studies Review* 4(2): 211–61.
Conrad, Bettina. 2006. "'We Are the Warsay of Eritrea in Diaspora': Contested Identities and Social Divisions in Cyberspace." In *Diasporas within and without Africa*, edited by Leif Manger and Manzoul A.A. Assal. Uppsala: Nordiska Afrikainstitutet.
Conrad, Bettina. 2006. "Out of the 'Memory Hole': Alternative Narratives of the Eritrean Revolution in the Diaspora." *Afrika Spectrum* 41(2): 249–71.
Conrad, Bettina. 2005. "From Revolution to Religion: The Politics of Religion in the Eritrean Diaspora in Germany." In *Religion in the Context of African Migration Studies*, edited by Afe Adogame und Cordula Welssköppel, 217–41. Bayreuth: Bayreuth African Studies Series, No. 75.
Farmer, Paul. 2004. "An Anthropology of Structural Violence." *Current Anthropology* 45(3): 305–25.
Feingold, David A. October 2005 "Human Trafficking." *Foreign Policy*, No. 150 (September–October 2005): 26–30, 32. Accessed August 8, 2011. http.www.justor.org.
Gutiérrez, Carlos González. 2009. "The Institute of Mexicans Abroad: An Effort to Empower the Diaspora." In *Closing the Distance: How Governments Strengthen Ties with Their Diasporas*, edited by Dovelyn Rannveig Agunias, 87–98. Washington, DC: Migration Policy Institute.
Hepner, Tricia Redeker. 2011. "Eritrean Immigrants." In *Multicultural America: An Encyclopedia of the Newest Americans*, Vol. 2, edited by Ronald H. Bayor, 617–55 Santa Barbara, CA; Denver; and Oxford: Greenwood Publishing.
Iyob, Ruth. 2000. "The Ethiopian-Eritrean Conflict: Diasporic vs. Hegemonic States in the Horn of Africa, 1991–2000." *The Journal of Modern African Studies* 38(4): 659–82.
Kibreab, Gaim. 2007. "The Eritrean Diaspora, the War of Independence, Post-Conflict (Re)-construction and Democratisation." In *The Role of Diasporas in Peace, Democracy and Development in the Horn of Africa*, edited by Ulf Johansson Dahre, 87–115. Lund, Sweden: Social Anthropology, Department of Sociology, and Department of Political Science; Lund University & Somalia International Rehabilitation Center. Research Report in Social Anthropology (Printed by Media-Tryck Sociologen, Lunds Universitet).
Mekonnen, Daniel R. "Pre- and Post-Migration Patterns of Victimisation among Eritrean Refugees in the Netherlands." Paper given at the panel, Eritrea—A Country Losing Its People, on June 18, 2011, at the Fourth European Conference on African Studies, the Nordic Africa Institute, Uppsala, Sweden, June 15–18, 2011.
Revelations, "Engaging the Eritrean Diaspora: Wikileaks." *Ethiopian Review*. Accessed December 17, 2011. http://www.ethiopianreview.com/forum/viewtopic.php?f=2&t=29059. June 30, 2011.
Schiller, Nina Glick, Linda Basch, and Cristina Szanton Blanc. "From Immigrant to Transmigrant: Theorizing Transnational Migration." *Anthropological Quarterly*, Vol. 68, No. 1 (January 1995): 48–63.
Sheffer, Gabriel. 1986. "A New Field of Study: Modern Diasporas in International Politics." In *Modern Diasporas in International Politics*, edited by Gabriel Sheffer. New York: St. Martin's Press.
Turner, Brian S. "Outline of a Theory of Citizenship." *Sociology*. Accessed May 31, 2012. http://soc.sagepub.com/content/24/2/189.short.

Newspaper Articles, News Magazines, News Services

"The Magic of Diasporas." Leader. *The Economist*. November 19, 2011, p. 13.
Sanders, Carol. "Eritreans in Canada Shaken Down by Despot Back Home." Winnipeg Free Press. November 25, 2011. Accessed November 27, 2011.
"Diaspora Politics: Returning Officers." *The Economist*, June 2, 2012, p. 74.

United Nations and Other International Organizations Reports and Documents

United Nations High Commission for Refugees. A Year of Crises Global Trends in 2011. Accessed July 4, 2012. http://www.unhcr.org/4fd6f87f9.html.
United Nations Security Council. Report of the Monitoring Group on Somalia and Eritrea Pursuant to Security Council Resolution 2002 (2011). July 13, 2012.

U.S. Government Documents

U.S. Census Bureau. By Elizabeth M. Grieco, Yesenia D. Acosta, C. Patricia de las Cruz, Christine Gambino, Thomas Gryn, Luke J. Larsen, Edward No. Trevelyan, and Nathan P. Walters. May 2012. "The Foreign-Brn Population in the United States: 2010." American Community Survey Reports.
U.S. Census Bureau. "Table FBP-1. Profile of Selected Demographic and Social Characteristics: 2000."
U.S. Department of Homeland Security, Office of Immigration Statistics. By Daniel C. Martin and James E. Yankay. "Refugees and Asylees: 2011."
U.S. Department of State, Bureau of Consular Affairs. "Travel Warning." April 18, 2012. Accessed August 12, 2012. http://travel.state.gov/travel/cis_pa_tw/tw/tw_5698.html.
U.S. Department of State."Us DoS Statement on Eritrean Recognition of Dual Citizenship." November 7, 2011. http://webcache.googleusercontent.com/search?rlz=1T4ADRA_enUS444US444&q=cache:2pbuzsDtU0QJ:http://travel.state.gov/travel/cis_pa_tw/cis/cis_1111.html%2Bdual+citizenship+eritrea&gs_upl=0l0l0l187343lllllllllll0&hl=en&ct=clnk.
NGO and Professional Association Reports, Documents, and Publications: Randy Capps, Kristen McCabe, and Michael Fix. "New Streams: Black African Migration to the United States." Washington, DC: Migration Policy Institute, 2011.
Kathleen Newland. 2010. *Voice after Exit: Diaspora Advocacy*. Washington, DC: Migration Policy Institute.
Schmitz-Pranghe, Clara. July 2010. "Modes and Potential of Diaspora Engagement in Eritrea." DIASPEACE Working Paper No. 3, July 2010.
Tezare, Kizanet, Tsehay Said, Daniel Bahets, Helen W. Tewolder, and Amanuel Melles, Selam Peacebuilding Network. October 2006. *The Role of the Eritrean Diaspora in Peacebuilding and Development: Challenges and Opportunities*. Toronto, Ontario.
Vertovec, Steven. June 2005. *The Political Importance of Diasporas*. Migration Information Source. Washington, DC: Migration Policy Institute.

Unpublished Papers

Cano, Gustavo and Alexandra Délano. 2004. "The Institute of Mexicans Abroad: The Day After . . . After 155 Years." Paper delivered at the 2004 Annual Meeting of the American Political Science Association, September 2–5, 2004.

Tricia Redeker Hepner. 2009. "Seeking asylum, autonomy, and human rights: Eritreans in Germany and the United States. Paper presented to the School of African Studies (University of London) conference. April 16, 2009.

Internet Resource Materials

Ashine, Argaw. "How Does 'Poor' Eritrea Afford to Fund Al-Shabaab?" *The Citizen.* November 9, 2011. Accessed March 24, 2012. http://thecitizen.co.tz/editorial-analysis/20-analysis-opinions/16938-how-does-poor-eritrea-afford-to-fund-al-shabaab.html.

Augustana Heritage Association. Accessed January 29, 2012. http://augustanaheritage.org/index.php.

Bell, Stewart. "Eritrea, Repressive African Dictatorship, Using Toronto Consulate to Bankroll Military: UN Report." July 23, 2012. Accessed July 24, 2012. http://assenna.com/eritrea-repressive-african-dictatorship-using-toronto-consulate-to-bankroll-military-un-report.

Bell, Stewart. "Eritrea Raising Money in Canada, Financing Terrorists to Attack Canada." *National Post.* November 5, 2011. Accessed March 25, 2012. http://news.nationalpost.com/2011/11/05/eritrea-is-raising-money-in-canada-and-financing-terrorists-that-want-to-attack-canada/. (Also published as "Eritreans Pressured to Pay 'Diaspora Tax' to Eritrean Diplomats and Agents in Canada to Finance Terrorist Groups to Attack Us." CIReport. Accessed March 23, 2012. http://www.cireport.ca/tag/eritrean-diplomats.)

Eritrean Community Center Links

Boston: Accessed January 18, 2016. http://www.eccboston.org/index.htmlhttp://www.eccboston.org/index.html; Washington, DC: http://www.ertra.com/dc/DC%20community%20home%20page.html.

Eritrean Orthodox Church, Diocese of North America. "Seattle Board Responds to Abba Sinoda's Illegal Interference in the Administration of the Church." August 17, 2006.

Eritrean Orthodox Church, Diocese of North America. "Resolutions on the Dangerous Developments in the Eritrean Orthodox Church." July 15, 2005.

Greenwood, Phoebe. "Eritrean Regime Cashes in on Arms and Human Trafficking, Says UN Report." *The Guardian.* July 17, 2012. Accessed July 23, 2012. http://www.guardian.co.uk/world/2012/jul/17/eritrean-regime-arms-human-trafficking.

Horn of Africa News. Various dates. Accessed January 18, 2016. http://hornofafricanews.blogspot.com.

In Chains for Christ.org. "An Eritrean Bishop's Game of Cat and Mouse—Special Report." October 20, 2011. Accessed June 22, 2012. http://www.inchainsforchrist.org/index.php?view=article&catid=35%3Aarticles-&id=103%3Aan-eritrean-bishops-game-of-cat-and-mouse-special-report&option=com_content&Itemid=54.

Hailbronner, Kay. "Nationality in Public International Law and European Law." Accessed May 31, 2012. http://www.law.ed.ac.uk/citmodes/files/NATACCh1Hailbronner.pdf.

Letter from Eritrean Orthodox Church, Diocese of North America, to the Embassy of Eritrea, Washington DC, February 9, 2008. Accessed July 19, 2012. http://tewahdo.org/Diocese/To%20Embassy%20of%20Eritrea%20Radio%20011808.pdf.

Teklemariam, Amanuel A. Summer 2005. "Understanding Abyssinian immigrants in the U.S.: Socio-cultural Background and Contemporary Experiences." *Western Journal of Black Studies.* Accessed June 14, 2012. http://findarticles.com/p/articles/mi_go2877/is_2_29/ai_n29240859/?tag=content;col1.

3

Africana Gender Studies: Toward Theorizing Gender without Feminism

Valethia A. Watkins

Introduction

Within the discipline of Africana Studies, an initiative is underway to systematically develop and infuse more concepts and information related to (Black) women's studies and gender content into the field. The emergence of (Black) women's studies as an area of specialization or a field of study within Africana Studies is one of the more significant outcomes of this infusion initiative. Understanding the intersection between the concepts of gender, (Black) women's studies, and feminism is imperative, if Africana gender studies is to avoid being reduced to functioning as a mere academic clone of and indistinguishable academic field from traditional women's studies, which is feminism dominated.

In significant ways, feminism is a hegemonic discourse. Feminist-derived concepts and assumptions have colonized discourses evoking the concept of gender as a category of analysis. The agenda of mainstreaming feminism as a conceptual paradigm beyond the field of traditional women's studies is motivated and informed not just by the intent of perpetuating the privileged status of feminism as an explanatory model, but by the animating idea of rendering feminism as a compulsory filter (i.e., universal interpretative lens) in all gender analyses and historical examinations of women, regardless of the academic discipline. This initiative poses a fundamental intellectual challenge for Africana Studies. I have used the term "compulsory feminism" to identify a type of feminism that seeks to privilege itself as the default and requisite normative lens and conceptual framework for guiding, framing, and determining how research is done on gender or in its use as an analytic category (Watkins 2006, 2010a, 2010b, 2011). The compulsory dynamic is primarily accomplished by constructing gender and feminism as indivisible.

The attempt to construct feminism as endemic to gender by rendering the two inseparable conceptually incarcerates gender as an analytical category. This tendency has, consequently, functioned to arrest the development (or at the very least compromise the viability) of nonfeminist explanatory models of gender as substantively distinct from feminism rather than mere adjuncts to its ideational genealogy. After stating the broad conceptual ground occupied by feminism (and its correlate "hyphenated feminism") as an academic discourse that obscures other potential discourses, this chapter identifies and examines a variety of rhetorical strategies used by compulsory feminism to repetitiously and perpetually recenter feminism in a monopolistic fashion vis-à-vis gender. It is through the co-optation of the concept of gender (e.g., treating gender as a euphemism for feminism) that feminists have sought to make their particular social construction a universal gender lens and the use of their explanatory model obligatory. This is a form of intellectual imperialism that discursively colonizes (i.e., acts as a mode of appropriation that dominates and circumscribes) the production of knowledge of Africana women and gender within a narrow mode of inquiry (Mohanty 1991; Nzegwu 2003; Okome 2003; Oyewumi 2005).

It may be hard to imagine feminism without gender. This, however, causes Africana Studies thinkers to wonder if the opposite, imagining gender without feminism, is possible within the discipline of Africana Studies. In other words, is it possible to theorize gender without undue deference to the constellation of normative theories and a priori assumptions indicative of the master narratives of the concept? How would a gender analysis within the discipline of Africana Studies differ from a gender analysis produced in other disciplines, in particular traditional women's studies? What would set the two analyses apart?

It is both necessary and possible for disciplinary Africana Studies to conceptualize gender as a tool of analysis without feminism. Creating discipline-specific normative theories of gender in Africana Studies unfettered by feminism will provide a more egalitarian foundation for the full spectrum of equally progressive nonfeminist, non-Eurocentric, and non-gender-biased perspectives to gain visibility that cease to be overshadowed by and subordinated to the production of knowledge on women and gender by feminists. Realizing the objective of reconceptualizing gender from Africana Studies perspectives is the leading challenge, which precedes the search for a new, different, and more appropriate name(s) to describe the intellectual enterprise of gender analysis within Africana Studies. The failure to seriously engage this challenge will result, intentionally or unintentionally, in doing feminist intellectual work by another name and thereby invariably replicating the Eurocentric conceptual system and bias in other guises.

Definitional Dilemmas: The Many Sides of Feminism

What is feminism? There is great debate over the meaning of the word feminism in the academy. However, outside of academia the meaning of feminism appears to be less ambiguous. For some, the answer to the aforementioned question seems so obvious that they never deeply contemplate the meaning of feminism. Popular culture and the media, for instance, represent the definition of feminism as simply the belief in women's equality. At the other end of the spectrum are professional gender academics who argue there does not exist a single feminism; instead there are multiple feminisms or many feminisms. This approach to conceptualizing feminism as a set of separate and discrete theories of feminism has come to be known as the hyphenated model of feminism or hyphenated feminism (Grant 1993).

Hyphenated descriptions of feminism emphasize alleged differences between various feminist schools of thought while simultaneously deemphasizing shared ideas common to each of them. The hyphenated model of feminism that emphasizes the plurality of feminisms delineate various schools of thought with an array of labels to denote various subgroups and their idiosyncratic and subjective articulations of the meaning of feminism to them (e.g., radical feminism, Marxist feminism, socialist feminism, liberal feminism, postmodern feminism, Black feminism, etc.). The meaning of feminism is constantly shifting and open to new interpretations. The promise is that each woman or group of women can personally define feminism for themselves, and each new version/iteration of feminism theoretically will share equal status or be equally valid within the continuum of feminist thought. This view is encapsulated in the following characterization of the internal debate over the meaning of the word:

> Feminists do not agree among themselves on one all-inclusive and universally accepted definition of the term feminism. Depending on a number of factors, feminism can mean different things and have a variety of functions. (Ruth 1990, 3)

Patricia Hill Collins writes about a similar definitional dilemma for those trying to define the term Black feminism. Her watershed text *Black Feminist Thought* describes the concept of Black feminism as a term "widely used but rarely defined . . . it encompasses diverse and contradictory meanings" (1991, 19). The case against a broadly shared and underlying consensus definition of feminism that provides the foundation for its coherence is overstated. Such a project would be more viable if the definitional focus were preceded by an effort to identify the common denominator between various versions of feminism.

The hyphenated approach described amounts to what Valerie Wagner (1995) and others have described as the "multiplication of feminism," a method by which I would argue compulsory feminism defends itself from accountability. It is a method by which feminism can appropriate, absorb, or even water down dissent. In doing so, dissent is disarmed and in some cases becomes completely invisible. This rhetorical strategy has served to neutralize critiques or disarm critical evaluations. Although there will always be differences within any group or political ideology, there are also fundamentally shared ideas that cause conceptual communities to be bound together under shared political labels as foundational principles. Valerie Wagner describes the process as follows:

> The multiplication of "feminism" is now read as a sign of healthy progress that feminism is making rather than as a sign of unbridgeable disagreements. In other words, all critiques of feminism and revindications of different feminism become feminism's self-critiques, where feminism, one suspects, still remains the copyright of a dominant group of people. (p. 123)

The strategic choice to emphasize differences and disagreements between different theories of feminism, coupled with the myth that each idiosyncratic and personalized definition of feminism has equal status, gives the illusion of nonexistence of a dominant feminism or no coherence between different schools of thought. This has allowed the Eurocentric constructions of feminism to remain privileged and centered in traditional Women's Studies and, in this light, the movement to infuse gender in all academic disciplines (including Africana Studies) at the most fundamental level becomes the means through which Eurocentric gender narratives become replicated as normative interpretations and hidden frames of reference. In this context "gender" and "gender analysis" becomes a euphemism for feminism. This is the quintessential means by which compulsory feminism is socially constructed and infused across the boundaries of different disciplines through the conflation of gender with feminism.

The Politics of Compulsory Feminism

One of the leading methods used to impose feminism on the study of gender outside the field of traditional women's studies involves the use of the concept of compulsory feminism. This concept promotes an unacknowledged movement to make feminism, as a unit of analysis, the only authentic and legitimate explanatory framework and lens to determine how research on gender and by extension women is framed and analyzed. The underlying assumption of compulsory feminism supports the notion that feminism and its constellation of concepts (e.g., gender and sexism, etc.) are indivisible. The seeming inseparability of gender from feminism's definition of this concept serves to reinforce the myth that, in some form or fashion, *every credible study of gender must be read through feminism and its discursive terrain* (i.e., accommodate its terms of debate and normative assumptions) in order to "properly" read and comprehend gender and, by extension, women in any given culture; to articulate the interest of women; and to address the special concerns or experiences of women. This premise sustains the dynamics of domination of feminist discourses in the analysis of gender across academic disciplines.

The dichotomous logic of "either/or" thinking reinforces the centrality of compulsory feminism. People are misled to believe they must make false choices. The message meant to be conveyed by the either/or logic in this context is conveyed as follows: a person is either a feminist or, by default, they are against women or oppose gender equality; either they defer to a feminist perspective on gender or they are collaborators in the abuse and subordination of women; either they use feminist explanatory models to analyze gender or they are accused of ignoring women or gender issues.

The underlying faulty premises behind these "either/or" assertions can be challenged on several grounds. First, these claims rest on the incorrect idea that the pursuit of knowledge and justice for women cannot be separated from feminism. To the contrary, a person can pursue justice on behalf of women or knowledge of women without doing so using a feminist-centered orientation. Concepts of freedom, equality, and justice are a part of the common heritage of humanity; therefore, no single ideological perspective or political group can credibly assert a proprietary claim to these concepts. Second, a person can be an advocate for women without simultaneously being an advocate for feminism. This is not a contradiction for those who see a distinction between "advocacy for women" and "advocacy for feminism."

We must challenge the faulty premise that advocacy for women presents prima facie evidence of de facto feminism. The concept of *"de facto" feminism* is a handmaiden of compulsory feminism. De facto feminism asserts that a person by virtue of agreement with the proposition that women should have the same rights as men automatically becomes a feminist, even if they deliberately refuse to identify themselves with the label. In fact, the concept of *de facto feminism* is a common rhetorical strategy and rebuttal used by self-named feminists to override the overt rejection of feminism (Watkins 2007). In common feminist discourse, this strategy is referred to as the "I'm not a feminist, but" counterargument. According to this line of thinking, if a person espouses certain allegedly feminist ideas (e.g., a belief in women's rights or gender equality), it is acceptable to infer they are in fact feminists by definition, despite their claiming otherwise.

In academia, particularly in the field of women's studies, it is common for the terms "women's studies" and "feminist studies" to be conflated. In fact, the intellectual genealogy and ideological paradigms of feminism are often equated and/or conflated with the subject matter field (and, equally problematically, inter and/or multidisciplinary project[s]) of women's studies. By this logic, traditional women's studies has been defined exclusively in terms of one ideological or theoretical perspective. In a clear attempt to reserve the intellectual genealogy and thereby discursive foundation of the field, women's studies is often defined as the academic arm of the feminist movement or the extension of this movement in the academy (Patai and Koertge 2003). Using the terms women's studies and feminist studies interchangeably has led to extremely narrow definitions of the field of women's studies as either the study of women from a feminist perspective or the study of women (and similarly oriented men) as feminists (Watkins 2007). This myopic conception of the field of traditional women's studies as essentially feminism by another name is a manifestation of the dynamic of compulsory feminism.

A discipline or academic field is larger than a single perspective within it and as an emerging discipline with its own normative theoretical contours and agendas largely unsettled beyond declaration of the necessity to undertake this work, Africana Studies must not concede its intellectual spaces on the subject of women to an ill-considered embrace of an aggressive, Western-oriented academic colonization presented by the women's studies feminist academic paradigm. Equating women's studies with feminist studies comes at the expense of other theoretical perspectives, draining the intellectual dynamism in the diversity of thought by papering over and covering up the intellectual, cultural, and/or political differences among and between communities as well as the women and men who study them.

The Invisible Majority: Nonaligned Women

While many academic feminists are women, it does not follow that most women (academics and, importantly, nonacademics) are feminists. When it comes to the subject of self-naming, large numbers of women consistently refuse to label themselves as feminist or choose not to advocate feminism, including substantial numbers of Black women. I refer to these women as "nonaligned women" (Watkins 2007). Nonaligned women intentionally choose to remain independent and "unaffiliated" with any subgroup of feminists or any version of feminism on the continuum of feminist thought. The refusal to define themselves as feminists is the most obvious way many nonaligned women manifest their deep reservations about, irreconcilable differences with, or rejection of feminism as a worldview as well as their reluctance to be viewed as in agreement with some of the extreme positions embedded in some articulations of feminism (i.e., men as the political enemies of women, gender separatism as political strategy, or male bashing) (Gordon 1987; Hudson-Weems 1993; Ani 1994; Aldridge 2003). Nonaligned women are neither monolithic nor a single group. Collectively, however, they constitute what can be referred to as an invisible majority.

The longstanding unpopularity of feminism among significant numbers of women and diverse groups of women is neither benign nor meaningless. It is, in fact, the Achilles Heel of feminism. The serious discrepancy between significant numbers of women disclaiming feminism on the one hand and the political fiction that feminist theoreticians represent and speak for all women as a group (i.e., women as women) is not always a readily apparent, but nevertheless a serious contradiction. What is the significance of the gap between the idea of feminism as *the* voice of women as a group and the fact so many women dissociate themselves from feminism? How does the myth of feminism as the "collective voice of women" endure when the very women feminists claim to speak for and represent dislike or disagree with enough elements associated with feminism to often shun the very word feminism itself? This is the irreconcilable contradiction of feminism and the challenge to Africana Studies scholars seeking to undertake intellectual work on this academically colonized terrain.

How has feminism responded to this contradiction and what are its implications for the credibility and probative value of feminism as an interpretative framework, both within and beyond Africana Studies? These questions have largely gone unanswered and ignored because feminist-oriented thinkers have been quite effective in keeping this grand contradiction hidden and therefore not properly accounted for in the master gender narratives. The political meaning of nonaligned women and the significance of their rejection of feminism is a phenomenon that calls for greater scholarly attention. In the normative discourses on gender, nonaligned women have been silenced and overshadowed by feminist women, a prime example of intragender inequality. They have not been silent as much as they are silenced by what I refer to as "master gender narratives." These thinkers have been intentionally erased through a conspiracy of silence as a consequence of their audacity to remain independent of feminism. This tendency is also exacerbated by the desire of many feminists to remain at the center of all gender analyses across academic disciplines. The imposition of invisibility on "nonaligned" women has created and perpetuated the mythology that all women are united by gender and in turn they are constructed as so-called sisters and inherent allies. This imagined unity, as a single gender group, is seen as translating into the authority of feminists to speak in the name of all women categorically, as if women have a singular voice. The pretense of homogeneity, based on this myth, reproduces the domination of feminism vis-à-vis the discourses on gender.

Despite their direct voices remaining largely invisible in master gender narratives, the ideas and critiques of feminism by nonaligned women are sometimes co-opted, appropriated, and incorporated in feminist-centered narratives. These ideas, in fact, are frequently repackaged and misleadingly represented without attribution as internal dialogue and internal critique among feminists, which also serves to erase any recognition of the nonaligned outsider orientation of the ideas. In rare instances when the rejection of feminism by nonaligned women is unavoidable and begrudgingly mentioned, it is done in a condescending and superficial manner that, in effect, serves to dismiss and trivialize nonaligned dissent.

Ironically, paternalistic explanations that rationalize the subordination of nonaligned women in feminist scholarship abound. By this logic, feminists are brave and courageous and nonfeminist women are cowards and fearful, too fearful to stand up for women. The well-founded skepticism of feminism by nonaligned women is usually not attributed to substantive political differences or disagreements but instead patronizingly characterized as the commentary of traumatized gender traitors or male-identified women too weak-willed to stand up for women. These thinkers' voices are, consequently, deemed justly subordinated to the views and voices of feminist women. The message meant to be conveyed is that the overt rejection of feminism is tantamount to disloyalty to women or inherently antiwoman. To be nonaligned with compulsory feminism is not to excuse or condone abuse, violence, exploitation, or unjust discrimination against women or anyone else and it certainly does not mean one is ignoring the problems of women. This is a deliberate and self-serving misreading of the meaning and significance of nonaligned women's well-founded skepticism of the construction of feminism as a universal explanatory model.

The views of nonaligned women are consistently represented in a negative light in feminist scholarship and they are too often caricatured or have their political acumen questioned in the scholarship on women. For example, nonaligned women are stereotyped as less intelligent or ignorant about feminism and this is posited as the basis for their disavowal of feminism. It is self-serving to dismiss female critics of feminism as uninformed. Indeed, many nonaligned women have done a critical assessment of this explanatory framework and have concluded it does not hold universal meaning for all groups of women; consequently, they conclude that it does not have the same probative value and explanatory power in every cultural context.

Some scholars of African descent are determined to confront and transcend this colonizing academic impulse to homogenize women based on gender. One of the most notable thinkers in this effort is Oyeronke Oyewumi, a leading theorist in African Women's Studies. Oyewumi, in her groundbreaking text *The Invention of Women* (1997), asserts that:

> In fact, the categorization of women in feminist discourses as a homogenous, bio-anatomically determined group which is always constituted as powerless and victimized does not reflect the fact that gender relations are social relations and therefore, historically grounded and culturally bound. If gender is socially constructed, then gender cannot behave in the same way across time and spaces. (p. 10)

The implication of Oyewumi's critical observation is that the gender stories of different groups of women are not and should not be treated as if they were interchangeable. All women do not have the same gender, if by gender we mean the cultural interpretations of gender as manifested in the social definitions, stereotypes, expectations, and assumptions that constitute the normative meanings of womanhood and manhood in a given society (Oyewumi 2011). Likewise, and consistent with worldview orientations across the subject matter range, gender questions and methodologies for interrogating the meaning of gender are not and will never be interchangeable across cultures, similarities, and convergences notwithstanding (Oyewumi 1997, 2003).

Is the reader of this chapter a feminist? Was Ida B. Wells Barnett or Frances Ellen Watkins Harper a feminist? What standards should Africana Studies scholars use before they impose on any given historical figure the label feminist? Within the context of compulsory feminism, the question of whether or not a person is a feminist is often rendered moot. The self-definition or rejection of feminism is rendered immaterial by the all-encompassing approach to feminism as an explanatory model, deployed as a universal gender lens to frame and control writ large the discourses on women as subject of study. Under current practices, no matter how much an individual person or different groups of women attempt to define themselves as nonfeminists or try to remain nonaligned, the very category of "women" itself and the interpretations of the gender of women has been discursively colonized by feminism, rendering the would-be subject's self-naming irrelevant. In other words, self-definitions are being consistently subordinated and supplanted to feminist definitions.

The rejection of feminism by women is a thorny problem that feminists could not and did not ignore, even if they rarely overtly acknowledge it. Disassociation from feminism by a critical mass of women is politically dangerous for feminism because it undermines the concept's credibility as reflecting the collective voice and political will of women as a group. Disarming or eliminating all together the option for rejection became a defensive response to the specter that challenges of large-scale rejection of academic domination by feminists of the discourse on women and gender represented. The nullification of the rejection of feminism by individual women thinkers or significant groups of women as subjects of historical and/or contemporary study, particularly on the part of Africana Studies scholars, is one of the driving forces behind the invention of compulsory feminism. The rhetorical evasion and reinscription of invisibility is the means to make disclaiming feminism a moot point. It also serves the purpose of rendering invisible resistance to feminism by women. To be sure, feminism concedes some differences among women. However, the kind of differences the paradigm is willing to concede is very narrow in scope. For example, feminist-oriented scholars have recognized internal differences among and between feminist women. By the same token, the political differences between nonaligned women and feminist women are hardly ever seriously engaged and are in fact consistently dismissed, trivialized, or erased with the possible exception of their acknowledgment of political differences with conservative women. As a consequence,

Africana gender studies scholars who are nonaligned have been relegated to an inferior status within the context of narratives on women and gender, and the women of feminism are privileged at their expense.

Africana Gender Studies: Beyond the Womanism/Feminism Dichotomy

Scholars of Africana studies, including Delores P. Aldridge, Clenora Hudson-Weems, La Frances Rodgers-Rose, and Dorothy Tsuruta, among others, have articulated a preference for theories of womanism over feminism (e.g., Africana womanism, African-centered womanism, African womanism, and/or womanism unmarked etc.) for analyzing and teaching (Black) women's experiences in the field and/or discipline (Aldridge and Young 2000; Tsuruta 2012). Clenora Hudson-Weems (1993) describes Africana womanism as "neither an outgrowth nor an addendum to feminism, *Africana Womanism* is not Black feminism, African feminism, or Walker's womanism" (p. 24). Diverse conceptions of womanism evolved in response to the conceptual weaknesses and disagreements with certain components of feminism's approach to gender in the context of Black women's lived experiences. Some schools of womanist thought concentrate on attempting to construct alternatives to feminism as well as challenging the domination of feminism in interpreting gender, particularly within the context of Africana Studies (Hudson-Weems 1993; Aldridge 2003). Other articulations of womanism, displaying conceptual similarities to the novelist Alice Walker's (1983) conception of "womanism," remain more or less supplemental (rather than oppositional) as a subsidiary of feminist thought and discourse.

Although the concept of womanism has now existed in various manifestations for decades, with new conceptualizations and definitions still emerging, it has yet to achieve conceptual parity with feminism as an intellectual thrust in the academy. In many regards, the subordinated status of womanism in discourses on gender reflects intragender disparity (unequal relations between different groups of women) in the construction and use of normative gender narratives. The reconceptualization of gender as explanatory model and analytical category for Africana Studies must take priority if this subordinated status in interpreting gender is to change. The uneven attempts of diverse schools of womanist thought to offer a paradigm-shifting critique of feminism is, of course, an indispensable development if for no other reason than the fact that it gives expression to the discontent of many Black women with feminism and reflects the fact that they are unwilling to concede gender studies to feminism. In addition, some versions of womanism represent increasingly salient attempts to construct explanatory models for analyzing Africana women as distinct and at once insoluble and interconnected communities within larger social, intellectual, cultural, and political spheres of Africana community rather than as decontextualized and isolated units of analysis who share contrived and artificial allegiances and similarities with "women" (marked by feminists with the cultural sensibilities and political allegiances of the West) over similarly externally defined notions of "race" and/or "class."

The discourses of womanism are growing in influence in the academy, especially within the field and discipline of Africana Studies. The proper role of feminism within Africana Studies, however, remains contested terrain (Watkins 2006). One of the impediments to womanist thought as an alternative is the fact that the demarcation between womanism and feminism is not clear-cut. In fact, given that Alice Walker, a devout feminist, is credited with coining the term, in many quarters womanism and (Black) feminism are conflated, or womanism is viewed as an expression of feminism by another name. In this view, womanism simply represents a different name and not a different conceptual paradigm or interpretative framework on gender. Another impediment to a conceptual break is the fact that womanism and feminism share an intellectual genealogy.

It is important to understand that the "womanist/feminist dichotomy" does not reflect the full range or the totality of gender perspectives within the field and discipline of Africana Studies. Although some of the nonaligned theorists in the field may be womanists, many nonaligned theorists and academics are neither feminists nor womanists, particularly the subset of this group devoted to exploring the possibilities of discipline-specific normative theory building. The attempt to privilege either womanism or feminism to the exclusion of other perspectives, both old and ever-emerging ones, oversimplifies the complexity of gender theory in Africana Studies and renders the diversity invisible.

Nor is it enough to rebrand discourses on gender within Africana Studies. The inauguration of new labels alone while simultaneously borrowing the entire underlying conceptual system of gender developed by traditional women's studies and feminist-centered academics bedevils the field with the very conceptual fetters it was created to reject (Watkins 1997). Rebranding amounts to label changing and does not go far enough. In many respects, reconceptualization must precede gender infusion as a category of analysis in Africana Studies scholarship and the reconstruction of gender in the study of Africana world communities. Simply rendering Black women more visible under these old regimes of gender and preexisting paradigms allows the Eurocentric biases of these normative theories to endure unadulterated. This is a major pitfall of current approaches to challenging the hegemony of feminism.

Defining Feminism through Africana Studies: Normative Challenges and Exemplars

Curiously, the complexity and definitional quandary of the word feminism disappears when feminists interface with women outside the academy, when they are seeking to recruit women to feminism and/or when they are redefining famous women in history as feminists. In their efforts to win the hearts and minds of ordinary women, feminists often represent feminism in the exact opposite way they do in the academy. Outside of the academy, in popular culture and social media, feminism is represented as an uncomplicated and simple idea. The radical oversimplification of the meaning of feminism is epitomized by the typical sanitized definition of feminism commonly found in the average dictionary. The standard dictionary defines feminism as simply the belief that women should have the same social, economic, and political rights as men; or the movement for equality between the sexes. The standard dictionary definitions of feminism are very misleading and ascribe an untenable meaning to this word. There is no hint of the definitional heterogeneity and competing social constructions of the concept posited by the hyphenated approach feminists have historically used to define feminism, nor are the contested aspects of the nature of the term reflected in the typical dictionary definitions of this word. There are a variety of shortcomings with these "definitions," and there is far more to feminism than these generic definitions imply. Dictionary definitions of feminism should not be accepted at face value for a variety reasons, including the fact that they are such pedestrian and politically self-serving representations of the meaning of this word. The average person uninitiated in the discourses of feminism would remain fundamentally unenlightened and misinformed about the deeper meaning of feminism. They would not acquire enough information to gain a proper and meaningful understanding of this term. Most significantly, these definitions fail to convey what is *unique* about feminism or what sets it apart from other theories or ideologies. What sets feminism apart or rather what is unique about feminism is not its advocacy for equality for women but rather its unique and distinctive approach to advocacy for women and more specifically its way of framing gender and the constellation of related issues.

The dictionary definitions of feminism are deficient and overreach because they convey the false idea that mere acceptance of the principle of equality between the sexes by definition makes a person a feminist and by extension an advocate of feminism. Automatically subsuming under the label of feminist everyone who believes in gender equality is an unacceptable approach to defining feminism. If we accept this as the litmus test for feminism then a person cannot be in favor of gender equality without being a feminist, a classic example of the compulsory dynamics of feminism. This is the faulty premise embedded in the misleading dictionary definitions that cede to feminism an unequivocal proprietary claim over the struggle for gender equality. This approach subordinates nonaligned women and progressive men, who without equivocation are equally committed to advancing the interests of women. The hegemonic definition of feminism endemic to dictionary formulations of this word that characterize the very belief in gender equality as de facto feminism is a quintessential example of the discursive colonization of gender. Because of this dynamic, it is not enough for nonaligned women to reject feminism without equally anticipating, counteracting, and accounting for how feminism is likely to respond in order to continually subvert discourses it views as oppositional to its continued hegemony over gender.

A more accurate and representative definition of feminism would not merely attempt to define feminism primarily in terms of its professed political aims or the perceived differences between various articulations of feminism but rather would pivot on what is *unique* to and about feminism. What is feminist about feminist theories? What is the sine qua non of feminism, the thing without which feminism would cease to exist and is shared in common by different versions of feminism? Identifying the unique and thus defining characteristics should be the point of departure for any good and competent definition of feminism. As stated earlier, the challenge facing Africana Studies scholars in this area is to stand apart from Western intellectual genealogies and normative assumptions and, in so doing, declare subject-oriented intellectual space out of which to theorize about Africana communities as well as other communities of meaning outside those communities, beginning with an interrogation of their normative assumptions.

On the basis of this criterion and grounded in the way the term has been operationalized in the academy, my own Africana Studies–oriented working definition of feminism would situate it as follows: *feminism is the study of gender pathology; it is the study of pathological models of gender to the exclusion of the study of positive, healthy, constructive, and more egalitarian models of gender.* Feminism is a worldview and set of theories that define women and men primarily as adversaries, political enemies, and rivals rooted in the premise that they are members of two separate and mutually exclusive groups on opposite sides politically. As a tool of analysis, feminism is a 'conflict model' of human relationships that presumes that all of human history is really the history of a universal gender war between women and men as two distinct and discrete oppositional groups. The gender conflict model tries to explain and make sense of the world through a "men versus women interpretative lens" (i.e., an adversarial consciousness) that perpetually and reflexively pits women as a group against men as a group and consistently represents them at odds and disconnected. Feminist discourses are organized around the notions of the "battle between the sexes" or "battle of the sexes"; this is the sine qua non to the feminist way of framing and making sense of gender.

Although it is no longer politically correct to refer to men as the enemy, nonetheless this sentiment was a founding idea of feminism and subsequently it has profoundly influenced the development and evolution of the social construction of gender in most feminist-centered scholarship. This way of framing gender potentially has serious implications for constructing gender as a category of analysis in Africana Studies. Many Africana scholars strongly disagree with the construction of gender as necessarily a wedge issue between African men and women. The politics of polarization that are endemic to feminism have led many to question if this is the most constructive or best approach to gender. Anna Julia Cooper's (1988) framing of the intergender interests of Africana people as indivisible along the lines of gender provides an important point of departure for Africana scholars seeking to reconceptualize gender and to reject the intransigent adversarial consciousness embedded in the "men versus women" interpretative lens. Cooper said it best when she wrote "for woman's cause is man's cause: (we) rise or sink together, dwarfed or godlike, bond or free" (p. 61). Why should Africana women frame their interests qua women and compartmentalize them along a discursively colonized gender line? This is one of the major points of disagreement and source of the fundamental differences between Africana Studies approaches to gender and the approach of traditional women's studies. The predisposition of many Africana Studies scholars to refrain from analytically segregating and conceptually isolating the interests of African people along a rigid and fundamentally unchallenged gender line and to emphasize the intersectionality of the interests of both genders, as a people or a collective whole, distinguishes (Black) women's studies within Africana studies from other approaches.

The rhetorical strategies employed to sustain feminism and impose compulsory feminism demonstrate the inability or unwillingness of many feminists to coexist, on an equal basis, with alternative perspectives on gender. The imperative to transcend this irreconcilable difference in conceptualization for framing gender is behind many of the efforts to develop alternative approaches and frameworks. Many of the critiques of nonaligned women were not driven by a desire to reform feminism or for inclusion. Instead, they were declarations of independence and self-determination. Those scholars seeking alternative explanatory models are coming to voice, unapologetically exercising their natural right to autonomously analyze gender not beholden to preexisting paradigms or to Eurocentric normative assumptions. The reconceptualization of gender from the distinct concerns, worldviews, and perspectives of African(a) people will be pivotal to distinguishing Africana gender studies. The creation of new conceptual frameworks is the preliminary challenge and the prerequisite for moving Africana Studies beyond asymmetrical gender questions and canned answers that characterize and produce cookie-cutter narratives across the other academic disciplines. This will free Africana Studies from the strictures of compulsory feminism and the master narratives and frames of reference of Eurocentric gender orientations.

Conclusion

A critical mass of scholars in Africana Studies are opposed to gender bias in all of its guises, without equivocation, and we are deeply committed to eradicating gender inequality. We all have a vested interest in the successful outcome of this struggle. It's a just and moral cause. Despite this fact, many remain unpersuaded that feminism represents the one and only or the best approach for collectively addressing and eradicating gender inequality, either internally or externally, for African people. As stated earlier, feminism has articulated an explanatory framework for analyzing pathological models of gender. Although this is important work, it is only one dimension of gender. The other dimensions (more constructive and egalitarian models of gender), on balance, remain underanalyzed and ignored. The normative approach of feminism produces one dimensional, essentialist, and incomplete explorations of gender, ignoring or attempting to subsume the full complexity of intergender and intragender relationships across time and space and between and among various human communities. Sexism is a subcategory of the larger category of gender but it is not to be equated with the category itself. Feminism produces a monolithic social construction of gender (gender as pathology only) because it conflates gender and sexism.

Although it is impossible to be in absolute disagreement with everything about feminism, the larger point of contestation is that the myth must be exploded that a single theoretical perspective or explanatory model holds all the legitimate insights on gender or that it is reasonable for this lens to try to dictate how gender is to be framed and analyzed universally (across cultures and academic disciplines). Decentering feminism as the privileged framework and normative lens is necessary for decolonizing the study of gender within Africana Studies. Feminism does not hold universal meaning for all women. It does not have the same probative value and explanatory power across cultures. To be clear, this chapter does not argue that feminism does not have a place within the genealogy of gender and the discourses on women; rather, in this area, Africana Studies must expose the subversive nature of the concept of compulsory feminism and how it operates to the detriment of nonaligned women and other perspectives on gender. Ideally this chapter will help to contribute to the development of more egalitarian contexts that provides the requisite intellectual space for a fuller range of disciplinary Africana Studies scholars (and others modeling our efforts and techniques) to participate in the production of knowledge about gender unfettered by feminism.

Demanding deference to feminist theories through the imposition of their normative assumptions is a form of intellectual imperialism. Decentering compulsory feminism is necessary if the full diversity of perspectives among women scholars is to be realized and represented in the scholarship on women and gender. The Achilles Heel of feminism is a ripe area for interrogation. The examination of the gap between how the majority of women perceive their relationship to feminism, in contrast to how feminism characterizes and represents its relationship with women in general, especially those who have disavowed feminism, will be very revealing about the nature of feminism. As a discipline, Africana Studies is committed to creating the intellectual conditions necessary for the continued development of a nonsexist and non-Eurocentric body of knowledge on gender and Black women that deliberately eschews an antimale orientation. (Black) Women's studies within Africana Studies has widespread support as an important component of the field because many Africana Studies scholars recognize the merit and indispensable role of this kind of scholarship for creating more holistic and comprehensive narratives of Africana people as a whole, leaving no gender behind. As an area of research, the development and evolution of (Black) women's studies provides the opportunity for the discipline to simultaneously rethink and interrogate the concept of gender.

There are competing conceptualizations of (Black) women's studies within the context of Africana studies. Some would like it to mirror traditional women's studies by utilizing identical analytical approaches and concepts. Others would like to see the field develop its own autonomous approaches to gender based on the distinct social and cultural imperatives of the global Africana world. A gender analysis in Africana Studies will be different from the one done in other academic fields, if and to the degree that the field develops a different conception of gender based on the uniqueness of Africana history and the distinct social and cultural imperatives that this gives rise to. Josephine St. Pierre Ruffin provides some guidance for conceiving a different approach that is not rooted in framing gender in adversarial terms, even as women are centered. In 1895, St. Pierre Ruffin (1992) cogently articulated the differences in Africana approaches to gender when she observed:

> Our woman's movement is a woman's movement in that it is led and directed by women of the race for the good of women and men, . . . we want, we ask the active interest of our men . . . we are not alienating or withdrawing, we are only coming to the front, willing to join any others in the same work and cordially inviting and welcoming any others to join us. (p. 443)

This ancestor's statement is based on an entirely different orientation and understanding of the intergender relationships between our women and our men, which is not viewed predominantly through the overarching prism of an adversarial gender frame of "men versus women." This is not an isolated view among African(a) people of both genders. Awareness of this premise, its intellectual genealogy, and the normative assumptions undergirding both is a prerequisite for the intellectual decolonization of the production of knowledge on women within disciplinary Africana Studies, foreshadowing a new chapter in the study of gender.

References

Aldridge, D. P. 2003. "Africana Studies and Gender Relations in the Twenty First Century." *The Western Journal of Black Studies* 27(3): 186–93.
Aldridge, D. P. and Young, C. 2000. *Out of the Revolution: The Development of Africana Studies.* Lanham, MD: Lexington Books.
Ani, M. 1994. *Yurugu: An African-Centered Critique of European Culture, Thought and Behavior.* Trenton, NJ: African World Press.
Cooper, A. J. 1988. *A Voice from the South by a Black Woman of the South.* New York: Oxford University Press. (Original work published in 1892).
Gordon, V. V. 1987. *Black Women, Feminism and Black Liberation: Which Way?* Chicago: Third World Press.
Grant, Judith. 1993. *Fundamental Feminism: Contesting the Core Concepts of Feminist Theory.* New York: Routledge.

Hudson-Weems, C. 1993. *Africana Womanism: Reclaiming Ourselves*, 3rd ed. Troy, MI: Bedford Publishers, Inc.

Mohanty, C. T. 1991. "Under Western Eyes: Feminist Scholarship in Colonial Discourses." In *Third World Women and the Politics of Feminism*, edited by C. Mohanty, A. Russo, and L. Torres, 51–80. Bloomington, IN: Indiana University Press.

Nzegwu, Nkiru. 2003. "O Africa: Gender Imperialism in Academia." In *African Women & Feminism: Reflecting on the Politics of Sisterhood*, edited by Oyeronke Oyewumi, 98–157. Trenton, NJ: African World Press.

Okome, Mojubaolu Olufunke. 2003. "What Women, Whose Development? A Critical Analysis of Reformist Feminist Evangelism on African Women." In *African Women & Feminism: Reflecting on the Politics of Sisterhood*, edited by Oyeronke Oyewumi, 67–98. Trenton, NJ: African World Press.

Oyewumi, O. 1997. *The Invention of Women: Making of African Sense of Western Gender Discourses*. Minneapolis: University of Minnesota Press.

―――, ed. 2003. *African Women & Feminism: Reflecting on the Politics of Sisterhood*. Trenton, NJ: African World Press.

―――, ed. 2005. *African Gender Studies: A Reader*. New York: Palgrave Macmillan.

―――, ed. 2011. *Gender Epistemologies in Africa: Gendering Traditions, Spaces, Social Institutions, and Identities*. New York: Palgrave Macmillan.

Patai, D., and Koertge, N. 2003. *Professing Feminism: Education and Indoctrination in Women's Studies*. Lanham, MD: Lexington Books.

Ruffin, J. S. 1992. "Address of Josephine St. Pierre Ruffin to the First National Conference of Colored Women." In *Black Women in White America: A Documentary History*, edited by G. Lerner, 440–3. New York: Vintage Books. (Original work published in 1895).

Ruth, Sheila. 1990. *Issues in Feminism: An Introduction to Women's Studies*. California: Mayfield Publishing.

Tsuruta, D. 2012. "The Womanish Roots of Womanism: A Culturally-Derived and African-Centered Ideal (Concept)." *The Western Journal of Black Studies* 36(1): 3–10.

Wagner, V. 1995. "In the Name of Feminism." In *Feminism Beside Itself*, edited by D. Elam and R. Wiegman, 119–30. New York: Routledge.

Walker, A. 1983. *In Search of Our Mothers' Gardens: Womanist Prose*. New York: Harcourt, Brace Jovanovich.

Watkins, V. 1997. "Womanism and Black Feminism: Issues in the Manipulation of African Historiography." In *The African World History Project: The Preliminary Challenges*, edited by J. H. Carruthers and L. C. Harris, 245–84. Los Angeles, CA: Association for the Study of Classical African Civilizations.

―――. 2006. "Dimensions of African Studies: Gender." In *Lessons in Africana Studies*, edited by G. E. Carr, 22–41. Philadelphia, PA: Songhai Press/School District of Philadelphia.

―――. 2007. "New Directions in Black Women's Studies." In *The African American Studies: A Reader*, 2nd ed., edited by N. Norment, Jr., 229–40. Durham, NC: Carolina Academic Press.

―――. 2010a, March. "Leave No Gender Behind: Reflections on the Non-traditional Gender Worldview of Radical Black Women." The Association for the Study of Classical African Civilizations Southern Regional Conference. Benedict, College, Columbia, South Carolina."

―――. 2010b, March. "Toward a Post-Feminist Orientation for the Study of Women in Africana Studies." The National Council for Black Studies National Conference. New Orleans, Louisiana.

―――. 2011, March. "Reflections and Remembrance: Re-Conceptualizing the Gender of Africana Women." The Association for the Study of Classical African Civilizations National Conference. Howard University, Washington, DC.

4

Africana Aesthetics: Creating a Critical Black Narrative from Photographs in South Texas

Alberto Rodriguez

After Reconstruction, leaders of the Black community sought to present a more assertive image to the Anglo world. Soon the United States and parts of the world were flooded with images of Blacks laboring at Hampton and Tuskegee University. Hampton and Tuskegee University presented Blacks doing manual labor, of course always directed by paternalistic Anglos. Many Blacks sought to express themselves in a more positive light and show themselves outside Anglo perceptions of their place in society. As Blacks acquired social and economic success, many Black leaders made it a goal to present Blacks in a new light under the Anglo racial structures.

With the help of W.E.B. Du Bois, the "New Negro" became featured at three events, The Atlanta Exposition of 1895, The Nashville Centennial Exposition of 1897, and The Paris Exposition of 1900. In most cases, the showcases displayed social mobility and a sense of acculturation acquired by Blacks both in the North and South after Reconstruction. The collection of photos showed Blacks reading, writing, and engaged in the world's current political issues. All three events became a celebration of Black Nationalism and presented a sense of autonomy from Anglo dominance. This image of the "New Negro" has become part of the South Texas image as collected by photographer Robert Runyon. Although it is not known if Runyon was aware of the new image Blacks wanted to portray, he managed to capture this dynamic change with his camera.

Robert Runyon was born on a farm in Kentucky on July 28, 1881. Even though he received a limited education, it did not keep him from becoming a successful businessperson. He became one of the most successful photo postcard distributors in South Texas. Runyon started taking photographs in 1907 in his home state of Kentucky. Runyon moved to Brownsville in 1909 after the death of his first wife. While working for the Gulf Coast News and Hotel Company in Brownsville he perfected his trade in photography. In his spare time, Runyon took photographs of local events and natural habitats of South Texas. What he originally called a hobby soon turned into a profitable business.[1]

In 1910, Mexico was encompassed in a bloody civil war that affected the South Texas border. As the revolution manifested itself, it was Runyon who had his photographs of the violence turned into postcards that he sold throughout the United States. Although photographs portraying the

Photo 1. Runyon Studio on 1140 Saint Charles Street opened in late 1917 because his demand for postcards had diminished. Even though he did not like the idea of being indoors, the studio would support him and his family. Runyon's first love was the outdoors and taking photos of real life situations. Although he disliked taking portraits he did it with great precision leaving an exclusive record of the local population in Brownsville and South Texas.[2]

Photo 2. A self-portrait of Robert Runyon after a long day of taking photos of the local South Texas population. Even though his new portrait studio did not allow him to work outdoors it kept him closer to his wife and six children.[3]

conflict and change on the border brought him fame, he also took photographs for land developments that had displaced Mexican landowners of South Texas in the early 1900s. With the end of the Mexican Revolution, Runyon sought a new avenue for income. He opened a portrait studio on 1140 Saint Charles Street in Brownsville. His photographs offer powerful views of South Texas society and culture. His collection of over 8,000 photographs was eventually donated by his children to the University of Texas at Austin.

The most important portraits taken by Runyon were those of the Mexican Revolution, border life, and Blacks in South Texas. Even though his work on Blacks is mostly portraits and not photographs of daily activities, they displayed Blacks living in and around the South Texas border and indicate a Black sense of self and level of prosperity. Unfortunately, his collection of portraits for the most part does not include the names of people photographed. But the many men, women, and children photographed offer a unique view into Black culture. Although males dominate the collection, most appears to have a "defiant" image that is perceived in many of the photographs. This image does not appear in the Hampton and Tuskegee photographs. With the help of the U.S. Census one can get the sense of Black communities, racial makeup, social class, and social mobility on the South Texas border.

Most Blacks that Robert Runyon photographed in South Texas from 1910 to 1920 had achieved a different structural position than Blacks had occupied in the past. Under the Antebellum Period, and with their involvement with the U.S. Military, Blacks were often in alliance with other Anglos or Mexicans. By the early 1900s, Blacks in South Texas were an integral part of the growing agro-business in the "Magic Valley." Many of them worked on the St. Louis Brownsville Mexican Railway where they formed unions and mutual aid societies to help the local Black community. Although Blacks were segregated in South Texas, the new structural position they took allowed their community to flourish. The need for labor also allowed them to enjoy a sense of economic success they had not had in the past.

Although the Black population of South Texas has not been studied in detail, the U.S. Census showed that free Blacks numbered from 72 individuals in 1850 to 1,672 in 1930. Even though the census is notorious for undercounting people, it still gives its users an insight to Black settlement in South Texas. Table 4.1 shows the Black population (1850–1930) for five counties of South Texas (Willacy would be added in 1920 from what was part of Cameron):

Table 4.1. Total black population in South Texas by county, 1850–1930.

	1850	1860	1870	1880	1890	1900	1910	1920	1930
Cameron	72	73	157	117	60	177	74	771	928
Hidalgo		35	41	114	31	110	62	87	491
Starr		10	18	211	4	141	21	1	1
Webb		0	2	184	126	205	38	41	153
Willacy								1	99
Totals	72	118	218	626	221	573	195	901	1681[4]

Many Blacks who moved into South Texas were interracially married or married into Mexican families. Blacks who could not disguise their interracial marriages found sanctuary on the U.S./Mexican border. But it also occasionally worked the other way. John Webber, an Anglo man, for example, married one of his former slaves and moved to Texas in 1832. He settled in Webberville (the city was named after him as the founder).[5] Webber and his interracial family were soon forced to move out of town due to some narrow-minded townspeople.[6] They came to settle in an area around what is now known as Donna, Texas. The Webber family eventually acquired some 27,000 acres of land along the Rio Grande.[7]

Once established, the family extended a helping hand to other interracial families like the Jacksons, Singletarys, and Rutledges.

Blacks like the Webbers, Jacksons, Singletarys, and Rutledges who acquired a large amount of wealth were able to influence their racial identity within the South Texas local community. According to the U.S. Census of 1860, all 37 members of the 4 families were documented as Mulatos and not Blacks.[8] All of the family members were free Blacks who moved from Alabama. By 1870, 33 out of 35 members of the Webber, Jackson, Singletary, and Rutledge families were documented as Mulatos, counting the pattern of social mobility and the redefining of their structural position within the South Texas racial hierarchy.[9]

Photo 3. Although the Jackson Chapel is known as a Black Church, it had both Mexicans and Blacks attending its services and school. On the far left of the church one can see a cemetery that has both Mexican and Black surnames.[10]

All four families were instrumental in the support of Blacks in South Texas. One of their most important contributions was Jackson Chapel. A Methodist Church was founded in 1874 on Jackson Ranch between Donna and Hidalgo. The one room ranch church served both as a school and community meeting center. It still stands today. Even though the church became the center of the community, it was the school that gave many Blacks mobility and fraternity. Jackson Chapel led the way for other Black churches. By 1930, areas like Brownsville, Raymondville, Harlingen, and Edinburg also had Black churches. Black churches built in South Texas allowed a sense of autonomy from both Anglos and Mexicans and in turn allowed Black communities to flourish and Black identity to become part of the South Texas racial makeup. As more and more Blacks arrived in South Texas in the early 1900s, many found a network of support that allowed them to assert a new structural position on the border.

Even though examples like Jackson Chapel give a positive and cooperative image between both Mexicans and Blacks in South Texas, they still faced serious disregard and hatred by Anglo segregationists.

Photo 4. Photograph of an interracially married couple taken at Runyon's studio. In the South, interracial couples could face serious punishment, even years of jail time, for such unions. The idea that a Black man would take a White women as a wife was outlawed in most parts of the South[11]

In most of the Southern States, laws were passed making it illegal for members of different races to marry.[12] Antimiscegenation laws were supported by the U.S. Supreme Court in *Pace v. Alabama* in 1883. The decision to overturn antimiscegenation did not happen until the Supreme Court ruled in the *Loving v. Virginia* of 1967. At the time, 16 states still had antimiscegenation laws in place.[13] Anglo Southerners sought to maintain their dominance over Blacks and other minorities through the enforcement of these discriminatory laws. Anglo males sought to maintain their long history of sexual privilege with Black females and social control of Anglo women. Even though laws had been passed to keep different ethnic groups apart, many times love and social mobility overruled the law.

Social status could be acquired by the marriage of both ethnic groups. In many cases one of the members had acquired some kind of social status that made him or her more desirable. There is no doubt that love also played a major part in interracial marriages, but social mobility was a factor for both ethnic groups.

According to the 1900 census, 177 Blacks formed 25 households in Cameron County.[15] Most Blacks came from the Deep South and were not native to Texas. For the most part, these families were farmers who lived off the land. Out of the 25 households, 9 families owned their land and

Photo 5. In this photograph taken by Runyon we see an older Black male with a younger non-Black female. From their dress we can tell that they are not from the lower working class. Both of them are wearing jewelry, nice hats and outfits. Social mobility could have been offered by the older Black male.[14]

Photo 6. Runyon's photograph of a Black male and Mexican woman. In most cases it was Black males who married Mexican women.[16]

16 families rented the land they farmed. If Blacks acquired land in South Texas, it happened one of two ways. One, they had acquired economic success giving them assets to purchase land; two, they may have married into some of the landed Mexican families of South Texas.

In 1900, Hidalgo County had 17 families that were interracially married. The interracial marriages for the most part were Black men marrying Mexican women or first generation Tejanas. For example, Louis Rutledge was a Black male born in Alabama who lived in the Second Precinct in Hidalgo County in 1900. Louis married Angle, a Mexican woman who was born to Mexican parents. The Rutledges had been married 14 years and had 7 children ranging from 2 years of age to 13 years of age.[17] The census also shows that all children of all ages attended school.[18]

Photographs such as the three presented earlier, and the use of the U.S. Census, show that the social position of Blacks in South Texas would have been closer to Mexicans than to Anglos. Social solidarity for Blacks would align itself with Mexicans once again for some Blacks in South Texas. Blacks, Mexicans, and Tejanos were fighting a losing battle against Anglo newcomers. Blacks were being segregated by Jim Crow Laws that had been imposed throughout the South and Mexicans in the South were losing their land to unscrupulous land developers of South Texas. The social position held by Anglos over both ethnic groups could have pulled many Blacks and Mexicans together.[19]

It was common for both groups to live with each other and to cross the racial lines that existed between Mexicans and Blacks in South Texas. In 1900, Juan Zuniga's daughter, Redacinde Jackson, lost her Black husband. She then returned with her children to her father's home. Interracial families often had stepchildren living in their households. Juan Singletary had two stepsons, Ballagar and Davie Solis, living with him. Both were sons of Antonia, his Mexican wife. Nagario Jackson also had a stepson living in his household. His name was Christ Visnuevo the stepson of his Mexican wife Eugiruia. In these instances, if one person had been

Photo 7. This particular Black man had lighter skin than most of the other portraits. He could have been an offspring of the many interracial marriages of South Texas.[20]

Photo 8. This well-dressed Black man also seems to be lighter skinned than most of the Black population and could have been of mixed blood.[21]

married before and had children from a previous union, they were still allowed in the same households. Many times people who crossed color lines were outcasts along with their children. Photographs 7 and 8 show two men who seem to have redefined their structural position on the South Texas border. Both men are light skinned and well dressed and could have been the offspring of the many interracial marriages between Blacks and Mexicans on the border.

One of Runyon's more impressive images is an unnamed Black male posing with a newspaper in his lap and wearing reading glasses. The image portrays intelligence, not similar to the photographs of the Hampton and Tuskegee collection. Rather than working with his hands, this Black male portrays that his mind is as powerful as his body.

Photo 9. Photograph of Black children could have been products of interracial marriages. An analysis of their physical features shows they are not as pronounced as other Southern Blacks. Their hair is not curly and their noses are also smaller than most Blacks. Although it is not known if the children lived in South Texas the photo was taken in Brownsville, Texas, in the early 1900s.[22]

Images of the "New Negro" appeared in South Texas. Photos 10–14 are examples of this image. Blacks on the border, like Blacks in the North, were changing their structural position within the Mexican and Anglo racial hierarchy. Whether it was through reading, education, dress, or occupation, many Blacks on the border were not the poor sharecroppers or tenant farmers that have been depicted throughout American history at his time. Many Blacks had changed structural positions and redefined their ranking on the border.

The following charts were compiled with the use of the U.S. Census. They demonstrate the total number of Blacks and their level of literacy in Cameron, Hidalgo, Starr, and Webb counties from 1900 to 1930. According to this particular information, most of the adult Black population was literate. Percentages of literacy for all five counties were around mid-80s, with the exception of 1920 when Willacy was added, which led to 68%.

Literacy rates did not drop below 81 percent in 30 years, with the exception of Willacy County. The high rate of literacy among Blacks of South Texas obviously brought social and economic mobility for many. It also shows that Blacks took a vested interest in teaching their young how to read and write. The four charts in Table 4.3 show a breakdown of the raw numbers. The numbers of illiterate Blacks ten years and over is small when compared to the overall Black population.

Photo 10. Photograph of a Black man making sure the world knew that he can read and is an intelligent person. Literacy had been a priority for Blacks in South Texas since emancipation.[23]

Table 4.2. Literate percentage of blacks ten years of age and over from 1900 to 1930.

	1900	1910	1920	1930	Average Percent Per County
Cameron	87.58	79.73	65.37	91.27	81
Hidalgo	81.87	80.65	82.76	96.34	85
Starr	82.98	95.24	100	100	95
Webb	90.25	84.21	92.69	90.85	90
Willacy			0	89.89	45
Average Percent Per Ten Years	85.67	84.50	68.16	93.67[24]	

Table 4.3. Literate and illiterate blacks from 1900 to 1930.

1900 Census	Black Males	Black Females	Illiterate Negroes Ten Years of Age and Over
Cameron	133	44	22
Hidalgo	51	59	20
Starr	118	23	24
Webb	149	56	20
Willacy	0	0	0
1910 Census	**Black Males**	**Black Females**	**Illiterate Negroes Ten Years of Age and Over**
Cameron	40	32	15
Hidalgo	33	29	12
Starr	13	8	1
Webb	17	21	6
Willacy	0	0	0
1920 Census	**Black Males**	**Black Females**	**Illiterate Negroes Ten Years of Age and Over**
Cameron	391	380	267
Hidalgo	55	32	15
Starr	1	0	0
Webb	17	24	3
Willacy			1
1930 Census	**Black Males**	**Black Females**	**Illiterate Negroes Ten Years of Age and Over**
Cameron	497	431	81
Hidalgo	239	252	—
Starr	0	1	0
Webb	79	74	14
Willacy	45	44	9[25]

The high literacy rate among Blacks in South Texas could have brought some social mobility within the local community. Many Blacks formed Black unions and mutual aid societies. A closer look at Runyon's collection of Black photographs shows a small round pin on the left lapel of most of the men. The pin could have been a Black Mason Society or a membership pin for the Colored Trainmen of America. Although its origins

Photo 11. Photograph of three well-dressed men taken outside of Runyon Studio sometime between 1913 and 1930. The middleman seemed to have a confidence that could only come from a person of status.[26]

are not known, it seems that many of the men who displayed the pin are well dressed and have a confident demeanor about them. Photographs 11–14 show well-dressed men who seemed to have acquired some kind of economic success.

Unions and mutual aid societies were not new to the border and South Texas. The first union and mutual aid societies were created by Mexicans to allow a sense of support for their communities and coworkers.[27] Much like Mexican unions and mutual aid societies, Black unions allowed support for locals that they could not find within the Mexican or Anglo structures. At the same time, unions allowed Blacks to improve their structural position by monopolizing jobs on the railroad. In addition, the need for labor on the border allowed Blacks to negotiate for better working conditions and higher wages. Even though the self-advancement of Blacks in the workplace allowed them better working conditions they were still segregated in their residential neighborhoods. For example, in Cameron County in 1900 most Blacks lived in the 3-Pct, in Hidalgo County most Blacks lived in the 2-Pct, in Starr County most Blacks lived in the 6-Pct.[28] Segregation would continue for Blacks in South Texas in 1910 and 1920 with the largest numbers of Blacks in Cameron County living in 7-Pct. In Hidalgo most Blacks would move into the cities of Edinburg and McAllen and in Starr Country they lived in the 5-Pct.[29] In

Photo 12. This photograph of a young Black male seemed to be out of place in the collection. His dress and hair are those of a person that would have been involved in the Harlem Renaissance. Although it is not known is this person lived in South Texas the photo was taken in Brownsville, Texas in the early 1900s.[30]

turn, Blacks did acquire economic success in South Texas but they were still limited in their daily life by Jim Crow segregation.

Although many of the Runyon photographs seemed to be of well-dressed Blacks, he did capture images of working-class Blacks. Runyon showed Blacks in different jobs that required some kind of manual labor. His photographs are much like the ones taken by Hampton and Tuskegee. There are nameless Blacks who seemed to have acquired a trade after emancipation and certainly not involved in the W.E.B. Du Bois image of the "New Negro."

Many Blacks who came to South Texas after 1903 worked for the railroads. Photos 15 and 16 are of two Black men who worked on the

Photo 13. Here we see an older Black male with a starched white shirt and a pocket watch. He also seems to have confidence.[31]

St. Louis Brownsville Mexican Railway as firemen. Jobs like the ones these two men held were at the lower end of the pay scale for Blacks and required a larger amount of manual labor. Even though these jobs were at the lower end of Black labor in South Texas they were still part of Black union labor. In turn, local unions like The Colored Trainsmen of America allowed workers like the ones mentioned earlier to enjoy better

Photo 14. A well-dressed older Black who that is also wearing a round pin of his left side.[32]

working conditions and privileges that other Blacks in the South did not have due to their lack of unions. Thus, Blacks in South Texas were able to redefine their ranking within the work force.

In 1918, Blacks of the St. Louis Brownsville Mexican Railway formed a chapter of Colored Trainmen of American in Kingsville. The union's purpose was "to promote the condition and welfare of colored trainmen and elevate their social, moral, and intellectual

Photo 15 and 16. Two Black males who worked as laborers on the St. Louis, Brownsville, Mexican Railway. The lamp and the dress of the two men tell us they were probably firemen in charge of keeping the engines running on trains. Both men do not possess the positive and defiant image that the other Blacks in Runyon's collection do have.[33]

standing and welfare."[34] With the large demand for labor in South Texas due to development of the "Magic Valley" and the "Great Black Migration," Blacks could enjoy a sense of economic opportunity not experienced before. According to Woodie Horn, a brakeman from Kingsville, "the railroad made such a big impact on the community . . . Even school teachers didn't make the kind of money we did on the railroad."[35] With the high literacy rates and the help of Black unions like the Colored Trainmen of America, Blacks negotiated for better working conditions and higher wages. This could be why so many of Runyon's Black portraits show a sense of economic mobility. But they also show that Blacks were structurally segregated into special occupations, such as brakemen or porters for the St. Louis Brownsville Mexican Railway. Even though they were denied a group dignity and civil rights, the Runyon Collection shows that Blacks in South Texas enjoyed a sense of mobility not experienced in other parts of the South.

Photo 17. Photograph of a Black break man who worked in Brownsville for the St. Louis Brownsville Mexican Railway. Black rail works like break men and porters could make a lot of money due to the labor shortage.[36]

Blacks also had a long history as cowboys in South Texas and Mexico. Black cowboys in Texas made up one-third of cattle drives in Texas.[38] Black cowboys outnumbered Mexican cowboys and many became the second in command among their outfits. Although history has glorified the Anglo cowboy and his journey throughout the West, many times it was the Black cowboy teaching Anglos the trade they had mastered.[39] Black cowboys in South Texas and Northern Mexico changed their structural position in both Mexican and Anglo hierarchy

Photo 18. On the right side of the photographs is a Black porter of St. Louis, Brownsville, Mexican railway assigning passengers at the Brownsville train station.[37]

as early as the antebellum period. As mentioned in Chapter 1, many fugitive slaves were engaged in the cattle industry, learning valuable trades that made it easier for them to penetrate Anglo society along the border. The need for labor in both peripheries allowed locals to overlook color if they could gain from the trades that many Black cowboys possessed. Photographs 19 and 20 are of two Black men who appeared dressed in cowboy garb and would have worked in the South Texas border.

With the growing Black population in South Texas and increasing economic opportunity, many Blacks looked to profit from the area. Not only were Blacks in South Texas acquiring economic success but many looked to celebrate their culture. In January 1921, Runyons photographed the King & Carter Jazzing Orchestra of Houston, Texas. The orchestra obviously visited Brownsville to play for the growing Black population in Cameron County and surrounding areas. The orchestra could have had

Photo 19. Photograph of a Black cowboy who would have been familiar with both South Texas and Northern/Central Mexico.[40]

a swinging 1920s sound, largely influenced by the Harlem Renaissance and the image of the "New Negro."

Robert Runyon obviously captured the image of the "New Negro" of Brownsville in the early 1900s. Blacks in the United States looked to change perceptions of themselves set out by training institutes like

Photo 20. This Black male could have been a retired cowboy who might have been involved in some kind of law enforcement.[41]

Hampton and Tuskegee. In the process, Blacks in South Texas seemed to have acquired a sense of kinship and status within their communities. Black mobility was largely due to the shortage of labor in South Texas between 1900 and 1930 and union organizing, which in turn allowed for some to acquire economic opportunity and success. There is no doubt that Blacks in South Texas enjoyed a true sense of group dignity. Proof of this activity can be seen in Robert Runyon's photographs. Blacks came together to form Black unions that allowed them to navigate the

Photo 21. King & Carter Jazzing Orchestra, Houston, Texas, January 1921, photographed at Robert Runyon studio.[42]

"racial power sharing" in South Texas between Mexicans and Anglos to include Blacks. They found that more could be accomplished if Blacks worked as a cohesive group, which in turn granted the group dignity, a more cohesive Black identity, and the maintenance of their culture on the South Texas border.

Notes

1. Paul J. Vanderwood and Frank N. Samponaro, *Border Fury: A Picture Postcard Record of Mexico's Revolution and U.S. War Preparedness, 1910–1917* (Albuquerque, NM: University of New Mexico Press, 1988), 1–14 and Paul J. Vanderwood and Frank N. Samponaro, *War Scare on the Rio Grande: Robert Runyon's Photographs of the Border Conflict, 1913–916* (Austin: Texas State Historical Association, 1992), 1–16.
2. The Robert Runyon Photograph Collection [image number, 02532], courtesy of the Center for American History, University of Texas at Austin.
3. Ibid. [image number, 09236].
4. Historical Census Browser. Retrieved January 1, 2005, from the University of Virginia, Geospatial and Statistical Data Center: http://fisher.lib.virginia.edu/collections/stats/histcensus/index.html.
5. Alwyn Barr, *Black Texans: A History of African Americans in Texas, 1528–1995* (Norman: University of Oklahoma Press, 1996), 4.

6. http://www.tsha.utexas.edu/handbook/online/articles/view/DD/hfd5.html. *The New Hand Book of Texas Online*, February 15, 1999.
7. John Webber, http://www.tsha.utexas.edu/handbook/online/articles/view/DD/hfd5.html.*The New Hand Book of Texas Online*, February 15, 1999.
8. The 8th U.S. Census of Hidalgo County.
9. The 9th U.S. Census of Hidalgo County.
10. Jackson Chapel photo taken by author.
11. The Robert Runyon Photograph Collection [image number, 07679].
12. Charles Frank Robinson II, *Dangerous Liaisons: Sex and Love in the Segregated South* (Fayetteville: University of Arkansas Press, 2003), 21–24.
13. Ibid.
14. The Robert Runyon Photograph Collection [image number, 07584].
15. The 12th U.S. Census of Hidalgo County.
16. The Robert Runyon Photograph Collection [image number, 07640].
17. Molie13, Louis 11, Lee 10, Nancy 8, Anna 7, John 4, Bert 2, The 12th Census of the United Series: T623, Roll: 1644, 230.
18. The 12th U.S. Census of Hidalgo County.
19. Arnoldo De Léon, *They Called Them Greasrs: Anglo Attitudes towards Mexicans in Texas, 1821–1900* (Austin: University of Texas Press, 1983), 49–62.
20. The Robert Runyon Photograph Collection [image number, 06790].
21. Ibid. [image number, 06494].
22. Ibid. [image number, 07506].
23. Ibid. [image number, 06823].
24. Historical Census Browser. Retrieved January 1, 2005, from the University of Virginia, Geospatial and Statistical Data Center: http://fisher.lib.virginia.edu/collections/stats/histcensus/index.html.
25. Historical Census Browser. Retrieved January 1, 2005, from the University of Virginia, Geospatial and Statistical Data Center: http://fisher.lib.virginia.edu/collections/stats/histcensus/index.html.
26. Ibid. [image number, 07499].
27. Emilio Zamora, *The World of the Mexican Worker in Texas* (College Station: Texas A&M University Press, 1993), 72–81.
28. The 12th U.S. Census of Cameron, Hidalgo and Starr Counties.
29. The 13th and 14th U.S. Census of Cameron, Hidalgo and Starr Counties.
30. Ibid. [image number, 06398].
31. Ibid. [image number, 06993].
32. Ibid. [image number, 06428].
33. Ibid. [image number, 06684 and 06346].
34. Jennifer Borrer, "Colored Trainman of America," in *Historic Kingsville, Texas: Guide to the Original Townsites Volume II* (Kingsville, TX: Kingsville Historical Development Board, 1997), 102.
35. Ibid., 101.
36. The Robert Runyon Photograph Collection [image number, 06219].
37. Ibid. [image number, 02909].
38. Kenneth W. Porter, "Negro Labor in the Western Cattle Industry, 1866–1900," *Labor History* 10 (1969), 346–364, 366–368, 370.
39. Ibid., 346.
40. The Robert Runyon Photograph Collection [image number, 06502].
41. Ibid. [image number, 06331].
42. Ibid. [image number, 05019]

5

Africana Perspectives in Criminal Justice: Are Black Women the New Mules of the Prison Industrial Complex?

Nishaun T. Battle

Introduction

The Trayvon Martin/George Zimmerman case will forever be remembered for provoking a nationwide conversation on the influence that the intersectional identities of race, class, and gender have on trial outcomes. The trial and verdict of the shooting death of Trayvon Martin was indicative of a larger societal narrative, identifying the ways in which some bodies are criminalized based solely on their race, class, and gender. Communities across the country were filled with hope about the possibility of achieving social justice on such a sensitive and highly racialized case. Restorative justice has been suggested by scholars and activists alike, in similar cases, to provide some form of justice and humanistic understanding for such tragic events (Lyubansky 2013). Many grassroots activists, criminal justice practitioners, and average citizens meekly assumed that the national outcry that resonated across the United States would be the last one necessary for what many considered to be a blatant display of legal injustice.

Roughly a year later, the country and the world would learn of the deaths of Michael Brown in Ferguson, MO, Eric Garner in New York, and Tamir Rice in Cleveland, who died senselessly at the hands of law enforcement. It appeared that communities across the country had reached a tipping point, and nationwide protests ensued to demand that law enforcement officials be held accountable for these deaths. Almost every week, there was a new story in the media about a young, Black male who died at the hands of law enforcement. The national protest, which came together around the phrase "Black Lives Matter," consisted of individuals from diverse racial and ethnic backgrounds. However, while there were news reports of Black women as victims of police violence, these reports were primarily from social media blogs, and there was no formal or informal social movement centered on the pervasive punishment of Black women by the hands of law enforcement.

While individuals across the country watched as Zimmerman was set free for killing an unarmed young, Black male, Marissa Alexander was sitting in a prison, separated from her children, for acting in self-defense against a husband she asserted was abusive. Why was there no public outcry for Alexander? Marissa Alexander did not have a national movement with t-shirts demanding justice. While her case garnered more attention than that of any other Black woman at the center of a court case for self-defense over the past few years, she did not receive the same level of social support from communities across the country that young, Black males have. In situations like this, society's nonvalidation of Black women, combined with the treatment Black women have received from the criminal justice system, has resulted in the mistrust of the criminal justice system as a whole, specifically the notion of equal protection under the law. This kind of treatment suggests that Black women are not worthy of social or legal protection, and it sends a societal message that it is normal for Black women to be punished and physically harmed by law enforcement.

Social Construction of Race and Gender

The fundamental premise of intersectionality is that the interconnected categories of race, gender, and class cannot be analyzed in isolation of one another. Therefore, the social experiences of women vary based on their race and class, leading to definitions of womanhood that are based on entirely different sets of questions and assumptions. The social construction of gender that sought to describe essential feminine characteristics was the prevailing ideology during the nineteenth century, often referred to as "true womanhood" or the "cult of true womanhood" (Welters 1966). "True" women were thought to embody proper feminine behavior that included piety, domesticity, submissiveness, and purity. This social construction was used solely to describe White, middle-class women.

The dominant racial ideology used to describe Black women included "Mammies," "Matriarchs," "Sapphires," and "Jezebels" (Collins 2000). Collins (2000) maintains that these stereotypical beliefs about Black women contributed to their devalued status in society and led to racial oppression that was justified through systemic practices. As Carpenter (2012) asserts in describing the plight of Black women due to societal misrepresentation, "slavery, Black codes, sterilization campaigns and Jim Crow laws" were only a few policies implemented and predicated on a generalized societal belief toward the deviant proclivities of the Black community. These controlling images of Black women have had lingering effects and are still responsible for the ways in which Black women are perceived in contemporary times.

While the social perception of Black women has improved significantly over the past few decades, the pervasive social perception of Black women is still attached to negative stereotypes and images. For instance, in an attempt to defeminize Black women in mainstream society, an influx of demeaning media characters promoting the historical "Mammy" character surfaced. In fact, cinematic portrayals of characters such as Tyler Perry's "Madea," Eddie Murphy's "Norbit," and Martin Lawrence's "Big Momma," among a host of other aggressive, threatening, and desexualized characters, have all contributed to the grossly negative depiction of Black women that has essentially stripped them of their social identity (Chen et al. 2012).

During the Zimmerman/Martin trial, Rachel Jeantel was called upon to be a key witness based on the fact that she was on the phone with Trayvon Martin during the time he was shot and killed by George Zimmerman. She did not fit into the box that defines appropriate demeanor nor society's accepted physical traits of womanhood and this may have impacted the way in which jurors viewed the validity of her testimony. Moreover, because she was unable to represent herself in a way that embodied a mainstream upbringing and culture, Jeantel was scrutinized and depicted as a joke and someone who could not be trusted to provide an accurate detailed account of what exactly happened during the death of Trayvon Martin. In fact, to illustrate the power that media images have in viewing ordinary citizens as stereotypical characters, Olympian athlete Lola Jones was quoted as saying "Rachel Jeantel looked so irritated during the cross-examination that I burned it on DVD and I'm going to sell it as Madea goes to court" (*Huffington Post* 2013). Consequently, Jeantel was not taken seriously as a witness and this could have shaped the verdict of the jury, which happened to consist of all White women, with the exception of one who was Hispanic. There is an implication that one's body size, skin color, and perceived negative body language determine if a person should be taken seriously or trusted.

Skin color is also associated with criminality and punishment in the United States. Darker skinned individuals are typically associated with a lower socioeconomic status, which is also associated with having a low intelligence level (Hochschild and Weaver 2007). While Rachel Jeantel was depicted as an aggressive individual who often scoffed at questioning she deemed annoying, her level of intelligence was highlighted throughout various media channels repeatedly, as well as by one of the jurors. A juror identified as Juror B37 associated the level of perceived intelligence of Jeantel with her credibility as a witness. Juror B37 was quoted in an interview with Anderson Cooper on CNN as saying she believed Rachel Jeantel "felt inadequate toward everyone because of her education and her communication skills. I just felt sadness for her" (ac360blogs.cnn.com 2013). The constant inundation of negative images can have a direct connection to systemic inequities that present themselves in spaces in which subjective beliefs held by those with a valued social, economic, and racial standing can result in biased punishment of groups that hold no collective social or economic power in this country. When one is "othered," they automatically occupy a space of invisibility, which reinforces dominant modes of social relations (Collins 1990). When a person is considered an "other" their narrative and their voice are typically already shaped for them. Their experiences are rarely heard, seen, or understood. On every institutional level in society, Blackness has been, and currently is, viewed as a crime.

Media images of African American girls and women are often used to create a societal depiction of deviant behavior. Metalanguage used to describe behavior associated with gender and race is often a result of negative images that result in the punishment of Black women on a daily basis. The face of policy discourse is often attached to a racialized and gendered body. The racialization of poverty and welfare is used as a euphemism for race and gender (Bridges 2007). At the same time many African American girls struggle to refute social identification with hypersexualization contextualized by the "Jezebel" stereotype (Townsend et al. 2010). There are social markers typically associated with particular populations, such as substance use among African American girls in urban communities (Wallace et al. 2011). These stereotypes and degrading images of Black women not only place Black women in a constant state of self-defense, but also illustrate the relationship between those who have the power to correlate the racial perception of particular bodies, with laws, policies, and procedures that are implemented to rectify a perceived social problem. Racial ideology not only influences the core of one's individual being, but it also impacts structural realities, leading to policy initiatives that are attached to the negative images promulgated in society (Carpenter 2012).

Black women's images have been used to justify suggested policies and practices for the African American community that denigrate African Americans and emasculate African American men (Moynihan 1964). According to these representations, Black women are the leading cause of the failure of the Black family. This seems improbable in a society created and dominated by patriarchal values, in which Black women are insignificant players within society's existing power relations. As Wyatt (2008) suggests in tracing the genealogy of the strong Black woman through the text of Patricia Hill Collins (1990), the intersection of race, class, gender, and sexuality is designed to uphold White dominance. While both of Trayvon Martin's parents were often interviewed in news media outlets, the mother of Trayvon was often highlighted as the primary spokesperson. This only becomes problematic when assumptions are made about parental involvement that does not fit within the constraints of the ideal American family. It perpetuates the myth of the dysfunctionality of the Black community, which usually justifies the punishment of young, Black bodies, who are automatically assumed to have criminal intent being viewed not only as racially inferior, but also as less than human, as legal outcomes and punishment in the court system have shown over time.

Under any typical circumstances, when asked a derogatory question, it is reasonable that an individual may express some form of frustration or anger. When asked about her daily observations of Trayvon Martin, Sabrina Fulton, mother of Martin, endured questions with racialized overtones such as whether Martin "enjoyed eating chicken." While remaining poised when faced with awkward questioning, Fulton may have wanted to debunk any notion of being an "angry Black woman." The politics of respectability are closely associated with a person's intersectional identities. While there is a pervasive belief that Black women hold and express overt and generalized anger, empirical evidence demystifies this assumption (Walley-Jean 2009).

Intersectionality and Social Group Behavior

Intersectionality emerged in the early 1990s, as a theoretical and methodological tool of analysis, to explore the production and maintenance of racial and sexist exclusivity. This notion originated in the critical legal studies movement, as a way to examine a justice system purportedly color-blind. Intersectionality scholarship draws upon tenets embedded in feminist and race studies in an effort to identify the ways in which structured inequality manifests as discrimination. As Anderson (2005) suggests, there is no particular form of power that dominates women but the population typically marginalized in a system of oppression overwhelmingly tends to be "women of color, poor women, and women not visibly attached to a heterosexual relationship" (p. 452). In fact, in general feminist studies, the principal argument of a host of Black scholars is that Black women have been excluded and marginalized from feminist arguments that do not always reflect experiences predicated upon the intersection of race and gender. Kimberle Crenshaw maintains that "because the intersectional experience is greater than the sum of racism and sexism, any analysis that does not take intersectionality into account cannot sufficiently address the particular manner in which Black women are subordinated" (Crenshaw 1989, 58). The Trayvon Martin/Zimmerman case highlighted the ways in which racial hierarchy is embedded in how key witnesses are characterized as credible or not, as a result of intersectional identities.

Inman and Baron (1996) studied how stereotypes often create a bias in how different groups view each other. Specifically, they investigate the potential of accurate or misled perceptions of prejudice. Discrimination and prejudice are thought to be part of a process that changes when power relations shift. It was clear that Rachel Jeantel did not fit into any mainstream social category that represented a standard ideal of womanhood. When socialized behavior that reinforces discriminatory behavior is ignored, the activity is thought to be supported. However, at the same time, precaution must be taken when identifying situations so as not to falsely make an accusation of bias when no racist or sexist intentions exist. The findings in Inman and Baron's (1996) study revealed that some individuals were "more likely to label certain perpetrator and victim configurations as prejudiced action an instance of prejudice if it involved a specific kind of perpetrator and specific kind of victim (with whites derogating Blacks and men derogating women" (p. 735). Their conclusion is that there is always a major struggle between those who have the power to inflict discrimination and those who are the recipients of the treatment.

Black women are part of a long historical tradition that places blame and shame upon them for being on the outside of dominant social categories (Harris-Perry). As such, Black women were included in the dominant societal belief that the majority of Black people, whether enslaved or free, were less than human (Fox-Genovese 1988). This social status was reflected in the laws and policies that were implemented specifically for people of color. The often cited feminist speech given by Sojourner Truth (Carby 1987) represented the challenges faced by Black women as a result of racial and gender bias. During Truth's speech in which she explained her exploitation as a Black woman and the lack of protection she was afforded, she was asked to bare her breasts to the White women who were present. It was partly due to the fact that they did not believe her physical or mental capability could inhabit the body of a woman. One study argues that there is a tendency to disregard the gender of a person based on their racial identity, as they often are not separated in considering Black individuals (Goff, Thomas, and Jackson 2008). The findings suggested that participants were more frequently wrong about the gender of Black women than about any other race/gender intersection when asked to identify a target gender. Not only were Black women categorized as Black men at a higher percentage than any other group, they were also viewed as more masculine than White women. The fact that Truth was not recognized as a woman illustrates the pervasive negative gendering of Black women that completely disregards their intersectional identities.

The examination of gender, race, class, and nation as a frame of understanding the functionality of traditional family ideals can lend insight into (1) the impact that the perception of womanhood has on members of particular families and (2) how the legal system comes to conclusions as a result of the framing of race, class, and gender (Collins 1998). There are scholars who warn against subscribing to the notion that intersectionality can be used only to explain the experiences of Black women. Some scholarship believes the way intersectionality is typically examined leads to a need for further exploration and new ways to interrogate issues. The conflicts that emerge within the tenets of intersectionality are thought to be obscured in the pursuit of achieving antiracist and antisexist goals (Nash 2008). Nash's (2008) study addressed four major themes that could lead to court bias: (1) the lack of a clearly defined methodology; (2) a theory developed primarily for Black women as subjects; (3) an ambiguous definition; and (4) grounding intersectionality within the lived experiences of multiple identities (p. 4). Essentially, the argument called for a more advanced level of clarity when examining subjective narratives with an intersectional approach. Unaligned with this line of thinking, Carbado (2013) maintains that intersectionality does not prioritize one social category over another. As Crenshaw (1989) delineated in her analysis of intersectionality at juridical sites of analysis, demarginalizing the intersection of race and gender was pivotal in identifying how racial hierarchy upholds itself. Carbado (2013) states: "'Demarginalizing the Intersection' was not simply to mark the unwillingness of courts to recognize Black women's discrimination claims based on race and sex: here, courts were essentially saying that Black women's experiences were the same as white women's (with respect to sex) and Black men's (with respect to race) and that there was therefore no juridical need to recognize Black women as a distinct social group" (p. 813).

Without the recognition of having separate experiences based on multiple subjectivities inherent in intersectional identities, women of color narratives are often marginalized. The lives and issues of women of color are not at the forefront of national discourse. As a result, their experiences are acknowledged only when there is relevance for White women (Southwell 1994). Southwell (1994) maintains: "Women of color can experience discrimination in a number of ways that are both similar to and different from those experienced by white women, or by men of color. Sometimes their experiences coincide with those of white women, at other times with those of men of color. Often they experience double discrimination—the combined effects of race and sex discrimination" (p. 361). If the norm and standard of womanhood is based on White women, the racial hierarchal ladder of Whites on top and people of color on the bottom remains in dominant institutions. Womanhood has its own set of assumptions and stereotypes, but the constant theme in intersectional studies is that women of color can never be divorced from race. Whether White women choose to ignore their race or not, the fact remains that they still hold an attachment to the racial hierarchy predominating society. In placing women of color at the center of the analysis a "fundamental paradigmatic shift" (Barnett, Brewer, and Kuumba 1999, 15) occurs. This understanding argues that race, class, and gender do not have a ranking in the experiences of African Americans but that oppression takes a variety of forms based on the mutual connectivity of each construct. Learning not how intersectionality operates, but how it is understood and influences decisions on a systematic level is vital to building toward an effort to foster social and legal justice that is not determined by racial and gender categories.

Socialization and Perception of Womanhood

How individuals contextualize race, class, and gender is often based on their unique lived experiences with groups inside and outside of their racial and gender identities. As such, in order to understand the process of identity development, it is important to take these constructed identities into consideration (Thomas, Hacker, and Hoxha 2011). Often how one group perceives the other is based upon their own racial identity association. As Heaven and Greene (2001) maintain, a major predictor of anti-White stereotypes among African American women is related to their own group identity and differences. Sociohistorical differences and experiences between White and Black women have framed the social perception of each group, often contrasted through their own understanding of intersectionality (Settles, Pratt-Hyatt, and Buchanan 2008). These authors suggest one primary difference in how Black and White women perceive the challenges of their daily lives. Although both African American and White women held general ideas about the concept of womanhood, the experiences differed between the two groups as informed by their different historical and socioeconomic situations. As such, although both women faced oppression under White male patriarchy, Black women were punished disproportionately in the criminal justice system. This constant juxtaposition of Black and White women serves to uphold an unequal balance of power and creates an atmosphere in which one group is considered the dominant model of respectability, while the group that lacks social standing is "Othered" (Collins 2000). Consequentially, the confounding societal perception that groups have of one another is attributed to the internalization of stereotypes. It has been suggested that discrimination and negative social evaluation of groups is a result of social categorization based on stereotype bias (Johnson, Freeman, and Pauker 2012).

Racial groups in society are inundated with both positive and negative perceptions toward generalized behavior and characteristics. The construction of womanhood is interlocked with the dominant social standing in relation to the race of their gender counterparts. While most White women believe that their race is not defined by any social markers, women of color generally perceived White women to be materialistic and self-absorbed (Conley 2013). Racial categorization is part of a larger framework of power dynamics that determines what and whom normalcy represents. It reflects the existence of racial dominance through social institutions, while positioning those who are deemed worthy at the center of analysis, and promotes the invisibility of marginalized groups (Carpenter 2012). The attitudes toward African Americans illustrate the development of social relations in the United States. As Simon and Abdel-Moneim (2010) suggest, race is a significant factor in the interplay of gender and class that shapes public opinion of certain racial populations.

Intersectionality in the Legal System

Culture is part of daily existence for individuals, communities, and social institutions. One particular site of cultural formation occurs in the courtroom, in which some socially constructed racial distortions are considered in judicial decisions. The legal system places a higher value on groups considered to uphold mainstream norms and values (Lawrence 2001). The notion that race and gender are socially constructed is not a new idea in American society. However, constructed identities continue to reproduce social injustices and inequities through often hidden systemic practices.

Speech that holds racist overtones and prejudicial beliefs is not as blatant as it was in historical times but race and gender are ubiquitous in the legal court system (Bridges 2007). Racial bias is not a sole action or the thought of primary actors in the courtroom such as judges, prosecutors, and defenders. It is much more likely to exist in jurors positioned to render judgment. Evidence shows that Black and White jurors are likely to judge against racial groups different from their own (Cohn et al. 2009). To understand the decision-making process of a juror is to understand the complexities of how race and gender are presented in mainstream media. In fact it is argued that African American juvenile offenders in particular often experience bias during the entire processing system (Stevenson and Bottoms 2009). The influence that intersectionality identities have on juror decision making encompasses a comprehensive belief about the entire racial framework of the family (Lane 2009).

Over the course of recent years, the issue of racial fairness in courtroom practices has been a primary concern in an attempt to build a more equitable inclusive courtroom. The importance of understanding the role the law plays in all of the various roles individuals have is important in learning how some groups are denied equitable treatment in the legal court system. Black women as a collective are regarded by their race and gender, and each takes on different assumptions. Crenshaw expounds upon this point highlighting the nature of discrimination faced by Black women in and outside the court room system. She also asserts that the narratives and experiences of Black women are typically examined only in a singular fashion and that intersectionality offers a more comprehensive analysis of different groups across race and gender.

Crenshaw's (1989) "Demarginalizing the Intersection" explores the role the legal court system has in creating identities and the influence this may have on court outcomes. As part of the critical race theory tradition, the ways in which those who hold power in the judicial system create subjective ideas that become realities for those who hold no power is the way the social construction of race surfaces and creates social categories. In the case of Trayvon Martin/George Zimmerman, the key eyewitness was Rachel Jeantel who was the last person to speak with Trayvon Martin before he was shot and killed. She was expected to recall crucial moments during her conversation with Martin, remember specific details, and had to defend her own credibility while on the stand. Eyewitnesses are a strong factor as jurors consider cases and they are generally accepted by those in the position to render a decision based on the testimony given (Wells, Memon, and Penrod 2006). The construction of womanhood, as a concept that upholds White male patriarchy, is pertinent in understanding how the perception and social status of women vary and influence decision making in social institutions.

Black Women and Leadership

Cooper (2014) questions if Black women are valued in society. She begins with a discussion of the persistent negative portrayal of Black women in the media and the lack of gender protection. She suggests that the politics of Black movement building and communities should reexamine where Black women are placed in the discussion of social justice. Furthermore, she argues that Black women are decentered from the Black political agenda that historically and in contemporary times has focused on Black males. Pratt-Clarke (2013) asserts that the development of the Transdisciplinary Applied Social Justice model moves theory to praxis by following principles from the Egyptian goddess Ma'at. She describes the transdisciplinary model as one that uses "multiple theories, methods, approaches, frameworks, and disciplines to understand, strategize, and implement transformative initiatives in society." Acknowledging the increasing female prison population, and most notably the overrepresentation of Black women, Pratt-Clarke argues that the racism and sexism experienced by Black women and girls should be examined when they are entangled with the criminal justice system. She goes further to illustrate how the principles of Ma'at, including restoring equality, justice, and harmony, can help to restore Black communities and foster self-empowerment. This community acknowledgment is akin to Black Feminist Criminology that draws from Patricia Hill Collins' tenets of community support and building. Radical Reconstruction of resistance strategies is the primary argument of this study. With Black women losing their lives at the hands of law enforcement on a regular basis with no public outcry from anyone, including Black men, it is essential that Black women identify ways of self-healing and empowerment. Taking a historical approach at studying social activism, Glass (2005) examined the works of Anna Julia Cooper. She argues that Cooper's writings illustrate the struggle of the nineteenth-century women and that her message for community empowerment embraced the Black liberation tradition. Furthermore, she maintains that Cooper's antiracist feminist position disrupted interlocking systems of oppression by calling out White women who did not use the power they had to uplift Black women and other women of color. Women have shaped social movements and organized community building efforts through direct participation and influence. Anna Julia Cooper consistently argued that women were able to influence their communities by their unique position as a woman. As McDuffie and Woodard (2013) maintain, Black male leaders were also heavily influenced by Black women. From his mother to his wife, his ideology toward community organizing and internationalism were shaped by Black women.

In a system designed to continue to keep Black women as the mules of the world through a variation of oppressive treatment, Black women have had to protect themselves and their communities, in part, due to structural inequalities built within the fabric of this country's social institutions. As a result, while the mode of exploitation may have changed from victimization during slavery to the overrepresentation of Black women in the criminal justice system, the narratives of Black women continue to go unheard informally or formally. Just in the last year, 15 Black women have died at the hands of police officers (*Huffington Post* 2015) in situations similar to the death of Black men, and yet to date, there still has not been any type of social movement to acknowledge the lives lost. According to an executive report by Kimberle Crenshaw, Black girls have higher suspension and expulsion rates than their White female counterparts. The report also highlights a variation of ways that Black girls and women are underprotected both socially and legally today. The manner in which Black girls were punished in the juvenile court system during the time period of Jim Crow is remarkably similar to the disproportionate confinement of Black girls today and the increased severity of punishment both physically and legally (Ward 2012). The numbers and incidents of Black women and girls being dehumanized at the hands of law enforcement is an issue that warrants a serious theoretical analysis in the academic field of criminal justice. Incorporating a historical overview that traces how and why Black women and girls have received a lack of protection and often unwarranted physical punishment can broaden intersectional analysis as a theoretical perspective. By reimagining and validating the experiences and narratives of Black women and girls, policies that address a comprehensive outlook of the historical and contemporary challenges faced can help to reshape how Black women as criminals and victims may be studied.

References

Anderson, M. L. 2005. "Thinking about Women: A Quarter Century's View." *Gender and Society* 19:437–55.

Barnett, B. M., Brewer, R. M., and Kuumba, M. B. 1999. "New Directions in Race, Gender, & Class Studies: African American Experiences." *Race, Gender, & Class* 6:7–28.

Bridges, K. M. 2007. "Wily Patients, Welfare Queens, and the Reiteration of Race in the U.S." *Texas Journal of Women & the Law* 17:1–65.

Carbado, D. W. 2013. "Colorblind Intersectionality." *Signs* 38:811–45.

Carby, H. V. 1987. *Reconstructing Womanhood: The Emergence of the Afro-American Woman Novelist.* New York: Oxford University Press.

Carpenter, T. R. 2012. Construction of the Crack Mother Icon. *Western Journal of Black Studies* 36:264–75.

Chen, G. M., Williams, S., Hendrickson, N., and Chen, L. 2012. "Male Mammies: A Social-Comparison Perspective on How Exaggeratedly Overweight Media Portrayals of Madea, Rasputia, and Big Momma Affect How Black Women Feel about Themselves." *Mass Communication & Society* 15:115–35.

Cohn, R., Bucolo, D., Pride, M., and Sommers, S. R. 2009. "Reducing White Juror Bias: The Role of Race Salience and Racial Attitudes." *Journal of Applied Social Psychology* 39:1953–73.

Colleen W. and Larissa K. 2012. "Back to and Beyond Berry's Basics: The Conceptualization, Operationalization and Classification of Acculturation." *International Journal of Intercultural Relations.* 36(4): 472–85.

Collins, P. H. 2000. *Black Feminist Thought: Knowledge, Consciousness, and the Politics of Empowerment.* New York: Routledge.

Collins, P. H. 1998. "It's All in the Family: Intersections of Gender, Race, and Nation." *Hypatia, Border Crossing: Multiracial and Postcolonist Feminist* 13:62–82.

Conley, T. D. 2013. "Beautiful, Self-Absorbed, and Shallow: People of Color Perceive White Women as an Ethnically Marked Category." *Journal of Applied Social Psychology.* 43:45–56.

Crenshaw, K. 1989. "Demarginalizing the Intersection of Race and Sex: A Black Feminist Critique of Antidiscrimination Doctrine, Feminist Theory, and Antiracist Politics." *University of Chicago Legal Forum* 140:139–67.

Fox-Genovese, Elizabeth. 1988. *Within the Plantation Household: Black and White Women of the Old South.* Chapel Hill, NC: The University of North Carolina Press.

Glass, Kathy L. 2005. "Tending to the Roots: Anna Julia Cooper's Sociopolitical Thought and Activism." *Meridians: Feminism, Race, Transnationalism.* (6) 23–55.

Goff, P. A., Thomas, M. A., and Jackson, M. C. 2008. "Ain't I a Woman? Towards an Intersectional Approach to Person Perception and Group-Based Harms." *Sex Roles.* 59:392–403.

Harris-Perry, M. 2013. *Shame, Stereotypes, and Black Women in America.* New York and London: Yale University Press.

Heaven, P. C., and Greene, R. L. 2001. "African Americans Stereotypes of Whites: Relationships with Social Dominance Orientation, Ring-Wing Authoritarianism, and Group Identity." *Journal of Social Psychology* 141:141–3.

Hochschild, J. L., and Weaver, V. 2007. "The Skin Color Paradox and the American Racial Order." *Social Forces* 86:643–70.
Inman, M. L., and Baron, R. S. 1996. "Influence of Prototypes on Perceptions of Prejudice." *Journal of Personality and Social Psychological* 70:727–39.
Johnson, K. L., Freeman, J. B., and Pauker, K. 2012. "Race Is Gendered: How Covarying Phenotypes and Stereotypes Bias Sex Categorization." *Journal of Personality & Social Psychology* 102:116–31.
Lane, Alycee. 2009. 'Hang Them if They Have to Be Hung': Mitigation Discourse, Black Families, and Racial Stereotypes." *New Criminal Law Review: In International and Interdisciplinary Journal.* (2): 171–204.
Lawrence, S. N. 2001. "Cultural (In)Sensitivity: The Dangers of a Simplistic Approach to Culture in the Courtroom." *Canadian Journal of Women & the Law* 13:107–36.
Lyubansky, M. 2013. "Restorative Justice for Trayvon Martin." *Journal for Social Action in Counseling & Psychology* 5:59–72.
McDuffie, E., and Woodard, K. 2013. 'If You're in a Country that's Progressive, the Woman Is Progressive': Black Women Radicals and The Making of the Politics and Legacy of Malcolm X." *Project Muse.* (3) 507–39.
Moynihan, Daniel P. 1965. *The Negro Family: The Case for National Action.* Washington, DC: US Department of Labor.
Nash, J. C. 2008. "Re-thinking Intersectionality." *Feminist Review* 89:1–15.
Perry, M. H. 2011. *Sister Citizen: Shame, Stereotypes, and Black Women.* New Haven, CT and London: Yale University Press.
Settles, I. H., Pratt-Hyatt, J. S., and Buchanan, N. T. 2008. "Through the Lens of Race: Black and White Women's Perceptions of Womanhood." *Psychology of Women Quarterly* 32:454–68.
Simon, R. J., and Abel-Moneim, M. 2010. "Does Gender Matter? Men and Women on Controversial Social Issues." *Gender Issues* 27:95–109.
Southwell, V. 1994. "The Case of the Invisible Woman: Essentialism, Intersectionality and Marginalization in Feminist Discourse." *The Comparative and International Law Journal of Southern Africa* 3:357–70.
Stevenson, M. C., and Bottoms, B. L. 2009. "Race Shapes Perceptions of Juvenile Offenders in Criminal Court." *Journal of Applied Social Psychology* 39:1660–89.
Thomas, A., Hacker, J., and Hoxha, D. 2011. "Gendered Racial Identity of Black Young Women." *Sex Roles* 64:530–42.
Townsend, T. G., Thomas, A. J., Neilands, T. B., and Jackson, T. R. 2010. "I'm No Jezebel; I Am Young, Gifted, and Black: Identity, Sexuality, and Black Girls." *Psychology of Women Quarterly* 34:273–85.
Wallace, S. A., Townsend, T. G., Glasgow, Y. M., and Ojie, M. J. 2011. "Gold Diggers, Video Vixens, and Jezebels: Stereotype Images and Substance Use among Urban African American Girls." *Journal of Women's Healthy* 20:1315–24.
Walley-Jean, J. Celeste. 2009. "Debunking the Myth of the 'Angry Black Woman': An Exploration of Anger in Young African American Women." *Black Women, Gender, and Families.* (2) 68–86.
Ward, T. 2012. Review of Gender, Shame and Sexual Violence: The Voices of Witnesses and Court Members at War Crimes Tribunals. *Journal of Gender Studies,* 21(3), 343–44. doi:10.1080/09589236.2012.715496
Wells, G. L., Memon, A., and Penrod, S. D. 2006. "Eyewitness Evidence: Improving Its Probative Value." *Psychological Science in the Public Interest* 7:45–75.
Welters, Barbara. 1966. "The Cult of True Womanhood: 1820–1860." *American Quarterly* 18(2), Part 1: 151–74.
Wyatt, J. 2008. "Patricia Hill Collins's Black Sexual Politics and the Genealogy of the Strong Black Woman." *Studies in Gender & Sexuality* 9:52–67.

6

Africana Studies and Diversity: All Shapes, Sizes, and Colors of HBCU Athletic Programs: The Sporting HBCU Diaspora—Cultural Convergence and Politics of Divergence

J. Kenyatta Cavil, Joseph Cooper, and Geremy Cheeks

Introduction

Historically Black Colleges and Universities (HBCUs) and their athletic programs are increasingly threatened by the sociopolitical construction of federal, state, and national athletic association legislative governance policies and politics. Among the most pronounced athletic reform in the past 15 years has been the Academic Progress Rate (APR), a team-based metric that accounts for both eligibility and retention across National College Athletic Association (NCAA) Division I institutions. The purpose of this study was to explore the diverse multifaceted collection of HBCU athletic programs throughout the sporting HBCU Diaspora, with credence to the cultural convergence and the politics of divergence. Much of the research on HBCU athletic programs has focused on HBCUs operating their athletic programs at the NCAA Division I classification and a dearth of the research has focused on HBCU athlete experiences at various classifications as members of the NCAA. However, HBCU athletic programs occupy space-operating athletic programs in the National Junior College Athletic Association (NJCAA), United States Collegiate Athletic Association

(USCAA), National Athletic Intercollegiate Association (NAIA), and NCAA across multiple operational divisional classifications throughout the athletic landscape. Prior to the 1950s HBCUs, athletic programs were unilaterally without the unifying national classification and prior to 1979 were primarily confined to the NAIA (small) and NCAA Division II (college) classifications, where sparse television appearances limited exposure. As HBCUs' athletic programs continue to grow, expand, and operate in either the NCAA or NAIA, and with the increased commitment to athletics from regional predominantly white institutions (PWI) programs, it is important to examine the current status of HBCUs' athletic programs in their national associations. This descriptive examination provides an illustration of each institution's athletic program and other program components such as the athletic programs operating membership alignment in which each program is operating, number of sports, classification level, and budget. Around 106 HBCU institutions were identified and examined using a content analysis methodology. Results revealed the percentage of athletic programs offering specific sports, as well as significant differences between programs based on the athletic programs operating membership in which the athletics program is an operating member institution, the status of the university (public or private), and the university size. For example, NCAA Division II now holds more HBCU athletics programs than HBCU athletic programs participating at the NCAA Division I Football Championship Subdivision (FCS) level. These findings are presented in the results and discussion sections. In synopsis, with the newly expanded NCAA governance policies for the NCAA Division I programs under the provision of autonomy associated with athletic programs most recently referred to as the Power Five Conference, a recommendation is for HBCUs to collectively create a global rebranding strategy.

Emergence of Sports and Athletics in the African American Community

The emergence of sport within the Black community, particularly at HBCUs, during the late nineteenth and early twentieth centuries in the United States served two vital purposes. One purpose sport served for Blacks during that time was an intransigent position for racial uplift and upward mobility (Miller 1995). Legendary sport administrator and African American activist, Edwin Bancroft (E.B.) Henderson, described the benefit of sport participation at HBCUs for Blacks when he said: "The glare and glamour [of athletics] attracted to scholastic halls many a backwoods boy and girl who would have been plowing and mating in the countryside untrained . . . now are being turned into high class more useful products of society" (Miller 1995, 112). These sentiments were echoed by Florida Agricultural and Mechanical University (FAMU) president John Robert Edward (J.R.E.) Lee Sr. who said, "No school in this day can expect to attract promising men or women that does not give organized athletics a foremost place. Where there is no athletics, it is very likely that only deadheads are attracted. Young men and women of promise desire to be connected with an institution that has spirit and force" (Miller 1995, 120). Moreover, not only did sport provide racial uplift for Blacks who participated, but also for those who were spectators of these athletic events. The racial solidarity associated with these events was reflected in the high attendance records at annual classics. For example, the annual Thanksgiving Day football games between different HBCUs such as Howard University and Lincoln (PA) University would routinely attracted thousands of attendees (Wiggins 2000). A heralded tradition at HBCU football games were the "rabbles" (Miller 1995, 119). These events would occur at half-time and involved each school's band performing a spirited musical and dance performance, which was reflective of the verve and soul of Blacks in the United States (similar to other forms of Black cultural expression such as jazz music).

The first recorded athletic event between HBCU teams was a baseball game between Morehouse College and Atlanta University (Hodge et al. 2013). However, football was the most popular sport during the late nineteenth and early twentieth centuries (Wiggins and Miller 2003). According to Saylor (2000), for 70 plus years, 1892–1964, there were colleges with football programs, which had only African American student athletes who competed against teams comprising African American student athletes, except on very rare exceptions. These colleges were throughout the southeast, southwest, midwest, and mid-Atlantic regions of the United States, an area bounded roughly by Daytona Beach, Florida, by Austin, Texas, by Kansas City, Missouri, and by Cheyney, Pennsylvania. In 1892, the men of Biddle Memorial Institute (now Johnson C. Smith University) met their counterparts from nearby Livingstone College for a "match game of ball" on a snow-covered field in Salisbury, North Carolina, 23 years after Princeton and Rutgers had inaugurated college football (Hawkins 2010). The Biddle and Livingstone players had no idea they were pioneering the sport for Black colleges, yet that is exactly what they did on December 27 of that year. Biddle took a controversial 5-0 decision and football at Black colleges was off and running (Saylor 2000).

Sports also served as a platform for assimilation for Blacks during a time when they were largely excluded from mainstream society. Several sport advocates such as Samuel Archer, former professor and the first football coach at Atlanta Baptist (now known as Morehouse College), and J.B. Watson promoted the idea that sports developed character, leadership, strong work ethic, and discipline among students who were athletes (Wiggins and Miller 2003). Samuel Archer explained how sports served as assimilation tool for Blacks because it challenged widespread myths about their ability to have self-control and integrity. He said, "The college man ordinarily has a high sense of honor and is very sensitive about fair play and acts that are not sportsmanlike. If left to himself he will insist on the principle,—first a gentleman, then an athlete" (as cited in Wiggins and Miller 2003, 44). Essentially, advocates of HBCU athletics felt even if by limited means, success in athletics would serve as a form of assimilation into America's national pastimes of sport and higher education (Miller 1995). Yet, in reality this idea of muscular assimilationism would meet resistance from the dominant White culture as Blacks were still viewed as intellectually inferior despite their pronounced athletic accomplishments. In addition, HBCU athletic programs during the 1920s and 1930s also faced rising public scrutiny (similar to the Historically White Colleges and Universities [HWCU] counterparts) regarding the lack of faculty oversight of their athletic programs, the questionable integrity of athletic contests (e.g., unethical officiating, recruiting, coaches' behaviors, etc.), under emphasis on academic preparation and performance, and the violent nature of football (Miller 1995; Wiggins 2000; Wiggins and Miller 2003).

Owing to the high visibility of athletics and increasing public outcry, several Black stakeholders (e.g., faculty, students, journalists, reformers, etc.) engaged in discussions to identify ways to improve the integrity and safety of intercollegiate sports at HBCUs. Many traditionalists at HBCUs viewed athletics as a diversion from educational pursuits and sought to limit student involvement in activities aside from academic classes (Miller 1995). Advocates of sport suggested athletic events enhanced campus spirit, institutional and cultural prestige, and students' overall development. One student captured this collective sentiment when he said "to excel in athletics as well as other things" would be to "raise the honor" of the school (Miller 1995, 117).

The History and Unique Role of HBCUs

HBCUs are institutions of higher education in the United States that were established since the early 1800s with the primary goal of educating African

Americans and serving the African American community. Although there are 24 HBCUs classified with the NCAA Division I affiliation, there are 106 HBCUs in the United States, the District of Columbia, and the U.S. Virgin Islands, including public and private, two-year and four-year institutions, medical schools, university law schools, business colleges, technical institutes, and community colleges. All are in the former states and territories of the United States that held Africans as slaves except for five—Central State University (Ohio), Cheyney University (Pennsylvania), Lewis College of Business (Michigan), Lincoln University (Pennsylvania), and Wilberforce University (Ohio) as well as the now-defunct Western University (Kansas).

The first HBCU to be established was Cheyney, located in Cheyney, Pennsylvania. It was founded in 1837. The First Morrill Act passed on July 2, 1862, made higher education available to Americans with federal support for state education. Ten years later, the Freedmen's Bureau helped to provide support to a small number of HBCUs (Brazzell 1992). Following the U.S. Civil War in 1865, the 13th Amendment abolished slavery, and reconstruction in the South began. While the 14th and 15th Amendments compelled states to provide public education for former slaves and other Black Americans (Brown 1999), HBCU struggled significantly with legislation and court decisions such as the Jim Crow laws in the South. These struggles led to the rise and fall of a number of HBCUs. The Second Morrill Act of 1890 mandated that those funds be extended to institutions that enrolled Black Americans and led to the establishment of an additional 19 HBCUs across the United States (Mance 2003). The Second Morrill Act of 1890 ultimately strengthened the prevailing doctrine of segregation.

In 1954, the U.S. Supreme Court's decision in *Brown vs. Board of Education* broke the barrier of separate but equal policy in schools. Even after that decision, HBCUs were the best opportunity for most blacks interested in attending college. This was during the civil rights movement era in the United States and Black colleges continued to produce successful African Americans, despite their fight for existence (Allen 1986).

According to the Higher Education Act of 1966 (U.S. Department of Education 2010), HBCUs are defined as:

> Any historically black college or university that was established prior to 1964, whose principal mission was, and is, the education of black Americans, and that is accredited by a nationally recognized accrediting agency or association determined by the Secretary [of Education] to be a reliable authority as to the quality of training offered or is, according to such an agency or association, making reasonable progress toward accreditation.

HBCUs have a strong and storied tradition with over 130 years of educational service to African American students. These universities operate all over the United States and the U.S. Virgin Islands.

The Formation of HBCU Athletic Conferences and National Association Membership

Before the Civil War, very few Blacks earned college degrees primarily from Northern colleges during the early 1800s as Southern states institutionalized and established Black Codes after the Civil War, and eventually, as the Jim Crow segregation laws of the late 1800s continued, the dominant ideology that Blacks were intellectually inferior to Whites led to establishment of HBCUs. As a result, several HBCUs formed intercollegiate athletic conferences to formalize competition rules and playing schedules (Hawkins et al. 2015). Several HBCUs hired part-time coaches and athletic trainers to assist with the day-to-day tasks of operating a well-organized athletic program (Miller 1995). The two major national athletic associations in the United States during the early 1900s were the NAIA and the NCAA. However, HBCU athletic programs were not admitted into the NAIA until 1953 and the NCAA until 1965 (Saylor 2000). Institutions also began to coalesce to form official conferences. The first HBCU athletic conference established in 1910 was the Georgia-Carolina Association (Hodge, Bennett, and Collins 2013). Member conferences included Allen University, Haines Institute, Morris College, Paine College, Savannah State University (formerly Georgia State Industrial), Walker Baptist Institute, and a handful of preparatory schools (Hodge et al. 2013; Saylor 2000).

Shortly thereafter, additional HBCU conferences began to emerge such as the Colored (now Central) Intercollegiate Athletic Association (CIAA) in 1912, the Southeastern (now Southern) Intercollegiate Athletic Conference in 1913, the Southwestern Athletic Conference (SWAC) in 1920, and later the formation of the Mid-Eastern Athletic Conference (MEAC) for Division I classification in 1969 (Borican 1963; Hunt 1996). Historically, this also includes such conferences as the NCAA of the 1930s, the Eastern Intercollegiate Athletic Conference (EIAC) of the 1940s, Southern Central Athletic Association (also known as the South Central Athletic Conference [SCAC 1942–1962]), and Midwestern Athletic Association (MWAA 1926–1967). Although these conferences governing HBCU athletic programs did not endure, they were part of the history and legacy of HBCUs. By 1940, there were six major conferences that housed HBCU athletic programs.

The founding fathers of the CIAA were Allen Washington of Hampton Institute, C.H. Williams of Hampton Institute, Ernest J. Marshall of Howard University, George Johnson of Lincoln (PA) University, W.E. Atkins of Shaw University, Charles Frasher of Shaw University, H.P. Hargrave of Shaw University, J.W. Barco of Virginia Union University, and J.W. Pierce of Virginia Union University (CIAA 2015). The CIAA charter member schools were Bowie State University, Elizabeth City State University, Fayetteville State University, St. Augustine's Normal School, St. Paul's University, Shaw University, Virginia Normal and Industrial Institute, Lincoln (PA) University, and Virginia Union University (Borican 1963). The first African American intercollegiate football game ever played was between CIAA members, Livingstone College and Biddle (now Johnson C. Smith University) in 1892 (CIAA 2015). In 1921, the CIAA was the first HBCU athletic conference to join the NCAA and in 1937 became the first HBCU athletic conference to be affiliated with the American Olympic Association (AOA) (Borican 1963). In 1970, the CIAA was the first HBCU athletic conference to implement the divisional football championship format. More recently, the CIAA Basketball Tournament was the first NCAA Division II conference to be televised as a part of the Entertainment and Sports Programming Network (ESPN) Championship Week (CIAA 2011).

In 1929, the conference changed its name from Southeastern to Southern Intercollegiate Athletic Conference (SIAC) (SIAC 2015). The founding member institutions of the SIAC were Morehouse College, Alabama State University, Atlanta University, Clark College, Morris Brown College, Talladega College (AL), and Tuskegee Institute. In 1978, Florida Agricultural and Mechanical University (then a member of the SIAC) became the first HBCU to win the NCAA Division I-AA national football championship when they defeated Massachusetts 35-28 in the championship game. In 1993, SIAC members competed for NCAA Division II championships in eight different sports, which remains a remarkable feat by any institution regardless of Division (e.g., I, II, or III) or institutional type (e.g., HBCU or PWI). In 1992 and 1993, the women's outdoor track and field teams from Alabama Agricultural and Mechanical University claimed back-to-back NCAA Division II National Championships. The SIAC is also home to the longest HBCU football rivalry between Morehouse and Tuskegee, which began in 1936. In addition, the Tuskegee football program has won 634 games, which is the first among all HBCUs (SIAC 2015).

The "Super Six" charter institutions of the SWAC were Bishop College, Paul Quinn College, Sam Houston College, Prairie View College,

Texas College, and Wiley College (Hunt 1996, 183). The founding fathers of the SWAC were C.H. Fuller (Bishop College), Red Randolph (Paul Quinn College), C.H. Patterson (Paul Quinn College), E.G. Evans (Prairie View Agricultural and Mechanical University), H.J. Evans (Prairie View Agricultural and Mechanical University), H.J. Starns (Prairie View Agricultural and Mechanical University), D.C. Fuller (Texas College), and G. Whitte Jordan (Wiley College) (SWAC 2015). Currently, nearly half of all HBCU athletic programs are members of the NCAA within the Division I (MEAC or SWAC) or Division II (CIAA or SIAC).

The original member schools of the MEAC were Delaware State University, Howard University, University of Maryland Eastern Shore, Morgan State University, North Carolina Agricultural and Technical State University, North Carolina Central University, and South Carolina State University (MEAC 2015). On June 8, 1980, the MEAC received acceptance into the NCAA's Division I (MEAC 2015). Since receiving Division I classification, the MEAC has produced automatic bids for the following NCAA championships: baseball (since 1994), men's basketball (since 1981), women's basketball (since 1982), football (since 1996), softball (since 1995), men's and women's tennis (since 1998), and volleyball (since 1994). In 1974, the Morgan State University men's basketball team claimed the NCAA Division II National Championship. In the same year, Howard University won the 1974 NCAA Division I Men's Soccer National Championship. In 1982, the South Carolina State University women's basketball team won the Association for Intercollegiate Athletics for Women (AIAW) National Championship. Also in 1982, the South Carolina State University women's outdoor track and field team won the AIAW Division II Outdoor Track and Field National Championship. More recently, in 2008, the University of Maryland Eastern Shore defeated Arkansas State 4-2 to claim the first NCAA Championship for the MEAC conference in women's bowling (MEAC 2015).

Current State of HBCU Athletics

College athletics in the United States has prospered significantly since its inception. American intercollegiate athletics has seen millions of spectators go through the turn styles each year. College football is an integrated part of campus activities positioning itself above other sports both in terms of revenues and expenses (Suggs 1998). According to Deschriver and Jensen (2002), NCAA universities such as the University of Tennessee attract over 100,000 attendees for each home football games, and ticket revenues alone can eclipse $3 million for a single game. In 2007, 619 schools combined for over 48 million people attending NCAA football games, which included all division levels: Division I—Football Bowl Subdivision (FBS), Division I—FCS, Division II, and Division III (Johnson 2008). NCAA Division I teams, with the exception of a few independent operating programs, are organized into conferences.

Attendance is a major component of sport consumption. Sport economic literature dealing with attendance has garnered a great deal of interest (DeSchriver 2007). According to Johnson (2007), although all-time records were not set in the Division I Football Championship Subdivision, classification's numbers were up for the second straight season. More than 5.5 million fans saw FCS games in 2007; this was the fourth highest total in that subdivision and was up 238 fans per game from the previous year. Historically, Black College "Classic" games have occurred for more than 80 years across America with large attended contests, as well. In fact, the Magic City Classic, the match-up of Alabama's two HBCU state schools, surpassed the Florida Classic (65,367) in attendance this year for the first time and it set an all-time record for game of 68,593 (Williams 2008). The top six attended HBCU "Classic" games each had attendance over 50,000 fans. While the SWAC, a conference made up of black universities and a FCS member, held on to its top spot once again with 15,614 fans per game (Johnson 2007) among all FCS members. Armstrong's (2002) research suggests that cultural factors significantly influence African Americans' motives for attending black college football games. McClelland (2011) suggests that the unequal distribution of resources has impacted the dynamics of HBCU academics and athletics.

A closer review of the financial gap associated with HBCU athletic programs and other athletic programs labeled as low-major Division I programs shows the importance of studying the financial challenges associated with all Division I athletic programs. The NCAA (2012) implemented the APR during the 2003–2004 academic year according to NCAA.org. It is a NCAA policy that measures term-by-term eligibility and retention of student athletes who participate in sports at the Division I level, to help with the graduation rates of college bound student athletes. In 2012, according to Hosick (2012), the NCAA Division I Board of Directors adopted a policy that would allow more time for institutions referred to as "limited-resource institutions" to meet the new minimum standards that increase from 925 to 930. As of 2014, additional measures were implemented to improve the overall graduation rates for all 340 NCAA Division I institutions (Reynolds, Fisher, and Cavil 2012). The original formula for determining limited-resource institutions included per capita expenditures on athletics, per capita educational expenditures for the student body, and average Pell Grant funds among all students according to Brown (2012). Most of the limited-resource labeled institutions are HBCUs that service mainly African Americans and therefore African American student athletes. According to Brown (2012), the Academic Performance Committee is considering whether the definition should include all Historically Black Colleges. The new standard of an APR of 930 predicts about a 50% graduation rate (Hosick 2012). Hence, these alarming statistics raise the concerns presented in the early twentieth century by traditionalists who challenged the role sport/athletic programs served within the context of Black educational institutions in quest for racial uplift.

Conceptual Framework: Education-Sports Symbiosis (ESS) Hypothesis

In analyzing the descriptive diversity of HBCU athletic programs, the current study also incorporated the Education-Sports Symbiosis (ESS) hypothesis to examine the role sport/athletic programs serve at HBCUs (Gawrysiak, Cooper, and Hawkins 2012) based on membership classification and sport management programs. The ESS refers to the process whereby educational institutions sponsor sport programs to enhance the attractiveness and visibility of its institutions and provide positive holistic (mental, physical, and social) development for its student athletes. In a study of Black baseball student athletes who attended HBCUs, Gawrysiak et al. (2012) found participants cited the athletic opportunity they were afforded at their schools motivated them to not only attend the school, but also persist through graduation. HBCUs that incorporate the ESS hypothesis "understand the significance sports can play in terms of attracting students to school in order to gain an education at a place that allows them the opportunity to participate in those activities that they value" (Gawrysiak et al. 2012, 21). The ESS echoes the sentiments of HBCU sport advocates Samuel Archer and J.B. Watson who supported the notion that sports build leadership, character, work ethic, and discipline among athletes including students who participate in intercollegiate athletics (Wiggins and Miller 2003). Using the ESS hypothesis, the researchers sought to examine the number of HBCUs that sponsored intercollegiate athletic programs as an extension of their educational institution to enhance institutional prestige and fulfill its missions of providing a well-rounded college experience for its students (athletes and nonathletes).

Even though previous research (Hodge et al. 2013) has documented the history and prevalence of HBCU sport programs, there is no study to date that has analyzed both the number of athletic programs as well as sport-related academic programs (e.g., physical education, human performance, kinesiology, recreation, and/or sport management programs). As a result, the current study seeks to fulfill this gap. This scholarship seeks to answer the question: What are the differences in HBCU athletic programs and sport-related academic programs?

Significance of Study

The purpose of this study was to provide an overview of each HBCU athletics program and other program components such as the athletics programs operating membership alignment, number of sports, classification level, and academic physical education, recreation, and/or sport management unit.

Method

This study incorporated a content analysis to evaluate HBCU athletic programs. The content analysis in the current study involved systematic examination of the literature on HBCU athletic programs and official institutional documents from HBCUs (Gratton and Jones 2010). The data obtained from the HBCUs' athletic program websites were systematically charted for ease of interpretation. The components of analysis for this study, as stated previously, were HBCUs' athletics program websites in correspondents with the Carnegie Foundation for the Advancement of Teaching website and the U.S. Census Bureau's regions and divisions.

Data were analyzed via descriptive statistics to identify key patterns across institution types (e.g., public vs. private, etc.) (Gratton and Jones 2010). Quantitative analysis generally involves a process or method of determining the value, significance, or difference of collected data by examining such variables that are involved in the overall purpose of the analysis to then lead to the conclusion. With this study, the variables include but are not limited to an overview of each institution's athletics program and other program components such as the athletic programs operating membership alignment, in which each program is operating, number of sports, whether the school is public or private, and each institution's region. To portray accurately the distribution and characteristics of HBCU athletic programs, the primary researcher analyzed the data using descriptive statistics. Charts and graphs for the collected data were used to ensure proper descriptive quantitative analysis was carried out.

Results

This study examined the total of athletic programs and academic athletic studies programs at 106 HBCU institutions in the United States and U.S. territories. These programs are identified as region, state, status, size, membership association, four sports programs, and athletic studies programs. Institutions labeled as Historically Black Colleges with membership association from the following governing bodies were identified and analyzed: (1) NCAA; (2) NAIA; (d) NJCAA; and (4) USCAA. As members of the aforementioned governing associations, HBCUs are located in different divisions within these associations including the NCAA Division I, NCAA Division II, NCAA Division III, NAIA Division I, and NAIA Division II.

Of the 106 HBCUs, several offer football, men's and women's basketball, and/or baseball programs as well as an academic physical education, recreation, and/or sport management unit. Among these schools, 53% (56 out of 106) sponsored football programs compared to 38% (40 out of 106) that did not offer a football program. Related to basketball, 88% (93 out of 106) schools sponsored men's basketball programs and 89% (94 out of 106) sponsored women's basketball programs. Regarding baseball, 55% (58 out of 106) offered it. From an academic program perspective, 53% (56 out of 106) offered at least one of the following academic programs: (1) physical education; (2) human performance; (3) kinesiology; (4) recreation; and /or (5) sport management programs. Specifically, there are a total of 26 HBCU institutions offering sport management programs at the 106 HBCU institutions in the United States and U.S. territories. Only a small portion of HBCU institutions offers sport management as a concentration or a minor; in particular, five HBCU institutions have the sport management program as a focus. There are 19 HBCU institutions that offer some form of the sport management degree at the undergraduate level. There are nine HBCU institutions that offer some form of the sport management program at the graduate level. No HBCU institution has yet to offer a doctoral program in sport management or physical education, human performance, kinesiology, recreation administration, recreation and leisure management, sports science, or sport administration for that matter

School Region

The 106 HBCU institutions evaluated in this study were coded according to the region in the United States and U.S. territories in which it resides. According to the U.S. Census Bureau, regions and divisions are defined as either: (1) Region 1—Northeast, divided between

Division 1, New England and Division 2, Middle Atlantic; (2) Region 2—Midwest, divided between Division 3, East North Central and Division 4, West North Central; (3) Region 3—South, divided among Division 5, South Atlantic, Division 6, East South Central and Division 7, West South Central; and (4) Region 4—West divided between Division 8, Mountain and Division 9, Pacific (U.S. Census Bureau 2010). The 106 HBCU athletic programs are distributed among three of the four different regions, six of the nine different divisions, and one is located outside the U.S. Census Bureau designation, located in a U.S. territory. In Region 1, there are two schools or 2%, with both HBCU institutions located in Division 2. In Region 2, there are five schools or 5%; 3 % of the HBCU institutions are located in Division 3 and the remaining 2% located in Division 4. Region 3 has the most schools located in this region with 98 HBCU or 92%. Of the 98 schools, 49 schools or 50% are located in Division 5, 29 schools or 30% in Division 6, and 20 schools or 20% in Division 7. There are no HBCU located in Region 4 or the two subdivisions, Division 8 and Division 9. There is one HBCU or 1% located in a U.S. territory.

School State

The 106 HBCUs are located in 20 States, the District of Columbia, and the Virgin Islands. This study found HBCU institutions' athletic programs in 19 of the 20 states or 95.0%, one in the District of Columbia and one in the Virgin Islands. As is shown in Table 6.1, Alabama had the greatest overall number of HBCU athletic programs with 15. The next two states with the highest number of HBCU athletic programs were North Carolina with 11 and Georgia with 10. Delaware, Michigan, and Oklahoma, with one institution each, were the states with the lowest number of HBCU athletics programs. In terms of public higher education institutions with HBCU athletics programs, Alabama ranked first with seven. Alabama also ranked first in the number of private higher education institution with eight HBCU athletics programs.

The Carnegie Foundation for the Advancement of Teaching website was used to profile each institution (The Carnegie Foundation 2010). The researcher was able to code whether the institution was public or private. The U.S. Department of Education website was used to code institutions as HBCUs) (U.S. Department of Education 2010). There were 51 or 48.1% public higher education institutions and 55 or 51.9% private higher education institutions designated as HBCUs.

Table 6.1. HBCU by state.

U.S. States/ U.S. Territories	Public Institutions N = 51 F	%	Private Institutions N = 55 f	%	Total Number of Programs N = 106 f	%
Alabama	7	13.5	8	14.5	15	14.2
Arkansas	1	2.0	3	5.4	4	3.8
Delaware	1	2.0	0	0.0	1	1.0
Florida	1	2.0	3	5.4	4	3.8
Georgia	3	5.9	7	12.7	10	9.4
Kentucky	1	2.0	0	0.0	1	1.0
Louisiana	4	7.8	2	3.6	6	5.7
Maryland	4	7.8	0	0.0	4	3.8
Michigan	1	2.0	0	0.0	1	1.0
Mississippi	5	9.8	3	5.4	8	7.5
Missouri	2	3.9	0	0.0	2	1.9
North Carolina	5	9.8	6	10.9	11	10.4
Ohio	1	2.0	1	1.9	2	1.9
Oklahoma	1	2.0	0	0.0	1	1.0
Pennsylvania	2	3.9	0	0.0	2	1.9
South Carolina	2	3.9	6	10.9	8	7.5
Tennessee	1	2.0	5	4.7	6	5.7
Texas	3	5.9	6	10.9	9	8.5
Virginia	2	3.9	4	7.2	6	5.7
West Virginia	2	3.9	0	0.0	2	1.9
U.S. Virgin Island	1	2.0	0	0.0	1	1.0
Washington, DC	1	2.0	1	1.9	2	1.9

School Size

Analogous to "School Status," the size of each institution was determined based on the Carnegie Foundation for the Advancement of Teaching website classification measure. Schools were classified as small two-year, larger two-year, very small four-year, small four-year, medium four-year, large four-year, or unknown. Of these classifications, medium four-year institutions ranked highest with 31 or 29.5% of higher education institutions with HBCU athletic programs fitting this category, followed by small four-year, 30 or 28.6%; very small four-year, 23 or 21.9%; medium two-year, five or 4.8%; small two-year, five or 4.8%; very small two-year four or 3.8%; large two-year, two or 1.9% and large four-year, one or 1.0%. There were four or 3.8% of the HBCU institutions that were not listed by size by the Carnegie Foundation for the Advancement of Teaching.

The difference between public and private designation in terms of size was analyzed. The results show that public institutions offering football programs were more likely to be medium or large four-year institutions, while private institutions offering football programs were more likely to be small or medium four-year institutions. The largest numbers of public institutions are labeled by institutional size as very small four-year schools with 22 or 43.1%. The largest numbers of private institutions are labeled as medium four-year schools with 26 or 48.1%. The second largest numbers of private institutions are identified as small four-year schools with 18 or 33.3%, while the second largest numbers of public institutions are listed as small four-year schools with 12 or 23.5%. The majority, 84 or 80%, of HBCUs are identified as very small, small or medium four-year-sized institutions.

Membership Association of the HBCU Athletic Programs

The researchers coded which association the HBCU athletic programs were a member of. The choices when coding this variable included NCAA Division I, NCAA Division II, NCAA Division III, NAIA Division I, NAIA Division II, and Unknown. Of these choices, NCAA Division II classification was the most popular for institutional membership association, with 32 or 30.5% of athletic programs as members. Table 6.2 showed the NCAA Division I classification with 24 or 22.9%, NAIA Division I with 17 or 16.2%, NJCAA with 13 or 12.4%, NAIA Division II with 5 or 4.8%, NCAA Division III with 2 or 1.9%, USCAA with 2 or 1.9%, and 10 or 9.5% are listed as Unknown. Of the 24 HBCUs that operate at the NCAA Division I classification, 22 operate football programs at the Football Championship Subdivision (formerly I-AA), while 2 do not offer football programs at the FCS. Currently, there are no HBCUs operating their football program at the highest level, as a member of the NCAA, at the FBS Division (Formerly I-A).

Football Program

This study found that 56 or 52.8% of the 106 HBCU institutions operate a collegiate football program. The largest numbers of HBCU institutions

Table 6.2. Differences in HBCU athletic programs based on institutional membership.

	N = 106	HBCU Institutions
Operational Membership	*F*	%
NCAA Division I FBS	0	0.0
NCAA Division I FCS	22	20.8
NCAA Division I AAA	2	1.9
NCAA Division II	32	30.2
NCAA Division III	2	1.9
NAIA Division I	17	16.0
NAIA Division II	5	4.7
NJCAA	13	12.3
USCAA	2	1.9
None	11	10.4

operating football programs are members of the NCAA Division II with 26 or 46.4%. The second largest number of football programs consists of programs operating at the NCAA Division I FCS (Formerly I-AA) level with 22 or 39.3% of the 56 that operate football programs. There are four or 7.1% of the HBCU programs operating their football programs as member of the NJCAA classification. There are three or 5.4% of the HBCU programs operating their football programs as member of the NAIA Division I classification. One HBCU program or 1.8% operates their football program as a member of the USCAA classification. There are no HBCU programs that operate their football program at the NAIA Division II, NCAA Division III, or NCAA Division I FBS (Formerly I-A) level.

In regard to the U.S. Census Bureau's regions and divisions classification, the region that consists of the majority of the football programs is the South, Region 3 with 52 or 92.9%. This South region consists of three divisions and is broken down as follows: Division 5—South Atlantic Division with 29 or 51.8% institutions; Division 6—East South Central Division with 15 or 26.8% institutions, and Division 7—West South Central Division with 8 or 14.3% institutions. The second largest region is the Midwest, Region 2 with three institutions or 5.4%. The Midwest Region consists of two divisions. Division 3—East North Central Division—has one or 1.8% institutions located in the division and Division 7—West North Central Division—with one or 1.8% institutions in the division. The Northeast, Region 1 has one institution operating a football program or 1.8% located in Division 2, the Middle Atlantic.

In regard to institution classification, the majority of institutions operating football programs, 33 or 58.9%, are labeled as four-year public institutions. There are 21 or 37.5% labeled as four-year private institutions. There are two or 3.6% labeled as two-year public institutions. There are no HBCU athletic programs labeled as a two-year private institution that operates a football program.

Men's Basketball Program

This study found that 93 or 87.7 % of the 106 HBCU institutions operate a collegiate men's basketball program. The largest numbers of HBCU institutions operating men's basketball programs are members of the NCAA Division II classification with 32 or 34.4% of the 93. The second largest number of men's basketball programs consists of programs operating at the highest level for HBCU divisional alignment as NCAA Division I members consist of 24 or 25.8% that operate men's basketball programs. There are 17 or 18.3% of the HBCU programs operating their men's basketball programs as member of the NAIA Division I classification. There are 13 or 14.0% of the HBCU programs operating their men's basketball programs as member of the NJCAA classification. There are five or 5.4% of the HBCU programs operating their men's basketball programs as member of the NAIA Division II classification. One HBCU program or 1.1% operates their men's basketball program as a member of the USCAA classification. Finally, there is one HBCU program or 1.1% that operates their men's basketball program as a member of the NCAA Division III classification.

In regard to the U.S. Census Bureau's regions and divisions classification, the region that consists of the majority of the men's basketball programs is the South, Region 3 with 86 or 92.5%. This South region consists of three divisions and broken down as follows: Division 5—South Atlantic Division with 43 or 46.2% institutions; Division 6—East South Central Division with 25 or 26.9% institutions, and Division 7—West South Central Division with 18 or 19.4% institutions. The second largest region is the Midwest, Region 2 with five institutions or 5.4%. The Midwest Region consists of two divisions. Division 3—East North Central Division—has two or 2.2% institutions located in the division and Division 7—West North Central Division with three or 3.2% institutions in the division. The Northeast, Region 1 has one HBCU institution operating a men's basketball program or 1.6% located in Division 2, the Middle Atlantic. Finally, there is one HBCU athletic program or 1.6%

Table 6.3. Differences in HBCU athletic programs based on size, membership, and region.

Institutional Size	Public Institutions N = 51 f	%	Private Institutions N = 55 f	%
Large Four-Year	1	2.0	0	0.0
Medium Four-Year	5	9.8	26	47.3
Small Four-Year	12	23.5	18	32.7
Very Small Four-Year	22	43.1	1	1.8
Large Two-Year	2	3.9	0	0.0
Medium Two-Year	5	9.8	0	0.0
Small Two-Year	4	7.8	1	1.8
Very Small Two-Year	0	0.0	4	7.3
Unknown	0	0.0	5	9.1
Operational Membership	f	%	f	%
NCAA Division I FBS	0	0.0	0	0.0
NCAA Division I FCS	19	37.3	3	5.4
NCAA Division I AAA	2	3.9	0	0.0
NCAA Division II	16	31.4	16	29.6
NCAA Division III	0	0.0	1	1.8
NAIA Division I	2	3.9	15	27.8
NAIA Division II	1	2.0	5	9.1
NJCAA	8	15.7	5	9.1
USCAA	0	0.0	2	3.6
None	3	5.9	8	14.5
Region			f	%	f	%
Northeast			2	3.9	0	0.0
	Division 1	New England	0	0.0	0	0.0
	Division 2	Middle Atlantics	2	3.9	0	0.0
Midwest			4	7.8	1	1.8
	Division 3	East North Central	2	3.9	1	1.8
	Division 4	West North Central	2	3.9	0	0.0
South			44	86.3	54	98.2
	Division 5	South Atlantic	21	41.2	27	49.1
	Division 6	East South Central 3	14	27.5	16	20.0
	Division 7	West South Central	9	17.6	11	0.0
West			0	0.0	0	0.0
	Division 8	Mountain	0	0.0	0	0.0
	Division 9	Pacific	0	0.0	0	0.0
U.S. Territory			1	2.0	0	0.0
		U.S. Virgin Island	1	2.0	0	0.0

that operates their men's basketball program in a U.S. territory in the U.S. Virgin Islands.

In regard to institution classification, the majority of institutions operating men's basketball programs, 44 or 47.3%, are labeled as four-year private institutions. There are 40 or 43.0% labeled as four-year public institutions. There are eight or 8.6% labeled as two-year public institutions. There is one HBCU athletic program or 1.6% labeled as a two-year private institution that operates a men's basketball program.

Women's Basketball Program

This study found that 94 of 88.7% of the 106 HBCU institutions operate a collegiate women's basketball program. The women's basketball programs that have the largest number of members of the 94 HBCU programs are in NCAA Division II classification with 31 or 33.0%. The second largest number of women's basketball programs consists of programs operating at the highest level for HBCU divisional alignment as NCAA Division I members consist of 24 or 25.5% that operate women's basketball programs. There are 17 or 18.1% of the HBCU programs operating their women's basketball programs as member of the NAIA Division I classification. There are 13 or 13.8% of the HBCU programs operating their women's basketball programs as member of the NJCAA classification. There are five or 5.3% of the HBCU programs operating their women's basketball programs as member of the NAIA Division II classification. Two HBCU programs or 2.1% operate their women's basketball program as a member of the USCAA classification. There are two HBCU programs or 2.1% that operate their women's basketball program as a member of the NCAA Division III classification.

In regard to regional and division classification and the U.S. Census Bureau, the region that consists of the majority of the women's basketball programs is the South, Region 3 with 87 or 92.6%. This South region consists of three divisions and broken down as follows: Division 5—South Atlantic Division with 44 or 46.8% institutions; Division 6—East South Central Division with 25 or 26.6% institutions; and Division 7—West South Central Division with 18 or 19.1% institutions. The second largest region is the Midwest, Region 2 with five institutions or 5.3%. The Midwest Region consists of two divisions. Division 3—East North Central Division—has two or 2.1% institutions located in the division and Division 7—West North Central Division—with three or 3.2% institutions in the division. The Northeast, Region 1 has one institution operating a women's basketball program or 1.1% located in Division 2, the Middle Atlantic. There is one HBCU institution operating women's basketball program or 1.1% located in the U.S. Virgin Islands. In terms of institution classification, the majority of institutions operating women's basketball programs, 45 or 47.9%, are labeled as four-year private institutions. There are 40 or 42.6% labeled as four-year public institutions. There are eight or 8.5% labeled as two-year public institutions. There is one HBCU athletic programs or 1.2% labeled as a two-year private institution that operates a basketball program.

Baseball Program

This study found that 58 (i.e., 54.7%) of the 106 HBCU institutions operate a collegiate baseball program. The largest numbers of HBCU institutions operating baseball programs are members of the NCAA Division II classification with 20 or 34.5% of the 58. The second largest number of baseball programs consists of programs operating at the highest level for HBCU divisional alignment as NCAA Division I members consist of 18 or 31.0% that operate baseball programs. HBCUs with baseball programs have the smallest difference margin of the two between all the athletic programs reviewed in this study at the NCAA Division I and Division II levels. There are nine or 15.5% of the HBCU programs operating their baseball programs as member of the NAIA Division I classification. There are eight or 13.8% of the HBCU programs operating their baseball programs as member of the NJCAA classification. Three HBCU programs or 5.1% operate their baseball programs as member of the three following classifications: NAIA Division II (one or 1.7%); USCAA (one or 1.7%); and NCAA Division III (one or 1.7%), respectively.

In regard to the U.S. Census Bureau's regions and divisions classification, the region that consists of the majority of the baseball programs is the South, Region 3 with 55 or 94.8%. This South region consists of three divisions and broken down as follows: Division 5—South Atlantic Division—with 23 or 39.7% institutions; Division 6—East South Central Division—with 22 or 37.9% institutions; and Division 7—West South Central Division—with 10 or 17.2% institutions. The second largest region is the Midwest, Region 2 with two institutions or 3.4%. The Midwest Region consists of two divisions. Division 3—East North Central Division—does not have an institution located in the division operating a baseball program and Division 7—West North Central Division—with two or 3.4% institutions in the division. The Northeast, Region 1 has one institution with a baseball program or 1.7% located in Division 2, the Middle Atlantic. The HBCU athletic program in the U.S. Virgin Islands does not offer a baseball program.

In regard to institution classification, the majority of institutions operating baseball programs, 44 or 47.3%, are labeled as four-year private institutions. There are 40 or 43.0% labeled as four-year public institutions. There are eight or 8.6% labeled as two-year public institutions. There is one HBCU athletic programs or 1.6% labeled as a two-year private institution that operates a baseball program.

Athletic Studies: Human Performance, Recreation, and/or Sport Management Programs

This study found that 56 of the 106 HBCU institutions have an academic physical education, recreation, and/or sport management unit in place, which accounts for 52.8% of the HBCUs. The highest number of HBCU institutions with an academic unit of physical education, recreation, and/or sport management operates their athletic departments as members of the NCAA Division I FCS (Formerly I-AA) level that consists of 21 or 37.5% of the 56 HBCU institutions. The second highest number of an academic physical education, recreation, and/or sport management unit consists of programs operating their athletic program at the NCAA Division II level with 20 or 35.7%. There are seven or 12.5% of the HBCU institutions with an academic physical education, recreation, and/or sport management unit operating their athletics programs as member of the NAIA Division I classification.

There are four or 7.1% of the HBCU institutions with an academic unit of physical education, recreation, and/or sport management that operates their athletic programs as member of the NJCAA classification. Two HBCU institutions or 3.6% with an academic unit of physical education, recreation, and/or sport management operates their athletics program as a member of the NAIA Division II classification. One HBCU institution or 1.8% with an academic unit of physical education, recreation, and/or sport management operates their athletics program as a member of the NCAA Division III classification. One HBCU institution or 1.8% with an academic unit of physical education, recreation, and/or sport management and does not operate an athletics program. There are no HBCU institutions with an academic unit of physical education, recreation, and/or sport management operating their athletics program as a member of the USCAA classification.

According to the U.S. Census Bureau's regions and divisions classification, the region that consists of the majority of the football programs is the South, Region 3 with 53 or 94.6%. This South region consists of three divisions and broken down as follows: Division 5—South Atlantic Division with 24 or 42.9% institutions; Division 6—East South Central Division with 17 or 30.4% institutions; and Division 7—West South Central Division with 12 or 21.4% institutions. The second largest region is the Midwest, Region 2 with two institutions or 3.6%. The Midwest Region consists of two divisions. Division 3—East North Central Division—has one or 1.8% HBCU institutions with an academic unit of physical education, recreation, and/or sport management operating an athletic program located in the division and Division 7—West North Central Division—with one or 1.8% HBCU institutions in the division. The Northeast, Region 1 has one HBCU institution with an academic unit of physical education, recreation, and/or sport management operating an athletic program or 1.8% located in Division 2, the Middle Atlantic.

In regard to institution classification, the majority of the HBCU institutions that have an academic physical education, recreation, and/or sport management unit, 29 or 51.8% are labeled as four-year public institutions. There are 23 or 41.1% labeled as four-year private institutions. There are four or 7.1% labeled as two-year public institutions. There are no HBCU institutions that have an academic physical education, recreation, and/or sport management unit as well as operate an athletic program labeled as a two-year private institution.

Classification Athletics Membership by Regions

The study reviewed the differences in the classification level of an institution in which the athletic programs are members. As noted in the previous section, differences were found between the athletics program in which the athletics program held association membership and the status of the institutions (public and private). In addition, the results shown in Table 6.4 prove that a significant difference exists between the regions that a HBCU is located in and the divisions the HBCU has as an association. Cross tabulation results showed that athletic programs located in the South in Region 3, Division 5: South Atlantic, Division 6: East South Central, and Division 7: West South Central according to U.S. Census Bureau's regions and divisions classification are the regions and divisions that HBCUs most often held memberships in all associations.

Table 6.4. Athletic programs differences based on classification of school in regions (%).

Region	DI FBS N = 0	DI FCS N = 22	DI AAA N = 2	NCAAII N = 32	NCAAIII N = 2	NAIA I N = 17	NAIA II N = 5	NJCAA N = 13	USCAA N = 2	NONE N = 11
R1 Northeast	0.0	0.0	0.0	6.2	0.0	0.0	0.0	0.0	0.0	0.0
Division 1	0.0	0.0	0.0	0.0	0.0	0.0	0.0	0.0	0.0	0.0
Division 2	0.0	0.0	0.0	6.2	0.0	0.0	0.0	0.0	0.0	0.0
R2 Midwest	0.0	0.0	0.0	6.2	0.0	0.0	40.0	0.0	0.0	9.1
Division 3	0.0	0.0	0.0	3.1	0.0	0.0	20.0	0.0	0.0	9.1
Division 4	0.0	0.0	0.0	3.1	0.0	0.0	20.0	0.0	0.0	0.0
R3 South	0.0	100.0	100.0	84.5	100.0	100.0	60.0	100.0	100.0	90.9
Division 5	0.0	50.0	100.0	65.6	50.0	23.5	40.0	23.1	50.0	27.3
Division 6	0.0	27.3	0.0	18.9	50.0	17.7	20.0	53.8	50.0	45.5
Division 7	0.0	22.7	0.0	0.0	0.0	58.8	0.0	23.1	0.0	18.2
R4 West	0.0	0.0	0.0	0.0	0.0	0.0	0.0	0.0	0.0	0.0
Division 8	0.0	0.0	0.0	0.0	0.0	0.0	0.0	0.0	0.0	0.0
Division 9	0.0	0.0	0.0	0.0	0.0	0.0	0.0	0.0	0.0	0.0
U.S. Territory	0.0	0.0	0.0	3.1	0.0	0.0	0.0	0.0	0.0	0.0
U.S. Virgin Island	0.0	0.0	0.0	3.1	0.0	0.0	0.0	0.0	0.0	0.0

Institutional Size by Sports (Football, Men's, and Women's Basketball and Baseball)

The differences in the size of the institution in which the sports are played were explored. After extensively analyzing the data small two-year and four-year HBCUs are less likely to provide athletic programs that require numerous participants and larger outdoor facilities, specifically for the sports of football and baseball. Overall, institutions labeled as small regardless of private or public status are less likely to provide all four athletic programs reviewed in this study. Of the 62 HBCU institutions listed as small or very small institutions, 31 or 50.0% offer three or less of the four athletic programs investigated in this study. This is significantly higher compared to institutions referred to as the medium and large institutions combined.

Medium and large two-year and four-year institutions are three and a half times more likely to provide more athletic programs than smaller HBCUs. While cost is a significant factor in the number of athletic programs offered by an institution, association membership guidelines also require a minimum number of men's and women's sports based on classification. Only 8 of the 39 or 20.5% institutions labeled as medium and large provide three or less of the four athletic programs evaluated in this study. This is a significantly lower percentage compared to institutions labeled as small institutions. Of the institutions listed as small HBCUs 31 or 50.0% do not have a physical education, recreation, and/or sport management academic unit.

Throughout HBCU campuses basketball has evolved into the dominant sport regardless of the size or gender identity base of the institution. There are only 13 out of 106 institutions or 12.3% that do not have a men's basketball program while there are only 12 out of 106 institutions or 11.3% that do not have a women's basketball program. Eleven of those institutions or 10.4% do not offer an athletics program. The sections that follow will discuss these results in greater detail and offer suggestions for future research in the area of HBCU athletic programs.

Discussion

As HBCU athletic programs continue to grow, expand, and operate in the NCAA, NAIA, NJCAA, or USCAA, and with the increased commitment to athletics from regional and national branded HWCU athletic programs operating at the highest level in the NCAA as member of the Division I

Table 6.5. Differences in HBCU athletic programs based on institutional status.

Institutional Size	Public Institutions (%) N = 51	Private Institutions (%) N = 55
Large Four-Year	2.0	0.0
Medium Four-Year	9.8	47.3
Small Four-Year	23.5	32.7
Very Small Four-Year	43.1	1.8
Large Two-Year	3.9	0.0
Medium Two-Year	9.8	0.0
Small Two-Year	7.8	1.8
Very Small Two-Year	0.0	7.3
Unknown	0.0	7.3
Operational Membership		
NCAA Division I FBS	0.0	0.0
NCAA Division I FCS	37.3	5.4
NCAA Division I AAA	3.9	0.0
NCAA Division II	31.4	29.6
NCAA Division III	0.0	1.8
NAIA Division I	3.9	27.8
NAIA Division II	2.0	9.1
NJCAA	15.7	9.1
USCAA	0.0	3.6
None	5.9	14.5
Region		
Northeast		3.9	0.0
Division 1	New England	0.0	0.0
Division 2	Middle Atlantics	3.9	0.0
Midwest		7.8	1.8
Division 3	East North Central	3.9	1.8
Division 4	West North Central	3.9	0.0
South		86.3	98.2
Division 5	South Atlantic	41.2	49.1
Division 6	East South Central 3	27.5	29.1
Division 7	West South Central	17.6	20.0
West		0.0	0.0
Division 8	Mountain	0.0	0.0
Division 9	Pacific	0.0	0.0
U.S. Territory		2.0	0.0
	U.S. Virgin Island	2.0	0.0

FBS, Bowl Championship Series (BCS), it is important to examine the current status of HBCUs' athletics programs and their national associations. By using an ESS conceptual framework and content analysis methodology, the objective of this study was to help illuminate the current status of HBCUs' athletic programs.

The first variable examined in this study, school region, revealed that the majority of historically Black institutions are located in the South, 97 or 92.4%, in Region 3, primarily in the South Atlantic area, 48 or 45.7% in Division 5 of the U.S. Census Bureau map. The majority of these institutions offer all five of the athletic programs analyzed in this study. The second variable analyzed in this study was size. This study revealed that size was highly relevant when comparing institutions and athletic programs. The data illustrate that HBCU institutions listed as small two-year or four-year offer fewer athletic programs as a whole and in many instances they fail to offer football and baseball programs.

Institutional status was explored that revealed that historically Black public institutions provided a wider range of athletic programs. Many of the of historically Black private institutions do not provide the larger outdoor athletic programs and participate in the lower NCAA divisional classification (i.e., NCAA Division II) as well as the NAIA Division I classification: 18 of the 54 or 33.3% of historically Black private institutions provide two or less of the five sports evaluated in this study. There are only 30 out of 106 or 28.3% historically Black institutions that offer all four athletic programs and 21 of those 30 or 70.0% are of historically Black public institutions. The final variable investigated is the significant difference found between two-year and four-year institutions offering athletic programs. Two-year historically Black institutions offer far fewer athletic programs than four-year historically Black institutions. There are 16 two-year historically black institutions and only 8 or 50.0% of these institutions offer two or more athletic programs. Among the 91 four-year historically Black institutions, 73 or 80.2% offer two or more athletic programs, and 3 of these institutions do not offer varsity athletic programs. Now, this 80.2% rate is significantly higher than the 50.0% rate found among the two-year historically Black institutions.

Conclusion

To conclude, this study showed that the athletic programs provided by HBCUs throughout the United States significantly vary at the present time. It is important for all universities to continually evaluate the status

Table 6.6. List of HBCU.

Institutional Name	Status	Founded	Size
ALABAMA			
1. Alabama A & M University	Public	1875	Four-Year
2. Alabama State University	Public	1874	Four-Year
3. Bishop State Community College	Public	1927	Two-Year
4. C.A. Fredd State Technical College	Public	1965	Two-Year
5. Concordia College	Private	1922	Two-Year
6. J.F. Drake Technical College	Public	1961	Two-Year
7. Lawson State Community College	Public	1965	Two-Year
8. Miles College	Private	1905	Four-Year
9. Oakwood College	Private	1896	Four-Year
10. Selma University	Private	1878	Four-Year
11. Shelton State Community College	Public	1952	Two-Year
12. Stillman College	Private	1876	Four-Year
13. Talladega College	Private	1967	Four-Year
14. Trenholm State Technical College	Public	1963	Two-Year
15. Tuskegee University	Private	1881	Two-Year
ARKANSAS			
16. Arkansas Baptist College	Private	1884	Four-Year
17. Philander Smith College	Private	1877	Four-Year
18. Shorter College	Private	1886	Two-Year
19. University of Arkansas at Pine Bluff	Public	1873	Four-Year
DELAWARE			
20. Delaware State University	Public	1891	Four-Year
DISTRICT OF COLUMBIA			
21. Howard University	Federal	1867	Four-Year
22. University of the District of Columbia	Private	1851	Four-Year
FLORIDA			
23. Bethune-Cookman College	Private	1904	Four-Year
24. Edward Waters College	Private	1866	Four-Year
25. Florida A & M University	Public	1877	Four-Year
26. Florida Memorial College	Private	1879	Four-Year

(*Continued*)

148 Africana Theory, Policy, and Leadership

Table 6.6 (Continued)

Institutional Name	Status	Founded	Size
GEORGIA			
27. Albany State College	Public	1903	Four-Year
28. Clark Atlanta University	Private	1989	Four-Year
29. Fort Valley State College	Public	1895	Four-Year
30. Interdenominational Theological Center	Private	1958	Four-Year
31. Morehouse College	Private	1867	Four-Year
32. Morehouse School of Medicine	Private	1975	Four-Year
33. Morris Brown College	Private	1881	Four-Year
34. Paine College	Private	1882	Four-Year
35. Savannah State College	Public	1890	Four-Year
36. Spelman College	Private	1881	Four-Year
KENTUCKY			
37. Kentucky State University	Public	1886	Four-Year
LOUISIANA			
38. Dillard University	Private	1869	Four-Year
39. Grambling State University	Public	1901	Four-Year
40. Southern University A & M College—Baton Rouge	Public	1880	Four-Year
41. Southern University at New Orleans	Public	1959	Four-Year
42. Southern University at Shreveport	Public	1964	Two-Year
43. Xavier University	Private	1915	Four-Year
MARYLAND			
44. Bowie State University	Public	1865	Four-Year
45. Coppin State College	Public	1900	Four-Year
46. Morgan State University	Public	1867	Four-Year
47. University of Maryland—Eastern Shore	Public	1886	Four-Year
MICHIGAN			
48. Lewis College of Business	Private	1874	Two-Year
MISSISSIPPI			
49. Alcorn State University	Public	1871	Four-Year
50. Coahoma Community College	Public	1949	Two-Year
51. Hinds Community College	Public	1954	Two-Year
52. Jackson State University	Public	1877	Four-Year

(*Continued*)

Table 6.6 (Continued)

Institutional Name	Status	Founded	Size
53. Mary Holmes College	Private	1892	Two-Year
54. Mississippi Valley State University	Public	1946	Four-Year
55. Rust College	Private	1866	Four-Year
56. Tougaloo College	Private	1869	Four-Year
MISSOURI			
57. Harris-Stowe State College	Public	1857	Four-Year
58. Lincoln University	Public	1866	Four-Year
NORTH CAROLINA			
59. Barber-Scotia College	Private	1867	Four-Year
60. Bennett College	Private	1873	Four-Year
61. Elizabeth City State University	Public	1891	Four-Year
62. Fayetteville State University	Public	1877	Four-Year
63. Johnson C. Smith University	Private	1867	Four-Year
64. Livingstone College	Private	1879	Four-Year
65. North Carolina A & T State University	Public	1891	Four-Year
66. North Carolina Central University	Public	1910	Four-Year
67. St. Augustine's College	Private	1867	Four-Year
68. Shaw University	Private	1865	Four-Year
69. Winston-Salem State University	Public	1862	Four-Year
OHIO			
70. Central State University	Public	1887	Four-Year
71. Wilberforce University	Private	1856	Four-Year
OKLAHOMA			
72. Langston University	Public	1897	Four-Year
PENNSYLVANIA			
73. Cheyney State University	Public	1837	Four-Year
74. Lincoln University	Public	1854	Four-Year
SOUTH CAROLINA			
75. Allen University	Private	1870	Four-Year
76. Benedict College	Private	1870	Four-Year
77. Claflin College	Private	1869	Four-Year
78. Clinton Junior College	Private	1894	Two-Year
79. Denmark Technical College	Public	1948	Two-Year

(*Continued*)

Table 6.6 (Continued)

Institutional Name	Status	Founded	Size
80. Morris College	Private	1908	Four-Year
81. South Carolina State University	Public	1896	Four-Year
82. Voorhees College	Private	1897	Four-Year
TENNESSEE			
83. American Baptist College	Private	1924	Four-Year
84. Fisk University	Private	1867	Four-Year
85. Knoxville College	Private	1875	Four-Year
86. Lane College	Private	1882	Four-Year
87. LeMoyne-Owen College	Private	1862	Four-Year
88. Meharry Medical College	Private	1876	Four-Year
89. Tennessee State University	Public	1912	Four-Year
TEXAS			
90. Huston-Tillotson College	Private	1876	Four-Year
91. Jarvis Christian College	Private	1912	Four-Year
92. Paul Quinn College	Private	1872	Four-Year
93. Prairie View A & M University	Public	1876	Four-Year
94. Saint Phillip's College	Public	1927	Two-Year
95. Southwestern Christian College	Private	1949	Four-Year
96. Texas College	Private	1894	Four-Year
97. Texas Southern University	Public	1947	Four-Year
98. Wiley College	Private	1873	Four-Year
VIRGIN ISLANDS			
99. University of Virgin Islands	Public	1962	Four-Year
VIRGINIA			
100. Hampton University	Private	1868	Four-Year
101. Norfolk State University	Public	1935	Four-Year
102. Saint Paul's College	Private	1888	Four-Year
103. Virginia State University	Public	1882	Four-Year
104. Virginia Union University	Private	1865	Four-Year
WEST VIRGINIA			
105. Bluefield State College	Public	1895	Four-Year
106. West Virginia State University	Public	1891	Four-Year

of their athletic programs in order to remain competitive. Doing so will be beneficial not only to the athletes and coaches, but also to the university as a whole in terms of recruiting athletes and nonathletes and appealing to the local public. The "Dr. Cavil's Ten Pillars for Active Engagement for Sport Leadership & Administration in Creating Athletic Organizational Success & Sustainability" provides a framework for HBCU athletic programs to enhance their collective brand and create positive outcomes for their educational stakeholders.

The Ten Pillars are split between two segments: the Five Internal Pillars of Engagement and the Five External Pillars of Engagement. The Five Internal Pillars of Engagement include Academic Alignment, Athletic Compliance, Media Solutions/Event Management, Alumni Activation/Community Engagement, and Corporate Fundraising/Capital Campaign. The Five External Pillars of Engagement include Critical Evaluation/Continuous Improvement, Strategic Planning/Tactical Analytics, Personal Mastery/Team Building, Shared Vision/Shared Governance, and System Thinking/Operational Practices. The pillars are not designed to be followed in any particular order. In a sporting organization, the pillar framework can be thought of as similar to the foundation of a building. It is necessary for all the areas of support to be impeded and reinforced to create the strength in order to make the building strong and not collapse. Therefore, the goal of Dr. Cavil's Ten Pillars framework is to focus the organization's attention on the areas that are key components to success and sustainability after analyzing the current status of HBCU athletics programs.

In addition, it should be noted that it was not the intent of this study to make an assertion on which HBCU athletic programs are good or bad, but rather to distinguish the differences among them and the causes for the differences. It is the researchers' hope that this study will ignite future conversations regarding HBCU athletic programs at national and regional gatherings of our colleagues. Organizers and administrators of HBCU athletic programs have a number of options when designing their programs and at what level they should operate their athletics programs, but sport managers and educational administrators have not undertaken much research to help them understand their choices. The results discussed in this chapter will at least allow policymakers to make an informed decision between such choices.

References

Allen, W.R. 1986. *Gender and Campus Race Differences in Black Student Academic Performance, Racial Attitudes and College Satisfaction*. Atlanta: Southern Education Foundation.

Armstrong, K.L. 2002. "An Examination of the Social Psychology of Black's Consumption of Sport." *Journal of Sport Management* 16:267–88.

Borican, J. 1963. "The Role of the Negro Colleges." In *Negro Firsts in Sports*, edited by A.S. Young, 88–97. Chicago, IL: Johnson Publishing Company, Inc.

Brazzell, Johnetta Cross. 1992. "Bricks without Straw: Missionary-sponsored Black Higher Education in the Post-emancipation Era." *The Journal of Higher Education* 63(1): 26–49.

Brown, M. C. 1999. *The Quest to Define Collegiate Desegregation: Black Colleges, Title VI Compliance, and Post-Adams Litigation*. Westport, CT: Bergin & Garvey.

Brown, Gary. 2012. "Executive Committee Funds Pilot to Help Limited-resource Schools Boost APR." Retrieved from http://www.ncaa.org/wps/wcm/connect/public/NCAA/Resources/Latest+News/2012/July/Executive+Committee+funds+pilot+to+help+limited-resource+schools+boost+APR

CIAA. 2015. The history of the CIAA. Retrieved from http://www.ciaatournament.org/about/ciaa-history

DeSchriver, T. D. 2007. "Much adieu about Freddy: The Relationship between mls spectator Attendance and the Arrival of Freddy Adu." *Journal of Sport Management* 21:(3): 438–51.

DeSchriver, T. D. and P. E. Jensen 2002. "Determinants of Spectator Attendance at NCAA Division II Football Contests." *Journal of Sports Management* 16(4): 311–30.

Gawrysiak, E. J., Cooper, J. N., and Hawkins, B. J. 2012. "The Impact of Baseball Participation on the Educational Experiences of Black Student-athletes at Historically Black Colleges and Universities." *Race, Ethnicity and Education*. doi:10.1080/1361 3324.2013.792795

Gratton, C., and Jones, I. 2010. *Research Methods for Sport Studies*, 2nd ed. New York: Routledge.

Hawkins, Billy. 2010. *The New Plantation: Black Athletes, College Sports, and Predominantly White Institutions*. New York: Palgrave Macmillan.

Hawkins, B., Cooper, J.N., Carter-Francique, A.R., and Cavil, J.K. (Eds.) 2015. *The Athletic experience at Historically Black Colleges and Universities (HBCUs): Past, Present, & Persistence*. Lanham, MD: Rowan & Littlefield Press.

Hosick, Michelle. 2012. Limited-resource Institutions Allowed Flexible Transition to Higher apr standards. NCAA.org. Retrieved from http://www.ncaa.org/wps/wcm/connect/public/NCAA/Resources/Latest+News/2012/April/Limited-resource+institutions+allowed+flexible+transition+to+higher+APR+standards

Hodge, S. R., Bennett III., R. A., and Collins, F. G. 2013. "Historically Black Colleges and Universities' Athletes and Sport Programs: Historical Overview, Evaluations, and Affiliations." In *Racism in College Athletics*, edited by D. Brooks and R. Althouse, 63–104. Morgantown, WV: Fitness Information Technology.

Hunt, D. 1996. *Great Names in Black College Sports*. Indianapolis, IN: Masters Press.

Johnson, G.K. 2007. Football attendance soars again. The NCAA News. Retrieved on March 6, 2008, http://www.ncaa.org/wps/ncaa?ContentID=4232

Mance, R. 2003 Thursday 1. The Morrill Act & 1862 & 1890 & HBCU's. Retrieved April 12, 2011, from http://emergingminds.org/The-MORRILL-ACT-of-1862-and-1890-and-HBCUs.html?format=pdf

McClelland, C.F. 2012. "Athletic directors' Perceptions of the Effectiveness of hbcu division I-AA Athletic Programs." Ph.D. dissertation, Texas A&M University MEAC.

2015. MEAC history. Retrieved from http://www.meacsports.com/ViewArticle.dbml?DB_OEM_ID=20800&ATCLID=1591845

Miller, P.B. 1995. "To Bring the Race along Rapidly: Sport, Student Culture, and Educational Mission at Historically Black Colleges during the Interwar Years." *History of Education Quarterly* 35:111–33.

Reynolds, Lacey, Dwalah Fisher, and Cavil, J. Kenyatta. 2012. "Demographic Variables Have a Significant Impact on African American Students Athletes Academic Performance." *Journal of Education Foundations* 26(no. 3–4) (Summer–Fall): 93–111.

Saylor, Roger. 2000. *College Football Historical Society Newsletter* 13(3). Retrieved from http://library.la84.org/SportsLibrary/CFHSN/CFHSNv13/CFHSNv13n3b.pdf

SIAC. 2015. SIAC history. Retrieved from http://www.thesiac.com/sports/2010/2/2/gen_0202103837.aspx?

Stuart, A., Ord, J.K., and Arnold, S. 1999. *Kendall's Advanced Theory of Statistics*, vol. 2A, 6th ed. London: Edward Arnold.

Suggs, W. 1998. "Only NCAA's State Schools Turn Profits." *Smith & Smith's Sports Business Journal* October (18–25): 5.

SWAC. 2015. SWAC history. Retrieved from http://www.swac.org/ViewArticle.dbml?DB_OEM_ID=27400&ATCLID=205246152

The Carnegie Foundation for the Advancement of Teaching. 2010. *Institution lookup*. Retrieved from http://www.classifications.carnegiefoundation.org/lookup_listings/institutions.php?key=732.

U.S. Census Bureau. 2010. *Census Bureau map products*. Retrieved from http://www.census.gov/geo/www/maps/CP_MapProducts.htm.

U.S. Department of Education. 2010. *List of HBCUs—White House initiative on Historically Black Colleges and Universities*. Retrieved from http://www2.ed.gov/about/inits/list/whhbcu/edlite-list.html.

Wiggins, D.K., and Miller. P. 2003. *The Unlevel Playing Field: A Documentary History of the African-American Experience in Sport*. Urbana, IL: University of Illinois Press.

Williams, L. (2008, January 1–7). Attendance Matters: Largest Attendance at Football Games of 2007. Black College Sports Page: 1.

7

The Afrocentric Idea in Leadership Studies

Abul Pitre

Introduction

Asante's (1988) historic text *Afrocentricity* reintroduced the concept of viewing the world from an African and Black American perspective. In *Afrocentricity* he highlights Booker T. Washington, W.E.B. Du Bois, Marcus Garvey, Dr. Martin Luther King Jr., Elijah Muhammad, Malcolm X, and Maulana Karenga. He specifically highlights the contributions that each of the aforementioned persons made to Afrocentricity. Although the text does not necessarily address leadership discourse found in leadership studies, it creates a space for Afrocentric discourse in leadership studies.

Leadership studies is a new field of study in academia dating back to around 60 years ago. It has been defined as an interdisciplinary field of study that examines leadership across disciplines. Similar to Africana/Black studies that is also an interdisciplinary area of study, scholars in leadership studies examine leadership from a wide range of academic disciplines. However, the majority of leadership studies discourse has been centered primarily on the management of businesses and large corporations. Scholars in leadership studies are beginning to explore a wide range of topics such as critical theory, religious studies, spirituality, popular culture, cultural diversity, and globalism, among others. Bryman et al. (2011) write, "Leadership perspectives and research increasingly draw on a broad range of disciplines, including (social) psychology, sociology, history, political science, anthropology, cultural studies, philosophy, education, military studies, health and social welfare and religious studies" (p. iv).

Despite the emerging discourse in leadership studies there is a dearth of information related to the Black American perspective of leadership. For example, in *The SAGE Handbook of Leadership* there is no discussion about leadership from a Black American perspective (Bryman et al. 2011). The handbook represents one of the dilemmas in leadership studies with regard to the limited discourse from diverse cultural perspectives. It is clear that this emerging and dynamic field misses the Afrocentric idea, a component that could inform the study of leadership enhancing the practice of leadership.

When James MacGregor Burns (1979) introduced his ground-breaking work in leadership it paved the way for leadership studies in academia. However, what is noticeably absent is an Afrocentric perspective of leadership. Walters (2007) writes, "Although there was not much in Burn's book about Black movements, his elucidation of the role of leaders gave me a useful framework for approaching a dynamic issue that seemed to account for some success" (p. 150). Thus students studying the varying leadership theories and topics in leadership studies will find virtually no discussion about what the Afrocentric idea means for leaders. Asante's (1991) article "The Afrocentric Idea in Education" as well as his book *Afrocentricity* can be used as a framework to examine the Afrocentric idea in leadership studies. In presenting the Afrocentric idea into the leadership studies discourse this article starts with a definition of Afrocentricity and later examines the varied ways it can be viewed in the leadership studies discourse. The article then explores Black leaders such as W.E.B. Du Bois, Elijah Muhammad, Louis Farrakhan, and Marcus Garvey in the context of leadership studies.

The Afrocentric Idea for Leadership Studies

Asante (2003) defines Afrocentricity in the following way: "Afrocentricty is a mode of thought and action in which the centrality of African interests, values, and perspectives predominate" (p. 2). He contends that "Afrocentricity reorganizes our frame of reference so that we become the center of analysis and synthesis" (1988, 39). This argument can be found in earlier Black American discourse such as Carter G. Woodson's *Mis-Education of the Negro* whereby Woodson argued that the education of Blacks gave them a perspective of the world that made them White in their thinking. Woodson (1933) argued, "THE 'educated Negroes' have the attitude of contempt toward their own people because in their own as well as in their mixed schools Negroes are taught to admire the Hebrew, the Greek, the Latin and the Teuton and to despise the African"

(p. 23). Woodson's argument demonstrates a logic that extends beyond education in schools per se and presents questions about leadership. If those who are considered well educated have been labeled as leaders or prospective leaders of Blacks, then Woodson's argument suggests that through education these leaders are leading in the interest of their oppressors.

Asante and Hall (2012) describes this kind of leadership as rooming in the master house. In other words, these types of leaders have a perspective or view of the world that is Eurocentric. Malcolm X described these types of Black leaders as house Negroes. He argued that their education and closeness to their slave masters resulted in them seeing the world from the perspective of their slave master. Using the example of a house fire he contends that if the master's house caught on fire the house Negro would attempt to put the fire out while the field Negro who sees the world from a more Afrocentric approach would pray for a strong wind to burn the master's house. The dualities that exist in the thinking of the house Negro and field Negro coincides with Du Bois' double consciousness where he argued that Blacks suffered from trying to stay connected with their Africaness while simultaneously trying to be American (Du Bois 1961).

Du Bois offered what Rabaka (2008) calls an Africana critical theory that is useful in the study of leadership. Rabaka writes that Du Bois' talented tenth represented a cadre of educated Blacks who would be educated for leadership. It was here that Du Bois and Booker T. Washington had opposing views about the future of Blacks. While Du Bois' talented tenth was only one aspect of his philosophical views about leadership Rabaka cogently argues that Du Bois' ideas were constantly evolving and that the talented tenth represented his earlier views about leadership.

Rabaka (2008) points out that later in his life Du Bois introduced the "doctrine of the Guiding Hundredth" that was centered more on group leadership: "the one hundred as broad group of leadership, not simply educated and self sacrificing, but with a clear vision of present world conditions and dangers, and conducting American Negroes alliance with culture groups in Europe, America, Asia, and Africa, and looking toward a new world culture" (p. 110). Over his lifetime Du Bois became disgruntled with his talented tenth who he felt betrayed Black America (Rabaka 2008). Perhaps much of Du Bois' frustration with the talented tenth was a result of the Eurocentered education that Blacks received. It has been argued that this Eurocentered education has indoctrinated Blacks to work in the interest of a White ruling class.

Du Bois' arguments regarding Black leadership and education raise salient points regarding the need to have Afrocentricity infused into the leadership studies discourse. If the majority of leadership studies discourse continues to be framed from the narrative of the dominant group, it is possible that students and practitioners of leadership may subconsciously perpetuate White supremacist perspectives. This became evident when I first introduced the concept of the Afrocentric idea in leadership studies to doctoral students who held leadership roles in diverse fields. Students were introduced to the writings of Asante that caused several to become angered, causing some students to ask: "How does Afrocentricity relate to the study of leadership?" These students also commented, "There is no need for an Afrocentric approach to the study of leadership?" Contrary to questioning the prevailing discourse in leadership studies that masks itself as universal and colorblind, these leaders represented a talented tenth that through years of mis-education were unable to recognize how leadership represents a frame of reference or as Asante argues a center from which one develops their leadership motive. These highly educated leaders represent Woodson's and Chomsky's notion of mis-education. Without a critical theory of leadership these leaders never ask deeper questions regarding the parameters that have defined how they lead or in many cases manage organizations and systems under the disguise of leadership.

The Afrocentric idea in leadership studies offers not only a Black American perspective about leadership but also represents an Africana critical theory for leadership (Rabaka 2008) and a critical Black pedagogy (Pitre 2011). Rabaka notes that Africana critical theory existed long before the Frankfurt school of critical theorists. Pitre (2011) similarly discusses a critical Black pedagogy that existed in education prior to the formal naming of critical pedagogy. Critical Black pedagogy represents the work of Black leaders and their critique of American education. Both Rabaka and Pitre's work present an Afrocentric approach to the study of critical theory in leadership. More importantly their works demonstrate that the Afrocentric idea in leadership studies presents a voluminous amount of knowledge that dates back to antiquity with regard to leadership (Warfield-Coppoack 1995). The ancient spiritual knowledge that emerged from Black peoples predates Socrates, Aristotle, Kant, and other European philosophers.

Drawing from the Africana Critical Theory tradition and the need for the Afrocentric idea in leadership studies, Asante (1988) brilliantly explains, "Breaking the mental chains only occurs when a person learns to take two sets of notes on almost everything encountered in the Western

World. If they say Shakespeare is the greatest writer, know Cesaire, Du Bois, Hughes, Soyinka, Gullien, Ngugu, Puskin. If they say that ballet is classical dance, know that is no more classical than Adowa or a Mfundalai Shairi Dansi. If they say Bach is universal, know that Bach cannot be anymore universal than John Coltrane or Duke Ellington" (p. 40). In contemporary leadership studies discourse when they mention Winston Churchill, John Kennedy, and Billy Graham, Blacks can point to Kwame Ture, Dr. Martin Luther King Jr., and Louis Farrakhan. Asante's two sets of notes would require an awakened consciousness among students and practitioners of leadership.

Regarding consciousness, it is here that the leadership of Elijah Muhammad catapults the Afrocentric idea in leadership studies. The son of a sharecropper in rural Georgia who only completed the third or fourth grade of school Elijah Muhammad's teaching raised the consciousness of Black peoples all over the world. Muhammad contended that Blacks in America needed to acquire the knowledge of self. The knowledge of self predates European leaders, transcended the physical world, and was connected to the spiritual. Muhammad argued that Black man is the original man who has his roots in the originator. Drawing from universal study or 360 degrees of knowledge that represents the entire universe, he argued that the entire universe comes out of the mind of the originator—"Black God." From his teachings he took the most downtrodden Blacks in the American society and produced a cadre of leaders that challenged the prevailing social norms.

Three good examples of his leadership are Malcolm X, Imam Warith Deen, and Louis Farrakhan of which none attained degrees from any university but yet the knowledge emanating from them created a groundswell among those in power as well as the oppressed and downtrodden in the society. During Elijah Muhammad's leadership of the Nation of Islam he created an entire nation within a nation. Under his leadership he argued that we don't wait for the White man to create jobs for us but we create our own jobs. Regarding Black leadership he was very critical of what he saw as blind leadership: "Look at the way in which the leadership yields to the wishes of the slave-master, even against their own life and against their people's lives. They don't want anything but the favor of the wicked world and it's leadership, not the favor of God, who offers them money, good homes, friendship in this world, and to set them in heaven at once . . . I want you to remember that the Bible plainly teaches you that the blind cannot lead the blind" (Hakim 1997, 93). Muhammad offered an Africana critical theory approach to leadership studies that involved critiquing the motives and desires of those Black leaders who were essentially being manipulated by a false consciousness that made them acquiesce to support the interest of their oppressors. He also knew that the problem of Black leadership resided in a White power structure that sought to divide and conquer Blacks.

In 1964, he met Dr. Martin Luther King Jr. and his wife Corretta Scott King in his Chicago home. During this meeting he noted that Dr. King agreed with him throughout the conversation (Hakim 1997). He also mentions that he was sure that the enemy heard King's agreement with him because their vans were parked across the street monitoring the conversation. Regarding the tactics of divide and conquer used against Blacks, he disclosed: "White America openly tries to divide Negroes, so-called Negro leaders, right in the face of each leader. We saw this going on, we hear it going on, we know it's going on. As soon as Dr. King and myself met together, there was a great stir to get to Dr. King. What is it they fear? They fear Dr. King will believe the truth, that's what they fear" (Hakim 1997, 93).

Elijah Muhammad's leadership represented a completely different kind of leadership as he started a nation, laid the foundation for a new civilization, and envisioned the creation of a new world. His leadership in the initial stages represents an Afrocentric approach that would awaken the consciousness in Blacks. Once equipped with the knowledge of self, Blacks would be able to recognize the divine force within. Being conscious of the divine force within would stimulate the creative mind in Blacks causing them to create a new world that would supersede the "White man's" world.

In *Our Savior Has Arrived*, he provides a picture of this new world emerging from Black people in America: "The new people that are to be made from us (Black Man of America). We will be made a new people, for we have been destroyed mentally and physically by the teachers and guides of this world of the White race. Therefore in order to renew us (the once servitude slave and now the free slave of our enemy), we must have a new spirit that will produce ideas in us to become a new people" (Muhammad 1974, 131). This is ultimately a discussion around leadership.

For Muhammad stimulating the creative mind in Blacks would cause them to produce a world that has not been experienced since the first creation of life that dates back into the trillions of years. Once awakened to this divine consciousness it ultimately means a paradigm shift in leadership. Thus, Muhammad's leadership was problematic to those in every circle of leadership both nationally and internationally. To date his well-known student Louis Farrakhan represents "the reproductive mind of Elijah Muhammad" (Asante 1988, 37).

Farrakhan's leadership has for over 50 years been concerned with the plight of Blacks. He has devoted his life to the mission of Elijah Muhammad, which is centered on the resurrection of Blacks in America. Over the course of his many years of service he has critiqued the leadership of diverse groups in America. He has also provided guidance and wisdom to a new generation of young leaders causing them to reject White dominance. In the largest gathering of men recorded in history, the 1995 Million Man March represented Minister Farrakhan's tremendous leadership ability. The knowledge emanating from Minister Farrakhan was a result of him seeing the problems affecting Black men in America from an Afrocentric approach. Regarding leadership and the study of leadership Minister Farrakhan's life contains jewels of knowledge that could be used to create new forms of leadership and leadership study.

In several of his speeches he has particularly addressed the issue of leadership. In a speech titled "Principles and Practices of Leadership to Suffice Our Needs," he highlights principles needed to effectively lead Black people. In describing the leadership principle he discloses that leadership is undergirded by a divine principle:

> Leadership" is undergirded by a Divine Principle. Some of us think that "good looks" make us "good leaders," and maybe that's why we're in the shape that we're in. "Leadership" is not for the arrogant. Some think that "great articulation of words" and "beautiful speech" is what makes "good leaders," and maybe that's why we're in the condition that we're in, because we always choose leaders that can speak well, but don't do well. And we always choose leaders sometimes that appeal to our fancy of what "leadership" is without ever considering the Divine Principle that undergirds real, and true, leadership. (Farrakhan 2011, 1)

The Afrocentric perspective is clearly at the forefront of Minister Farrakhan's (2011) principles of leadership as he points out, "Black people today don't need leaders who 'wanna be': Who are seeking somebody to carry their bags and to help us live better with finer cars and clothes, and homes in good neighborhoods—Black people don't need that; enough of that"! (p. 2). For Minister Farrakhan leadership is not about individual power for vane purposes but it is about service to one's fellows. Similarly, Robert Greenleaf in his theory of servant leadership cogently writes: "It begins with the natural feeling that one wants to serve, to serve first. Then conscious choice brings one to aspire to lead" (p. 27). Speaking on servant leadership Greenleaf contends that the servant leader aspires to "make sure that other people's priority needs are being met" (p. 27). Farrakhan

(2011), speaking on the issue of leadership, highlights, "The Principle of Leadership is based on serving, and seeing that the people whom you're serving value the service, benefit from the service and grow from the service; in order, then, that they become that to others as you have become that to them" (p. 3). Both Farrakhan and Greenleaf view servant leadership as a major area of discourse for those aspiring to leadership. In addition, a study of both men's teaching on leadership confirms why there is a need to take two sets of notes. While Greenleaf is a major figure discussed in leadership studies Farrakhan is virtually absent in the leadership studies discourse despite his 50 plus years of leadership.

Servant leadership is not new among Black leaders and has been put into practice by distinguished Black leaders such as Dr. Martin Luther King Jr. and Marcus Garvey. Dr. Martin Luther King Jr. in one of his speeches captures the servant leadership principle. Making reference to biblical text, he declared that the "greatest among you shall be your servant." Leaders like Marcus Garvey, the founder of the United Negro Improvement Association, practiced servant leadership by placing the needs of Blacks as a collective group before his personal needs. Dr. Martin Luther King Jr. spoke to the significance of Garvey's leadership for Blacks: "Marcus was the first man of color in the history of the United States to lead and develop a mass movement. He was the first man, on a mass scale, and level, to give millions of Negroes a sense of dignity and destiny, and make the Negro feel that he was somebody" (Haugen 2008, 95). Garvey's extraordinary leadership was rooted in the Afrocentric idea.

Scholars in leadership studies could draw from Garvey's ability to navigate through hostile territory while keeping a commitment to enhance the lives of people of African descent. Garvey's leadership like other Black leaders provides a framework for understanding the challenges of leading for liberation. Unlike the majority of leadership studies discourse that is primarily concerned with management and leadership within a business model, which seeks to make profits, Afrocentric leadership is transformative leadership. Transformative leadership is concerned with a critique of the society, social justice, and liberation from oppressive structures (Shields 2011).

In addition to transformative leadership practice among Black leaders, there is a need to explore the challenges of leading oppressed peoples. Thus leadership studies should examine those who have undertaken liberatory approaches to leadership. Although leadership might appear to be an easy task within the dominant literature there is a need to explore the opposition faced by leaders who were truly committed to the practice of Afrocentric leadership.

Black leaders with an Afrocentric frame of reference faced extreme opposition from a wide range of groups and organizations. One example is J. Edgar Hoover's counterintelligence program that sought to destroy Black leadership that advocated for freedom, justice, and equality. Kenneth O'Reilly (1994), speaking on the challenges faced by Black leaders in his book *Black Americans: The FBI Files*, writes: "My view, simply put, is that Hoover targeted both King and Malcolm for what he called "neutralization," and his men, in effect, did their best to incite the killings short of actually pulling the trigger" (p. 7). Regarding Garvey he writes: "J. Edgar Hoover, eight years Garvey's junior but already General Intelligence Division Chief by 1919, led the government's charge. Having first decided that Garvey ought to be jailed, the future FBI director then searched for an appropriate crime. He hired four black men to work the case and sent one of them to infiltrate the UNIA and other shadow 'the Negro Moses'" (p. 139). Thus leading from an Afrocentric framework has different challenges that might require the leader to become a sacrificial lamb.

The history of Black leadership is replete with leaders who have led from the Afrocentric center described by Asante (1991). These leaders also put into practice concepts found in servant leadership and transformative leadership. As servant leaders they were willing to give their lives for the cause of justice. The contemporary discourse in leadership studies would do well to revisit the lives of great Black leaders and the wealth of knowledge they have bequeathed to those aspiring to leadership roles as well as those seeking to become scholars of leadership studies.

References

Asante, M. K. 1988. *Afrocentricity*. Trenton, NJ: Africa World Press.
Asante, M. K. 1991. "The Afrocentric Idea in Education." *The Journal of Negro Education* 60(2): 170–80.
Asante, M. K. 2003. *Afrocentricity: The Theory of Social Change (revised and expanded)*. Chicago, IL: Black Images.
Asante, M. K., and Hall, R 2012. *Rooming in the Master's House*. Boulder, CO: Paradigm Publishers.
Bryman, A., Collinson, D., Grint, K., Jackson, B., and Uhl-Bien, M. 2011. *The SAGE Handbook of Leadership*. Thousand Oaks, CA: Sage Publication.
Burns, J. M. 1979. *Leadership*. New York: HarperCollins.
Cuoto, R. (Ed.). 2007. *Reflections on Leadership*. Lanham, MD: University Press of America.
Du Bois, W. E. B. 1961. *The Souls of Black Folk*. Greenwich, CT: Fawcett.
Farrakhan, L. 2011, October 8. Principles and practices of leadership to suffice our needs. *FinalCall.com*. Retrieved March 5, 2012, from http://www.finalcall.com/artman/publish/Minister...9/article_8369.shtml

Greenleaf, R. K. 2002. *Servant Leadership: A Journey into the Nature of Legitimate Power and Greatness*. Mahwah, NJ: Paulist Press.
Hakim, N. (Ed). 1997. *The Theology of Time*, 3rd ed. Atlanta, GA: M.E.M.P.S. Publication.
Haugen, B. 2008. *Marcus Garvey: Black Nationalist Crusader and Entrepreneur*. Minneapolis, MN: Compass Point Books.
Muhammad, E. 1997. *Our Savior Has Arrived*. Chicago, IL: Final Call.
O'Reilly, K. 1994. *Black Americans: The FBI Files*. New York: Carroll & Graf.
Pitre, A. 2011. *Freedom Fighters: Struggles Instituting Black History in k-12 Education*. San Francisco, CA: Cognella Academic Publishers.
Pitre, A., Allen, T., and Pitre, E. 2015. *Multicultural Education for Educational Leaders: Critical Race Theory and Antiracist Perspectives*. Lanham, MD: Rowman and Littlefield.
Rabaka, R. 2008. *Africana Critical Theory: Reconstructing the Black Radical Tradition*. Lanham, MD: Lexington Books.
Shields, T. (Ed.). 2011. *Transformative Leadership*: *An Introduction*. California: Peter Lang.
Walters, R. 2007. "Leadership from the Bottom Up." In *Reflections on Leadership*, edited by R. Couto, 149–62. Lanham, MD: University Press of America.
Warfield-Coppoack, N. 1995. "Toward a Theory of Afrocentric Organizations." *Journal of Black Psychology* 21(1): 30–48.
Woodson, C. G. 1933. *The Mis-education of the Negro*. New York: Tribeca Books.

Notes on Contributors

Nishaun T. Battle, PhD, earned her Doctorate in Sociology with special focus on Criminology and Social Inequality in 2014 at Howard University where she also received a graduate certificate in Women's Studies. Currently, Dr. Battle is Assistant Professor of Criminal Justice at Virginia State University. Her research and teaching interests include examining the relationship between activism and social and legal outcomes. Her most recent publication is "Assata Shakur: A Black Political Revolutionary," in *African Americans and Criminal Justice: An Encyclopedia*, coauthored with Delores Brown. Committed to social justice, Dr. Battle is also involved in community engagement efforts that promote fairness and equality on various issues within the criminal justice system.

Irvin H. Bromall, PhD, received his doctorate degree from the University of Wisconsin-Madison in 1967. He was a senior federal manager in transit-related civil rights and former political science professor at several higher education institutions. Dr. Bromall also worked as a consultant on community development and civil society for many NGOs both in the United States and other countries. After years of voluntary service to hundreds of asylum seekers and immigrants mostly from Eritrea, Ethiopia, and Mexico Dr. Bromall passed away on March 23, 2014, at his home in Moab, UT, where he was living since he retired from the federal government two decades ago. Dr. Bromall was a very dedicated civil right advocate, who dedicated his entire life to promoting social and economic justice for all.

J. Kenyatta Cavil, EdD, MBA, born in Norman, Oklahoma, and reared in Waco, Texas, is a graduate of Prairie View A&M University's Roy G. Perry College of Engineering, holding a Bachelors of Science in Mechanical Engineering (1994) and the Whitlowe R. Green College of Education with a Master of Education Mathematics with special focus on Applied

Mathematics in Scientific Computation (2004) degree. He continued his education at Texas Southern University's Jesse H. Jones School of Business with a Masters in Business Administration (2008) degree and holds a Doctorate in Education Administration (2009) degree and a Master of Science in Human Performance/Kinesiology (2009) degree from Texas Southern's College of Education. Dr. Cavil has completed postgraduate studies in Sport Management from Sam Houston State University. Dr. Cavil is currently Associate Professor at Texas Southern University in Houston, TX, and is one of the preeminent voices on HBCUs sport business and a scholar on HBCU sports culture theory, the "Sporting HBCU Diaspora" and sport leadership. He is the Executive Director of the HBCU Athletic Research Consortium Conference. He has published research articles and book chapters. His most recent book publication as one of the four authors along with Billy Hawkins, Joseph Cooper, and Akilah Carter-Francique is *The Athletic Experience at Historically Black Colleges and Universities—Past, Present, and Persistence*, published in 2015. Dr. Cavil has written articles for *College Sporting News (CSN)* magazine. His newest venture is the *Dr. Cavil's "Inside the HBCU Sports Lab"* radio show. He is a member of the North American Society for Sociology of Sport (NASSS), North American Society for Sport Management (NASSM), and a Board Member for the *Journal of HBCU Research + Culture* in conjunction with the HBCUStory Symposium.

Geremy Cheeks, MBA, is currently a doctoral candidate at Texas A&M University in the Department of Health and Kinesiology. He obtained his baccalaureate and Master's degrees in Business Administration from Florida A&M University in Tallahassee. His research and scholarship focuses on HBCU athletics and revenue generation disparities between HBCUs and PWIHEs, based on his experiences as a former intercollegiate athletics administrator.

James L. Conyers, Jr., PhD, is the Director of the African American Studies Program, Director of the Center for African American Culture, and Professor of African American Studies at the University of Houston. He serves as editor of the Africana Studies series at Transaction Publishers.

Joseph Cooper, PhD, MBA, is a native of Greensboro, North Carolina. He has a Bachelor's in Sociology and Recreation Administration from the University of North Carolina at Chapel Hill, a Master's in Sport Administration from the University of North Carolina at Chapel Hill, and a Doctorate in Kinesiology (Sport Management and Policy) from the University of Georgia. Dr. Cooper is currently Assistant Professor at the University of Connecticut in the Department of Educational Leadership (sport management program). His research interests focus on the nexus between sport, race, education, and culture. His current research agenda investigates the relationship between postsecondary environments in the United States and Black student athletes' educational experiences and outcomes. He is a member of the North American Society for Sociology of Sport (NASSS), North American Society for Sport Management (NASSM), the Association for the Study of Higher Education (ASHE), and the American Educational Research Association (AERA). He has published several articles that examine the experiences of Black male athletes at HBCUs.

Abul Pitre, PhD, is Professor and department head of educational leadership and counseling at Prairie View A&M University, where he teaches Multicultural Education for Educational Leaders and Leadership. He was appointed Edinboro University's first named professor for his outstanding work in African American education and held the distinguished title of the Carter G. Woodson Professor of Education.

Alberto Rodriguez, PhD, is currently Assistant Professor of History at Texas A&M University Kingsville and managing editor of *The Journal of South Texas History*. Rodriguez has published *Mexican American Baseball in the Alamo Region* (Charleston: Arcadia Publishing, 2015), "*Ponte El Guante!* Baseball on the US/Mexican Border: The Game and Community Building, 1920s–1970s," *The Journal of the West* (Fall 2015), "Spanish Southern States Recording Expedition," with Rene Torres, *Journal of Texas Music History* (Spring 2016). His upcoming project *Urban Borderlands: Situating Race, Class and Ethnicity in South Texas 1910–1960* is a comparative multiethnic analysis of the Lower Rio Grande Valley, focusing on race relations in American and Borderland society with a specialty in Mexican American and African American encounters.

Christel N. Temple, PhD, is Associate Professor of Africana Studies at the University of Pittsburgh where she teaches and researches comparative global African literature, cultural theory, cultural memory, and the intersection of history and literature. She is the author of *Literary Pan-Africanism: History, Contexts, and Criticism* (2005), *Literary Spaces: Introduction to*

Comparative Black Literature (2007), and is currently advancing research on the topic of *Black Cultural Mythology*.

Valethia A. Watkins, PhD, JD, is Assistant Professor in the Department of Afro-American Studies at Howard University and the Director of the Women's Graduate Certificate Program. She holds a Law degree from the Ohio State University College of Law and her PhD is in African American Studies (Temple University). Her research interests include Black women's intellectual history, feminism, and efforts toward conceptualizing Africana Studies–specific approaches to gender. Currently she is completing a book entitled *Africana Studies and Gender: Black Women, Power, and the Politics of Knowledge Production,* which explores the contentious and historical relationship between Black women and feminism and the implications for Black Women Studies and the analysis of gender within Africana Studies.

Dawit O. Woldu, PhD, is Assistant Professor of Anthropology and Cross-cultural Studies at the University of Houston Clear Lake who teaches courses on social medicine, community health, and topics on African Studies. He received his PhD from the University of Florida (Gainesville) in Medical Anthropology in 2012. A native of Eritrea, he has done extensive research on the cultural, biological, and ecological dimension of malaria and HIV/AIDS in Kenya. Dr. Woldu has also done research on Eritrean refugees and immigrants in the United States. Before moving to the University of Houston, Clear Lake, Dr. Woldu did his postdoctoral work at Ohio University, African Studies Program, working on HIV/AIDS and substance abuse project and teaching a course on Health Research in Africa. Dr. Woldu also assisted teaching a global health course with the Global Health Initiative at Ohio University. Dr. Woldu recent publication 2015 titled "Gender Roles and Perceptions of Malaria Risk in Agricultural Communities of Mwea Division in Central Kenya" in the *Journal of Women's Health*, a peer-reviewed and Pubmed indexed journal. Dr. Dawit Woldu can be contacted at Woldu@uhcl.edu or dawito2001@yahoo.com.

Index

Names of plays are in italic font.

A
Abdel-Moneim, M.A., 115
Academic Progress Rate (APR), 121, 129–30
Africana aesthetics. *See* Black narrative, from photographs; South Texas, Blacks in
Africana ethnography. *See* Eritrea
Africana gender studies, without feminism
   decolonization of gender, within Africana studies, 79
   feminism, definition using, 75–78
   gender analysis in, 64–65
   nonaligned women, definition, 69
   pathological models of gender, 76–77, 78
   womanism *vs.* feminism dichotomy, 73–75
   See also feminism
Africana perspectives in criminal justice, of Black women, 107–20
   Marissa Alexander, incarceration of, 108
   Black Lives Matter, 108
   Black women, leadership and, 117–19
   deaths of young Black males, by law enforcement, 107–8
   legal system, intersection in, 116–17
   Trayvon Martin/George Zimmerman case, 107, 109–10
   race/gender, social construction of, 108–11
   social group behavior, intersectionality and, 111–14
   womanhood, socialization/perception of, 114–15
Afrocentric leadership perspectives, 155–64
   of Molefi Asante, 156, 157, 158–59, 163
   of W.E.B. Du Bois, 157–58
   of Louis Farrakhan, 161–62
   FBI, opposition to Black leadership by, 163
   of Marcus Garvey, 162
   of Robert Greenleaf, 161–62
   of Dr. Martin Luther King, Jr., 160, 162
   of Elijah Muhammad, 159–61
   of Abul Pitre, 158
   of Reiland Rabaka, 158
   in scholarship, 155–56
   servant leadership, 161–62
   transformative leadership, 162–63
   of Carter G. Woodson, 156–57
   of Malcolm X, 157
Afrocentricity (Asante), 155
"The Afrocentric Idea in Education" (Asante), 156
Agunias, Dovelyn, 58 n.59
AIAW (Association for Intercollegiate Athletics for Women), 128
Alabama, HBCUs in, 127, 133, 134 *Table 6.1,* 147 *Table 6.6*
Aldridge, Delores, P., 69, 73
Alexander, Marissa, case of, 108
Allen, W.R., 125
Anderson, M.L., 112
Ani, M., 69
antimiscegenation laws, 89
Abune Antonios, deposing of, 43–44, 57 n.46
Archer, Samuel, 124, 130
Arkansas, HBCUs in, 134 *Table 6.1,* 147 *Table 6.6*
Armstrong, K.L., 129
Asante, Molefi K.
   Afrocentricity, 155
   on Afrocentricity, 3, 156, 158–59, 163

"The Afrocentric Idea in Education," 156
on Black leadership, 157, 161
Ashine, Argaw, 52 n.11
athletic conferences. *See* AIAW, NAIA, NCAA, NJCAA, USCAA
athletic programs, at HBCUs. *See* HBCU athletic programs
Atlanta University, Morehouse College *vs.* (baseball game), 123

B
Barnett, B.M., 114
Baron, R.S., 112
baseball
  Atlanta University *vs.* Morehouse College, 123
  at HBCUs, statistics, 132, 140–41, 144
  as motivation, in HBCUs, 130
basketball
  AIAW National Championships, 128
  at HBCUs, statistics, 132
  at HBCUs (men's), statistics, 137–39, 144
  at HBCUs (women's), statistics, 139–40, 144
Battle, Nishaun T., 107
Bennett, R.A., III, 126
Black Americans: The FBI Files (O'Reilly), 163
Black Feminist Criminology, 117–18
Black Feminist Thought (Collins), 66
Black Freedom Movement, in *Two Trains Running*, 20
Black literature, DLS in
  concept, 2–4
  intellectual/academic benefits of, 25–26
  limitations of, 25
  Parks' play, application to, 4–8
  procedural elements of, 2–4
  questions/observations on, 26–27
  Wilson's plays, application to, 8–25
Black Lives Matter, 108
Black music
  Black music culture, in South Texas, 102–3, 105 *photo 21*
  "rabbles," college bands at half time, 123
  tradition, DLS elements and, 16, 17–19
Black narrative, from photographs, 83–106
  Black children, 93 *photo 9*
  Black cowboys, 101–2, 103 *photo 19*, 104 *photo 20*
  Black railway workers, 97–100, 100 *photo 15*, 100 *photo 16*, 101 *photo 17*, 102 *photo 18*
  interracial marriages, 88 *photo 4*, 89 *photo 5*, 90 *photo 6*, 91 *photo 7*, 92 *photo 8*
  King & Carter Jazzing Orchestra (Houston, Texas), 102–3, 105 *photo 21*
  "New Negro," 83–84, 92–93, 94 *photo 10*, 96 *photo 11*, 97 *photo 12*, 98 *photo 13*, 99 *photo 14*, 103–4
  Robert Runyon, 84–85, 85 *photo 2*
  Runyon Studio, 84 *photo 1*
  See also South Texas
Black women
  leadership and, 117–19
  legal system and, 116–17
  as playwrights, tradition of, 6
  race/gender, social construction of, 108–11
  social devaluation of, 107–8, 118–19
  social group behavior, intersectionality and, 111–14
  womanhood, socialization/perception of, 114–15
(Black) women's studies, 63–64, 79–80
Blackmon, Douglas A. *(Slavery by Another Name)*, 14
Borican, J., 126, 127
Bottoms, B.L., 116
bowling, NCAA Championships in, 128
Brazzell, Johnetta Cross, 125
Brewer, R.M., 114
Bridges, K.M., 110, 116
Bromall, Irwin H., 31
Brown, Gary, 130
Brown, M.C., 125
Brown-Guillory, Elizabeth, 6
Brown *vs.* Board of Education (1954), 125
Bryman, A. *(The SAGE Handbook of Leadership)*, 155, 156
Buchanan, N.T., 115
Burns, James MacGregor, 156

C
Cameron County, Texas, Black households in, 89–90
Carbado, D.W., 113, 114
Carby, H.V., 113

Index

Carpenter, T.R., 109, 111, 115
Cavil, J. Kenyatta, 121, 129
Chait, Sandra M., 59 n.60
Cheeks, Geremy, 121
Chen, G.M., 109
Cheyne (HBCU), 125
Chicago, setting for *Ma Rainey's Black Bottom* (Wilson), 16
Chomsky, Noam, 158
CIAA (Central (Colored) Intercollegiate Athletic Association), history of, 126, 127
Civil Rights Movement, influence on Eritrean students, 36
Cohn, R., 116
Collins, F.G., 126
Collins, Patricia Hill, 66, 109, 110, 111, 113, 115
Colored Trainsmen of America (union), 98–99
community centers (Eritrean-American), 45–46
Conley, T.D., 115
Conrad, Bettina, 47
Cooper, Anna Julia, 77, 117, 118
Cooper, J.N., 130
Cooper, Joseph, 121
Crenshaw, Kimberle, 112, 113–14, 118
"Demarginalizing the Intersection," 116–17
criminal justice system, Black women in, 107–20
 Marissa Alexander, case of, 108
 Black Lives Matter, 108
 Black women, leadership and, 117–19
 deaths of young Black males, by law enforcement, 107–8
 legal system, intersection in, 116–17
 Trayvon Martin/George Zimmerman case, 107, 109–10
 race/gender, social construction of, 108–11
 social group behavior, intersectionality and, 111–14
 womanhood, socialization/perception of, 114–15
cyber Eritrea, websites, 32

D

Delaware, HBCUs in, 133, 134 *Table 6.1*, 147 *Table 6.6*
DeLeon-Granados, William (survey), 7

"Demarginalizing the Intersection" (Crenshaw), 116–17
DeSchriver, T.D., 129
diaspora Eritrea
 associations, 48
 characteristics, 33–35
 community centers, 45–46
 diaspora, definition, 52 n.10
 diasporic elite, 36
 Eritrean Orthodox Church, regime "capture" of, 42–45
 ethnic/religious groups, in U.S., 33
 exodus, reasons for, 32
 festivals, sports, seminars and, 46
 homeland surveys, 49–50
 as invisible entity, 35–36
 jasus, PFDJ cells and, 41–42
 military personnel, registration of, 49
 Office for Eritreans Residing Abroad, 55 n.39
 politics, attitudes towards, 35
 population concentrations, in U.S., 33, 52–53 n.18
 population in U.S., statistics/estimates, 32–33, 51 n.2, 52 n.17
 public gathering spots, role of, 41, 56 n.43
 RCBs (regime-controlled benefits), 38–39
 regime oppression, in host country, 47–48
 regime policies, 40, 55 n.34, 55 n.38
 regime tracking, of diaspora population, 48–50
 revolutionary groups, 35
 summer trips back, 46–47
 tax collection/national ID cards, 48–49, 56 n.41
 taxes/levies, RCBs and, 39–41
Abune Dioscoros, 44
DLS (demographic literary standard), 1–30
 concept, 2–4
 intellectual/academic benefits of, 25–26
 limitations of, 25
 Parks' play, application to, 4–8
 procedural elements of, 2–4
 questions/observations on, 26–27
 Wilson's plays, application to, 8–25

Dr. Cavil's Ten Pillars framework, 151
Du Bois, W.E.B., leadership perspective of, 157–58

E
Eastern Intercollegiate Athletic Conference (EIAC), 126
Education-Sports Symbiosis (ESS) hypothesis. *See* ESS
ELF (Eritrean Liberation Front), 35
English, Diane J. (survey), 7
EPLF (Eritrean Peoples Liberation Front), 35
Eritrea, 31–62
   Isaias Afwerki (president), 31
   conclusion, 50
   cyber Eritrea, websites, 32
   diaspora Eritrea, 32–50
   Eritrean citizenship, 38
   future research directions, 50–51
   homeland Eritrea, demographics/religion, 31–33
   Human Rights Watch report on, 31
   political/social problems in, research methodology, 37–38, 53–54 n.29, 54 n.30
   political/social problems in, theoretical perspective, 36–37
   religious freedom in, 32
   travel warning, for Eritrean-U.S. dual citizens, 54 n.32
   yike'alo, definition, 34
   See also diaspora Eritrea
Eritrean Orthodox Diocese of North America, 42–44, 48, 57 nn.46–47
ESS (Education-Sports Symbiosis) hypothesis
   athletic programs, by region, 142, 143 *Table 6.4*
   athletic studies, at HBCUs, 141–42
   baseball programs, 138 *Table 6.3,* 140–41
   football programs, 135–37, 136 *Table 6.1*
   institutional size/ type of sport, 144, 145 *Table 6.5,* 146
   membership associations, of athletic programs, 135
   men's basketball programs, 137–39, 138 *Table 6.3*
   methodology, 131
   overview, 132
   school region, 132–33, 146
   school size, 134–35
   school state, 133, 134 *Table 6.1*
   study framework, 130–31
   study significance, 131
   women's basketball programs, 138 *Table 6.3,* 139–40
Ethiopia. *See* Eritrea

F
Farmer, Paul, 37
Farrakhan, Louis, leadership of, 161–62
FBI, opposition to Black leadership by, 163
feminism
   Black feminism, definition, 66
   Black Feminist Criminology, 117–18
   compulsory feminism, 63–64, 67–69, 72–73
   de facto feminism, definition, 68
   definition, debate about, 66–67
   feminism, definitions, 63, 65–66, 75–78
   hyphenated feminism, definition/debate about, 65–66
   "master gender narratives," 70–71
   "multiplication of feminism," 66
   nonaligned women and, 69–73
   pathological models of gender, 76–77, 78
   rejection of, 72–73
   Sojourner Truth, feminist speech by, 113
   womanism, (Black) feminism and, 74
   womanism/feminism dichotomy, in Africana gender studies, 73–75
   See also Africana gender studies, without feminism
Fences (Wilson), DLS considerations of, 19–20
Fisher, Dwalah, 129
Florida, HBCUs in, 134 *Table 6.1,* 147 *Table 6.6*
Florida Agricultural/Mechanical University, 127
Florida Classic, current attendance at, 129
football
   Samuel Archer, football coach, 124
   college football, popularity of, 128–29
   HBCU rivalry, Morehouse *vs.* Tuskegee, 127

at HBCUs, statistics, 129, 132, 135–37, 144
Fox-Genovese, E., 113
Freedmen's Bureau, 125
Freeman, J.B., 115
Fulton, Sabrina (mother, Trayvon Martin), 111

G
Garvey, Marcus, leadership of, 162, 163
Gawrysiak, E.J., 130
Gem of the Ocean (Wilson), DLS considerations of, 12–14
Georgia, HBCUs in, 133, 134 *Table 6.1*, 148 *Table 6.6*, 149 *Table 6.6*, 150 *Table 6.6*
Glass, K.L., 118
Goff, P.A., 113
Gordon, V.V., 69
Grant, Judith, 65
Gratton, C., 131
Great Migration, in *Joe Turner's Come and Gone* (Wilson), 14–16
Greene, R.L., 115
Greenleaf, Robert, leadership of, 161–62

H
Hacker, J., 115
Hakim, N., 159, 160
Hall, R., 157
Hampton University, public image of Blacks at, 83
Harlem Renaissance, 97 *photo 12*
Harris-Perry, M., 112
Haugen, B., 162
Hawkins, B., 123, 126, 130
HBCU athletic programs, 121–53
  ESS (Education-Sports Symbiosis) hypothesis, 130–31
  global rebranding strategy, argument for, 121–22
  HBCU athletic conferences and association memberships, 126–28
  HBCU athletics, current state of, 128–30
  HBCUs, history and role of, 124–26
  "limited-resource institutions," NCAA policy for, 129–30
  methodology, 131
  recommendation, for brand enhancement, 146, 151
  sports/athletics, in African American community, 122–24
  study results, 132–44
  study results, discussion of, 144–46
Heaven, P.C., 115
Henderson, Edwin Bancroft ("E.B."), 122–23
Hepner, Tricia Redeker, 33, 34
Hidalgo County, Texas, interracial households in, 90
Historically Black Colleges and Universities (HBCUs), 124–28. *See also* HBCU athletic programs
Hochschild, J.L., 110
Hodge, S.R., 123, 126, 131
homeland Eritrea, 31–33, 35
Hoover, J. Edgar, opposition to Black leadership by, 163
Hosick, Michelle, 129, 130
Howard University, 128
Hoxha, D., 115
Hudson-Weems, Clenora, 69, 73
human performance programs, at HBCUs, 132
Hunt, D., 126

I
Impact of Immigration on Ethnic-Specific Violence in Miami, Florida (Martinez, Jr.), 7
Inman, M.L., 112
interracial marriage, in South Texas, 88 *photo 4*
intersectionality
  in the legal system, 116–17
  social construction of race/gender, 109–11
  social group behavior and, 111–14
  socialization, perception of womanhood and, 114–15
Intimate Partner Homicide in California (Wells and DeLeon-Granados), 7
The Invention of Women (Oyewumi), 71–72
IRS reporting forms, use by Eritrean regime, 47–48

J
Jackson, Eugiruia (South Texas), 91
Jackson, James S. (survey), 7
Jackson, M.C., 113
Jackson, Nagario (South Texas), 91

174   Africana Theory, Policy, and Leadership

Jackson, Redacinde (South Texas), 91
Jackson family, in South Texas, 87
   photo 3, 88
jasus, PFDJ cells and, 41–42
Jeantel, Rachel, credibility of, 109–10, 112, 117
Jitney (Wilson), DLS considerations of, 21–22
Joe Turner's Come and Gone (Wilson), DLS considerations of, 14–16
Johnson, G.K., 129
Johnson, K.L., 115
Jones, I., 131
Jones, Lola, 109

K
Karenga, Maulana, 1–2, 5–6
Kdst Selassie Eritrean Orthodox Tewahedo Church, 44
Kentucky, HBCUs in, 134 *Table 6.1,* 148 *Table 6.6*
Kidisti Selassie Orthodox Tewahedo Church, 43–44
kinesiology programs, at HBCUs, 132
King, Martin Luther, Jr., 160, 162
King & Carter Jazzing Orchestra, 102–3, 105 *photo 21*
King Hedley II (Wilson), DLS considerations of, 22–23
Koertge, N., 68
Kolin, Philip, 5
Kuumba, M.B., 114

L
la voix érythrée, 36
Lawrence, S.N., 116
Lee, John Robert Edward, Jr., 123
Levine, Donald N., 51 n.1
literary analysis/study, within Africana Studies, 1–27
   DLS, applied to August Wilson's plays, 8–25
   DLS, applied to Suzan-Lori Parks' *365 Days/365 Plays,* 4–8
   DLS, intellectual/academic benefits of, 25–26
   DLS, limitations of, 25
   DLS, questions/observations on, 26–27
   DLS concept, 2–4
   literature *vs.* social science, 1–2
Livingstone College, Johnson C. Smith University *vs.,* 123

Louisiana, HBCUs in, 134 *Table 6.1,* 148 *Table 6.6*
Loving v. Virginia (1967), 89
Abune Lukas, 43–44
Lyubansky, M., 107

M
Ma Rainey's Black Bottom (Wilson), DLS considerations of, 16
Magic City Classic, current attendance at, 129
Malcolm X, leadership perspectives of, 157
Mance, R., 125
Martin, Trayvon, case of, 107, 109–10, 111
Martinez, Ramiro, Jr. (survey), 7
Maryland, HBCUs in, 134 *Table 6.1,* 148 *Table 6.6*
McClelland, C.F., 129
McDuffie, E.S., 118
McMullen, Ronald K. (ambassador), 34
Memon, A., 117
Michigan, HBCUs in, 133, 134 *Table 6.1,* 148 *Table 6.6*
Mid-Eastern Athletic Conference (MEAC), 126, 128
Midwestern Athletic Association (MWAA), 126
Miller, P.B., 122, 123, 124, 126, 130
Mis-education of the Negro (Woodson), 156–57, 158
Mississippi, HBCUs in, 134 *Table 6.1,* 148 *Table 6.6*
Missouri, HBCUs in, 134 *Table 6.1,* 149 *Table 6.6*
Mohanty, C.T., 64
Morehouse College, 123, 124, 127
Morrill Act of 1862, 125
Morrill Act of 1890, 125
Moynihan, D.P., 111
Muhammad, Elijah, leadership of, 159–61
   Our Savior Has Arrived, 160

N
NAIA (National Athletic Intercollegiate Association)
   academic physical education/sport management programs, at HBCUs, 141–42
   baseball, at HBCUs, 140–41

basketball (men's), at HBCUs, 137–38, 138 *Table 6.3*
basketball (women's), at HBCUs, 139–40
HBCU athletic programs, admission of, 126
HBCUs and, 122
HBCUs in, by Division, 135, 136 *Table 6.2*
HBCUs in, by institutional size, 144, 145 *Table 6.5*, 146
HBCUs in, by region, 142, 143 *Table 6.4*
Nash, J.C., 113
NCAA (National College Athletic Association)
  academic physical education/sport management programs, at HBCUs, 141–42
  APR policy, on graduation rates, 121, 129–30
  baseball, at HBCUs, 140–41
  basketball (men's), at HBCUs, 137–38, 138 *Table 6.3*
  basketball (women's), at HBCUs, 139–40
  Division II competitions, SIAC in, 127
  football game attendance, statistics, 129
  HBCUs and, 121, 122
  HBCUs in, by Division, 128, 135, 136 *Table 6.2*
  HBCUs in, by institutional size, 144, 145 *Table 6.5*, 146
  HBCUs in, by region, 142, 143 *Table 6.4*
  MEAC Division I membership, 128
Neighbors, Harold W. (survey), 7
NJCAA (National Junior College Athletic Association), 121
  academic physical education/sport management programs, at HBCUs, 141–42
  baseball, at HBCUs, 140–41
  basketball (men's), at HBCUs, 137–38, 138 *Table 6.3*
  basketball (women's), at HBCUs, 139–40
  HBCUs in, by Division, 135, 136 *Table 6.2*
  HBCUs in, by institutional size, 144, 145 *Table 6.5*, 146
  HBCUs in, by region, 142, 143 *Table 6.4*
North Carolina, HBCUs in, 133, 134 *Table 6.1*, 149 *Table 6.6*
Nzegwu, Nkiru, 64

O
Ohio, HBCUs in, 134 *Table 6.1*, 149 *Table 6.6*
Oklahoma, HBCUs in, 133, 134 *Table 6.1*, 149 *Table 6.6*
Okome, Mojubaolu Olufunke, 64
O'Reilly, Kenneth *(Black Americans: The FBI Files)*, 163
Orthodox Church, in Eritrea, 42–45
Our Savior Has Arrived (Muhammad), 160
Oyewumi, Oyeronke, 64
The Invention of Women, 71–72

P
Pace v. Alabama (1883), 89
Parks, Suzan-Lori, 4–8
  365 Days/365 Plays, concepts/themes in, 4–5
  365 Days/365 Plays, literary analysis of, 5–6
  brief biography, 4
  collection of plays, data set for, 6–8
  on commitment to write a play/day, 6
Patai, D., 68
Pauker, K., 115
Pennsylvania, HBCUs in, 134 *Table 6.1*, 149 *Table 6.6*
Penrod, S.D., 117
PFDJ (People's Front for Democracy and Justice), in Eritrea
  associations, 48
  community centers in U.S. and, 45–46, 48
  festivals, sports and seminars, by PFDJ, 46
  genesis of, 31, 35
  jasus and, 41–42
physical education programs, 132, 141–42
The Piano Lesson (Wilson), DLS considerations of, 17
Pitre, Abul, 155, 158
Pittsburgh, as setting for Wilson's plays
  century cycle, DLS and, 11–12
  Fences, 19–20

Gem of the Ocean, 12–14
Jitney, 21–22
Joe Turner's Come and Gone, 14–16
King Hedley II, 22–23
The Piano Lesson, 17
Radio Golf, 23–25
Seven Guitars, 17–19
as source, for quantitative/qualitative data sets, 10–11
Two Trains Running, 20–21
Power Five Conference, 122
Pratt-Hyatt, J.S., 115, 117
"Principles and Practices of Leadership to Suffice Our Needs" (Farrakhan), 161
prison industrial complex, Black women and. *See* Africana perspectives in criminal justice, of Black women

R
Rabaka, Reiland, leadership perspectives of, 157, 158
racism, in the legal system, 116–17. *See also* intersectionality
Radio Golf (Wilson), DLS considerations of, 23–25
railroad workers/railroad union, in South Texas, 97–100, 100 *photo 15,* 100 *photo 16,* 101 *photo 17,* 102 *photo 18*
Reconstruction, HBCUs and, 125
recreation programs, at HBCUs, 132
religious freedom, Eritrea and, 32, 42–45
Reynolds, Lacey, 129
Rodgers-Rose, La Frances, 73
Rodriguez, Alberto, 83
Ruffin, St. Pierre, 80
Ruggeach, Rebecca Ann, 5
Ruth, Sheila, 66
Rutledge family, in South Texas, 87, 90

S
The Sage Handbook of Leadership (Bryman), 156
Saylor, Roger, 123, 126
servant leadership, 161–62
Settles, I.H., 115
Seven Guitars (Wilson), DLS considerations of, 17–19
Sheffer, Gabriel, 52 n.10, 59 n.59
Shields, T., 162
SIAC. *See* Southern (Southeastern) Intercollegiate Athletic Conference

Simon, Hanna (ambassador), 55 n.39
Simon, R.J., 115
Singletary family, in South Texas, 87, 91
Abune Sinoda, 43–44, 58 n.51
Slavery by Another Name (Blackmon), 14
Johnson C. Smith University (Biddle Memorial Institute), Livingstone College *vs.*, 123
social science research, application to plays, 7–8, 10
Solis, Ballagar (South Texas), 91
Solis, Davie (South Texas), 91
South Carolina, HBCUs in, 134
Table 6.1, 149 *Table 6.6*
South Carolina State University, 128
South Texas, Blacks in, 83–106
antimiscegenation laws in, 89
Black churches in, 87–88
Black cowboys, 101–2
Black households, 89–90
Black literacy rates, 93–95, 94 *Table 4.2*
Black literacy rates/county, 95 *Table 4.3*
Black music culture in, 102–3, 105 *photo 21*
Black population/county, 86 *Table 4.1*
Black railway workers/unions, 97–100
Black unions/mutual aid societies, 95–96
Hampton University, 83
interracial marriages, 91–92
segregated neighborhoods, 96–97
social mobility in, 89–90, 100, 104
social position, of Blacks, 90–92
Tuskegee University, 83
See also Black narrative, from photographs
Southern Central Athletic Association (SCAC), 126
Southern (Southeastern) Intercollegiate Athletic Conference, history of, 126, 127
Southwell, V., 114
Southwestern Athletic Conference (SWAC), history of, 126, 127–28, 129
sport culture, Black male experience and, 19–20, 122–24. *See also* HBCU athletic programs
sport management programs, at HBCUs, 132

St. Louis Brownsville Mexican Railway, 98, 99–100, 101 *photo 17*
stereotypes, of Black women, 111–14
Stevenson, M.C., 116
Stewart, James, 2, 5–6
Suggs, W., 128

T
Tekeste, Tesfamariam (ambassador), 55 n.39
Temple, Christel N., 1
Ten Pillars framework (Dr. Cavil's), for athletic program brand enhancement, 151
Tennessee, HBCUs in, 134 *Table 6.1*, 150 *Table 6.6*
Texas, HBCUs in, 134 *Table 6.1*, 150 *Table 6.6*
Thomas, A., 113, 115
365 Days/365 Plays (Parks), 4–6
 concepts/themes in, 4–5
 literary analysis of, 5–6
 website, 5
Townsend, T.G., 110
track and field, 127, 128
transdisciplinary applied social justice model, 117
transformative leadership, 162
Truth, Sojourner, feminist speech by, 113
Tsuruta, Dorothy, 73
Tuskegee University, 83, 127
Two Trains Running (Wilson), DLS considerations of, 20–21

U
Underground Railroad, in *Gem of the Ocean* (Wilson), 12–14
U.S. Virgin Island, HBCUs in, 134 *Table 6.1*, 150 *Table 6.6*
USCAA (United States Collegiate Athletic Association), 122
 HBCUs in, by Division, 135, 136 *Table 6.2*
 HBCUs in, by institutional size, 144, 145 *Table 6.5*, 146
 HBCUs in, by region, 143 *Table 6.4*

V
Virginia, HBCUs in, 134 *Table 6.1*, 150 *Table 6.6*
Visnuevo, Christ (South Texas), 91

W
Wagner, Valerie, 66
Walker, Alice, 73
Wallace, S.A., 110
Walley-Jean, C., 111
Walters, R., 156
Warfield-Coppoack, N., 158
Washington, D.C., HBCUs in, 134 *Table 6.1*, 147 *Table 6.6*
Watkins, Valethia A., 63
Watson, J.B., 124, 130
Weaver, V., 110
Webber family, in South Texas, 86–87
Wells, G.L., 117
Wells, William (survey), 7
Welters, B., 108
West Virginia, HBCUs in, 134 *Table 6.1*, 150 *Table 6.6*
White women, socialization/perception of, 114–15
Widom, Cathy Spatz (survey), 7
Wiggins, D.K., 123, 124, 130
Williams, L., 129
Wilson, August, DLS considerations of plays by, 8–25
 on Afrocentricity, 9
 brief biography, 9
 DLS century cycle and, 11–12
 Fences, 19–20
 Gem of the Ocean, 12–14
 Jitney, 21–22
 Joe Turner's Come and Gone, 14–16
 King Hedley II, 22–23
 literary analysis, of play collection, 9–10
 Ma Rainey's Black Bottom, 16
 The Piano Lesson, 17
 Pittsburgh, as play setting, 10–11
 play list, 8–9
 Radio Golf, 23–25
 Seven Guitars, 17–19
 Two Trains Running, 20–21
Woldu, Dawit O., 31
womanhood
 Black women, social perceptions of, 109
 race/gender, social construction of, 108–11
 social group behavior, intersectionality and, 111–14
 socialization/perception of, 114–15

"true womanhood," definition, 108–9
  White women and, 114–15
women's studies (traditional), 68
Woodard, K., 118
Woodson, Carter G. *(Mis-education of the Negro),* 156–57, 158
Wyatt, J., 111

Y
Young, C., 73

Z
Zimmerman George, case of, 107
Zuniga, Juan (South Texas), 91
Zura n' Hagerka, 46–47